MS World History I
Student Guide

Second Edition

Illustrations Credits
All illustrations © K12 Inc. unless otherwise noted

About K12 Inc.
K12 Inc., a technology-based education company, is the nation's leading provider of proprietary curriculum and online education programs to students in grades K–12. K¹² provides its curriculum and academic services to online schools, traditional classrooms, blended school programs, and directly to families. K12 Inc. also operates the K¹² International Academy, an accredited, diploma-granting online private school serving students worldwide. K¹²'s mission is to provide any child the curriculum and tools to maximize success in life, regardless of geographic, financial, or demographic circumstances. K12 Inc. is accredited by CITA. More information can be found at www.K12.com.

ISBN: 978-1-60153-496-5
Printed by RR Donnelley, Kendallville, IN, USA, September 2016

Table of Contents

Unit 4: Civilization Spreads

Unit 5: Writing About the Past

Unit 6: Some Lasting Ideas

Unit 7: More Lasting Ideas

Unit 8: Write Again

Unit 9: Classical Greece

Unit 10: Rome: Republic and Empire

Unit 11: Empires

Unit 12: In Western Europe

Unit 13: From East Asia to Western Europe Again

Unit 14: Seeking the Silk Road

Unit 15: Finishing

Student Guide

Unit 1: History: The Map of Time
Lesson 1: History and You

History is the study of the human past--the story of change over time. It's a story based on evidence. Our physical world is the setting that helps shape the story, real people are its heroes, and time and space are its anchors. Historians ask questions about all of these elements. How did the Egyptians build pyramids? When and where did democracy begin? Why are most of the world's great cities located on rivers? Join our odyssey through history. The questions are endless, and the answers amazing.

You will be helped along in your journey through history by a book--*The Human Odyssey: Prehistory Through the Middle Ages*. In it you will find out how the Egyptians built their amazing pyramids. You'll discover when and where democracy began. You'll meet extraordinary leaders and ordinary people. This book will be your passport to faraway places and long-ago times.

Lesson Objectives

- Locate selected information in *The Human Odyssey: Prehistory Through the Middle Ages*.
- Discuss reasons for studying history.
- Define *history*.

PREPARE

Approximate lesson time is 60 minutes.

Materials

For the Student

Your Passport to The Human Odyssey

The Human Odyssey: Prehistory Through the Middle Ages edited by Klee, Cribb, and Holdren

History Journal

LEARN

Activity 1: Your Passport to *The Human Odyssey* *(Online)*

Let's get started by reviewing what you'll encounter on your odyssey through history. Click Introduction to History to get an overview of the course. Then, print the materials and continue the lesson offline.

Activity 2: History: What Is It and Why Study It? *(Online)*

Name Date

Your Passport to *The Human Odyssey*

Before you begin your odyssey through history, start by going on a little odyssey through your book. Use *The Human Odyssey: Prehistory Through the Middle Ages* to help you answer some questions.

The book has four parts, and each part is divided into chapters. Use the table of contents to help you find the answers to the following questions:

1. On what page does Part 4 begin? ________

2. In the Introduction to Part 2 there is a photograph showing a Hindu praying in a river. What river is it? ________________

3. What is Part 3, Chapter 5, about? ______________________

You may find that some of the words in the book are hard to pronounce. For help, look for the pronunciations in parentheses right after the word. You can use these, along with the Pronunciation Guide on page 650, to help you sound out the words.

4. Look at the following word in the first column of page 478--*Umayyads*. Use the pronunciation in parentheses after the word to sound out *Umayyads*. Check the Pronunciation Guide on page 650 to help you recognize the sounds associated with specific letters and letter combinations used in word pronunciations.

The book is full of photographs, illustrations, maps, and other pictures. All pictures have captions, although the caption may not always be right below the image.

5. What does the map on page 180 show?
____

6. Who are the two figures in the image to the left of the first column on page 50, and what are they doing?
____

There is a time line at the end of each part. Use the time line for Part 2 to answer the following questions:

7. Which of the following three events happened first? __________________

   - Herodotus writes his histories.
   - Aryans migrate to India.
   - Saul, David, and Solomon rule the Hebrews.

8. In what year were the first recorded Olympic Games held? _____________

The book includes an atlas that starts on page 623. Use the atlas to answer the following questions:

9. In what direction (north, west, northeast, etc.) would you be heading if you traveled from Kandahar, Afghanistan, to Ahmadabad, India? ____________________

Name ______________________ Date ______________________

10. What map projection is an elliptical equal-area projection that distorts shapes near the edges? ______________________

11. What two climate zones comprise most of Australia? ______________________

What was the Black Death? When did Socrates live? What is the definition of *millennium*? Two sections of the book can help you find the answers to questions like these: the Glossary and the Index. Use these two valuable resources to help you find the answers to these two questions:

12. Write the definition and pronunciation for *oligarchy*.
____

13. On what two pages can you read about Ganesha? ______________________

Nothing helps us understand the past quite like a good story. In your book you'll find lots of good stories, including some in special sections called "Imagining the Past." Some are myths, and some are fiction based on historical truth. Look on page 491.

14. What is the name of the boy featured in this story? ______________________

Check your answers with those in the Lesson Answer Key.

You have completed your short odyssey through the book! There is a lot of history in this book, and ahead of you lies an entire year of world history. Why should people study history? And what exactly IS history?

Go back online and complete the History: What Is It and Why Study It? activity to help you find the answers to those last two questions.

Student Guide
Lesson 2: When?

What do we mean when we say we live in the twenty-first century? Did people who lived in the first century know it was the first century? What about all the years before then? Why do we even measure time? Thousands of years ago, farmers needed to know when to plant and to be able to predict the annual floods. Observant people noticed that some events kept happening over and over again. They noticed that the sky changed in a fairly predictable way and they began to track the cycle we call a year. Their careful observations and calculations led to the development of the earliest calendars.

Lesson Objectives

- Recognize time-related terms and how they are used in the study of history.
- Use time-related terms correctly and in context.
- Describe the purposes and evolution of the calendar.

PREPARE

Approximate lesson time is 60 minutes.

Materials

For the Student

The Human Odyssey: Prehistory Through the Middle Ages edited by Klee, Cribb, and Holdren

History Journal

Keywords and Pronunciation

A.D. : the abbreviation for the Latin words *anno Domini* ("in the year of the Lord"), used to date events that took place after the birth of Jesus Christ

B.C. : the abbreviation for "before Christ," used to date events that took place in the years before the birth of Jesus Christ

B.C.E. : the abbreviation for "before the common era," sometimes used instead of B.C.

C.E. : the abbreviation for "common era," sometimes used instead of A.D.

century : a period of 100 years

decade : a period of 10 years

millennium : a period of 1,000 years

LEARN

Activity 1: The Curious Calendar *(Online)*

Activity 2: Keeping Track *(Offline)*

Read

Read the Introduction, from the beginning to "Locating Ourselves in Space: Grid Lines," pages 9-13. As you read, define the following terms in your History Journal:

century
decade
millennia
millennium
A.D.
C.E.
B.C.
B.C.E.

Note: Refer to the Lesson Answer Key to find the answers to the bulleted questions in today's reading.

Use What You Know

Create a time line of "Me." Think about the significant events in your life. Then see what kinds of things were happening elsewhere in the world at the same time.

Directions:

1. Ask an adult to help you list important events in his or him life or in the world (and the dates of those events) in the five years before you were born.
2. Now make a list of important events in your life and their dates. Don't forget to include the year you were born. Ask an adult to help you.
3. Draw a vertical line on a piece of plain paper or a sheet in your History Journal.
4. Draw a small horizontal line every two inches. These lines will indicate years. Remember, even when several things happen in the same year and nothing in another year, a time line shows equal increments of time.
5. Leave five lines for the years before you were born. Label the sixth horizontal line "A.M.B. 1." This is the year you were born. (in this activity, A.M.B. stands for "after my birth.")
6. On the right-hand side of the time line, add important events from your life. For example, if you started walking the day after your first birthday, list that event in the year A.M.B. 2.
7. Now add the events that occurred in the five years before you were born. The years before your birth are noted as B.M.B. (before my birth). For example, your parents might have gotten married in 4 B.M.B.
8. Last, choose five or six of the events listed below and place them on the left side of the time line. If you prefer, you may refer to an almanac or ask an adult to help you choose world events in your lifetime.

Suggested World Events:

- 1989 - Fall of the Berlin Wall
- 1990 - Reunification of Germany
- 1991 - Desert Storm (Gulf War in Iraq)
- 1993 - Czechoslovakia split into two nations: Czech Republic & Slovakia
- 1994 - Nelson Mandela elected president of South Africa
- 1995 - Prime Minister of Israel assassinated
- 1997 - Hong Kong "reunited" with China
- 2001 - World Trade Center attacked
- 2003 - War in Iraq

Review

Click Flash Cards for a quick review before taking the Lesson Assessment.

ASSESS

Lesson Assessment: When? (*Online*)

You will complete an online assessment covering the main points of this lesson. Your assessment will be scored by the computer.

LEARN

Activity 3. Optional: When? *(Online)*

This activity is OPTIONAL. It's provided for enrichment or extra practice, but not required for completion of this lesson. You may skip this activity.

If you have some time, explore the fascinating history of calendars at these websites:

- Calendars Through the Ages
- A Brief History of the Calendar

Student Guide
Lesson 3: Where?

The study of history cannot be separated from geography. Events are often shaped by the location and the physical, environmental characteristics of a place. But how do we describe location? Geographers have come up with handy "tools" to help us locate and describe where in the world events happen.

Lesson Objectives

- Use longitude and latitude to determine absolute location.
- Define latitude, longitude, parallel, and equator.
- Recognize the purposes of maps, globes, and lines of longitude and latitude.
- Identify the seven continents and four oceans.
- Define *latitude, longitude, parallel,* and *equator.*

PREPARE

Approximate lesson time is 60 minutes.

Advance Preparation

- If you don't already have it, you will need to gather a world atlas.

Materials

For the Student

Location: Relative and Absolute

The Human Odyssey: Prehistory Through the Middle Ages edited by Klee, Cribb, and Holdren

atlas - world

art supplies

History Journal

paper, 8 1/2" x 11"

Keywords and Pronunciation

equator : the imaginary line that circles Earth halfway between the North Pole and the South Pole
latitude (LA-tuh-tood) : a distance in degrees north and south of the equator
longitude (LAHN-juh-tood) : A distance in degrees east and west of the prime, or zero, meridian.
parallels : another name for latitude; every point on a parallel is an equal distance north or south from the equator

---

LEARN

Activity 1: Absolute and Relative Location *(Online)*

Location, Location, Location

The world is a big place. How do we know exactly where we are on the planet? How do we describe to someone else how to find a particular spot? How do we explain the relationship between one place and another?

Geographers refer to the concept of *location* in two ways--*absolute location* and *relative location.*

Absolute Location

Absolute location is the precise location of a particular place. Latitude and longitude allow us to pinpoint absolute location. No two places on Earth have exactly the same latitude and longitude. A ship at sea that radios its position as 20°N, 60° E, for example, will not be confused with a ship somewhere else. There is only one city--New Orleans--located at 30°N, 90°W.

Activity 2: Where in the World? *(Offline)*

Read

Read the Introduction, from "Locating Ourselves in Space: Grid Lines" to the end, pages 13-15 in *The Human Odyssey: Prehistory Through the Middle Ages*. As you read, define the following terms in your History Journal:

latitude

longitude

parallel

equator

Note: Refer to the Lesson Answer Key to find the answers to the bulleted questions in today's reading.

Focus on Geography

Use your knowledge of absolute and relative location and a world atlas to complete the Location: Relative and Absolute sheet.

ASSESS

Lesson Assessment: Where? (*Online*)

You will complete an online assessment covering the main points of this lesson. Your assessment will be scored by the computer.

LEARN

Activity 3. Optional: Where? *(Online)*

This activity is OPTIONAL. It's provided for enrichment or extra practice, but not required for completion of this lesson. You may skip this activity.

What does time have to do with longitude? Learn how a clockmaker helped solve

The Longitude Problem

Name Date

Location: Relative and Absolute

Part 1: Absolute Location

Directions: Use a world atlas to identify each place. Where appropriate, give the city and the country.

You are part of a worldwide spy operation. You've just been given your new assignment. You and your partner are to track and capture Mr. X who is on the run. You pack your bags—taking clothes for both warm and cool weather since you aren't sure where you will end up—and fly to ____________________, located at 36° N and 140° E. There you meet up with your partner. You decide to split up because you've heard two rumors about where Mr. X is holed up. Your partner catches a boat to ____________________, at 25° N and 122° E. Meanwhile, you catch an airplane and head to the continent of ____________________, where China is located. Mr. X was there—cold and using bottled oxygen—hiding out in the ____________________, which border China to the west. Unfortunately, you just missed him. You and your partner decide to regroup, so you rendezvous in ____________________, located between 15° and 30° N and between 150° and 170° W. You spend several days surfing and talking to the locals. Word on the street is that Mr. X is cruising in the middle of the ____________ ____________, located at 20° S and 70° E. You haven't heard exactly where he is going, so you head to ____________________, located at 1° S and 37° E, where one of your satellite offices is located. Meanwhile, your partner takes off for Cape Town, South Africa located at ____________ (latitude/longitude) to visit with an old friend while awaiting Mr. X's next move. Within days you learn that your information was incorrect. Mr. X was last located on a boat at 40° S and 20° W in the ____________ ____________, and the boat is traveling west toward the ____________ ____________ continent. You and your partner charter an airplane and are waiting for him at ____________________, located at 23° S and 43° W. Your mission is almost complete. You transport him back to the United States, located on the ____________ ____________ continent, and turn him over to the head of the spy ring, whose home base is in ____________________, located at 39° N and 89° W. You say goodbye to your partner and head home to wait for your next assignment.

Part 2: Relative Location

Directions: The following places are identified by their relative locations. Use the clues (and a world map if necessary) to name each country.

1. This country/continent is located in the Pacific Ocean. New Zealand lies southeast of it.

   ____

2. This Asian country is between Russia and China. ______________________

3. This African country is bordered by the Democratic Republic of the Congo on the north, Tanzania on the northeast, Angola on the west, and Namibia and Botswana on the south.

   ____

4. This country is in Europe. Germany is to the north, Italy to the south, France to the west and Austria to the east of the country. ______________________

5. This country is north of the United States on the North American continent.

   ____

6. This country borders the Atlantic Ocean on the South American continent. Guyana, Suriname, and French Guiana are to the north. ______________________

Student Guide
Lesson 4: Maps, Maps, Maps

Maps help us understand the Earth by giving us a picture of the size and shape of land and water. Globes can show the Earth fairly accurately. But it is impossible to transfer the round Earth onto flat paper precisely. Since every flat map has to be distorted in some way, mapmakers always have to compromise. They have to decide the best way to show the Earth. Some map projections are better for some purposes, others are better for other purposes.

Lesson Objectives

- Recognize the limitations of maps.
- Analyze map projections to discern their differences.
- Recognize major map projections and their purposes.

PREPARE

Approximate lesson time is 60 minutes.

Materials

For the Student

The Human Odyssey: Prehistory Through the Middle Ages edited by Klee, Cribb, and Holdren

Keywords and Pronunciation

Mercator (muhr-KAY-tuhr)
Mollweide (mohl-VID-uh)

LEARN

Activity 1: Flattening Out the Earth *(Offline)*

Do you want to see for yourself why a flat map will always have some distortion?

1. Blow up a balloon.
2. Draw an outline of North America on it, using most of the balloon from top to bottom.
3. Pop the balloon and flatten out your drawing. Does it still look like North America?

If you don't have a balloon, draw on an orange, and then peel it and flatten the peel. Now answer the following questions in your history journal.

1. Which area of the map remains the most accurate--the center, the northernmost and southernmost areas, or the easternmost and westernmost areas?
2. If you could zoom in on a small location on your map, would it be more or less distorted than the entire map?
3. On the basis of your observations, which would you say would be more accurate and less distorted--a street map of your neighborhood or a road map of Canada? Why?

Activity 2: Map Projections *(Online)*

When cartographers make a map, they project the geographic grid of the round Earth onto a flat sheet of paper. To deal with distortion, cartographers have devised special ways of representing the round Earth on a flat surface. These are called *map projections.* There are many different projections. Let's consider the strengths and weaknesses of some of the most popular ones.

Activity 3: Choosing the Right Projection *(Online)*

Step into the role of a cartographer! Use the knowledge you have gained in this lesson to select the right projection for each use. You can also use the atlas in your book as a reference.
Click The Right Projection to begin.

ASSESS

Lesson Assessment: Maps, Maps, Maps (*Online*)

You will complete an online assessment covering the main points of this lesson. Your assessment will be scored by the computer.

LEARN

Activity 4. Optional: Maps, Maps, Maps *(Online)*

The next activity is OPTIONAL. It's provided for enrichment or extra practice, but not required for completion of this lesson. You may skip this activity.
Mapping the oceans and seas was especially important for early explorers and adventurers.

Student Guide
Lesson 5: Thinking Geographically

Each place on Earth has a unique blend of human, physical, and environmental characteristics. When several places share one or more similar characteristics, they form a *region.*

Lesson Objectives

- Recognize examples of the geographic concepts of place and region.

PREPARE

Approximate lesson time is 60 minutes.

Materials

For the Student

History Journal

LEARN
Activity 1: Place and Region *(Online)*

Activity 2: Home *(Offline)*

Home: Place

What makes your home area unique? Is there a landmark building that is easily recognizable? Are there mountains where you live? Do you live near the ocean or another large body of water? What is the climate like? How is your area different from other areas in your state? All of these things make up a place--your home.

Follow these directions to make a My Home collage:

1. Find pictures and words from your local newspaper or a regional magazine that show the uniqueness of your city, town, or area. If you prefer, you can draw pictures that represent your home area.
2. Cut out the pictures and glue them on a sheet of construction paper. Remember, the pictures should show characteristics that combine to make the place you live unique.
3. Write a few sentences at the bottom of the collage explaining how your small part of the world is unique.

Home: Region

Geographers and cartographers divide the United States into regions. Each region is an area defined by certain unifying human and physical characteristics. These features make one region different from another region.

Not all geographers divide the country into the same regions. You'll see the United States divided up in several different ways. The following regions are commonly used:

- Northeast
- Mid-Atlantic
- Southeast
- Midwest
- Southwest
- West

Do you live in one of these regions? Which one? The Northeast? The Midwest? The West? If you're not sure, use a resource such as an atlas to help you find out.

Now write a paragraph explaining what you think makes the area in which you live a region. Is it because all the places in the region have a similar climate? If so, what is the climate? Is the economy in the area based on agriculture? If so, what is grown? Is the land flat? Hilly? Mountainous?

ASSESS

Lesson Assessment: Thinking Geographically (*Online*)

You will complete an online assessment covering the main points of this lesson. Your assessment will be scored by the computer.

Student Guide
Lesson 6. Optional: Your Choice

You may use today's lesson time to do one or more of the following:

- Complete work in progress.
- Complete the Beyond the Lesson activity in any lesson in this unit.
- Go on to the next lesson.

Please mark this lesson complete to proceed to the next lesson in the course.

Lesson Objectives

- Explore knowledge and skills taught in this course.

PREPARE

Approximate lesson time is 60 minutes.

Student Guide
Lesson 7: Unit Review and Assessment

You've finished the unit! Now it's time to review what you've learned and take the Unit Assessment.

Lesson Objectives

- Demonstrate mastery of important knowledge and skills in this unit.
- Define history and identify reasons for studying it.
- Recognize time-related terms and their uses.
- Use maps, globes, latitude, and longitude to determine absolute and relative locations.
- Recognize examples of major geographical concepts, including place and region.
- Define *history* and identify reasons for studying history.
- Demonstrate familiarity with the organization and format of *The Human Odyssey: Prehistory Through the Middle Ages.*
- Identify on a map the seven continents and four oceans.

PREPARE

Approximate lesson time is 60 minutes.

Materials

For the Student

History Journal

Question Review Table

LEARN

Activity 1: Offline Review *(Offline)*

Start off by reviewing your History Journal. You should:

- Look at activity sheets you completed for this unit.
- Review Keywords from this unit.
- Read through any writing assignments you completed during the unit.
- Review any offline assessments you took.

When you've finished, come back online to finish the review.

Activity 2: A Look Back *(Online)*

ASSESS

Unit Assessment: History: The Map of Time (*Offline*)

You will complete an offline assessment covering some of the main points of this unit. Your assessment will be scored by the teacher.

LEARN

Activity 3. Optional: Unit Assessment Review Table *(Online)*

If you earned a score of **less than 80%** on the Unit Assessment, complete the activity.

If you earned a score of **80% or greater**, you may skip this activity.

Let's prepare to retake the Unit Assessment:

- Identify the questions that you answered incorrectly.
- Complete the appropriate review activities listed in the table.

Assessment Date

Unit 1: History: The Map of Time

Before you retake the Unit Assessment, use the table to figure out which activities you should review.

Question Review Table

Circle the numbers of the questions that you missed on the Unit Assessment. Review the activities that correspond with these questions.

Question	Lesson	Review Activity
1,2	1: History and You	History: What Is It and Why Study It?
3,4,5,6,7,8,9,10,11,12,13	2: When?	Keeping Track
14,15	3: Where?	Where in the World? Absolute and Relative
16	5: Thinking Geographically	Place and Region Home

Student Guide

Unit 2: From Gathering to Growing
Lesson 1: How Long Is Long?

Imagine finding food, clothes, and shelter if there were no stores, factories, or farms. Long ago, everyone constantly struggled to survive. Today, in much of the world, only a few people produce food; most are involved in other activities. We create cities, art, and governments--all part of civilization. But what is civilization? How did it begin? How do we know what happened before people kept records? Historians and archaeologists help answer these and thousands of other questions.

You are studying history--the story of the human past and of change over time. One way to study history is to read a history book. But what if there were no history books? What if people didn't even know how to write? There *was* a time when writing did not exist. Historians call this period *prehistory*--the time before written records. They use the term *history* to describe the period from which we *do* have written records. And believe it or not, prehistory covers a much, much longer span of time than history does!

Lesson Objectives

- Describe prehistory and history in terms of written records.
- Compare prehistory with history in terms of span of time.
- Identify spans of time between the emergence of hunting-gathering societies and the beginning of agriculture, the beginning of civilization, and the twenty-first century.
- Recognize that early humans were nomadic hunter-gatherers and cave dwellers.
- Describe characteristics of hunter-gatherers.
- Identify the period of time when humans made tools from stone.
- List examples of ways early humans used and adapted to their environment.
- Describe the importance of the human discovery of the use of fire.
- Explain the main reasons for human migrations at the end of the Ice Age.

PREPARE

Approximate lesson time is 60 minutes.

Materials

For the Student

Visualizing Time

The Human Odyssey: Prehistory Through the Middle Ages edited by Klee, Cribb, and Holdren

History Journal

LEARN

Activity 1: Long Ago *(Offline)*

Use What You Know

Complete the Visualizing Time sheet.

ASSESS

Lesson Assessment: How Long Is Long? (*Online*)

You will complete an online assessment covering the main points of this lesson. Your assessment will be scored by the computer.

LEARN

Activity 2: How Long is Long? *(Offline)*

What was life like 5,300 years ago? Did humans use fire or tools? Did they hunt or farm? To find out, read Chapter 1, the beginning to "The Move to Mesopotamia," pages 17-20. Then, answer these questions in your History Journal:

1. Where did early humans seek shelter?
2. What is a *hunter-gatherer*?
3. Why is the era of early humans called the Stone Age?
4. Name at least three ways that people of the Stone Age used their environment.
5. Name at least three ways that early humans adapted to their environment.
6. Why was the use of fire an important discovery?
7. Why did early humans travel in bands, or groups?
8. What happened during the last ice age that allowed people to migrate, or move, to new places in search of food? Why wouldn't you be able to follow their routes today?

Name ______________________________ Date ______________________________

Visualizing Time

Figuring Time

Number the dates in chronological order. Recognize that all dates are approximate. Refer to the book's introduction if you need a refresher on how to order dates.

_____ 1. The practice of agriculture begins – approximately 8000 B.C.

_____ 2. The Sumerians develop writing – approximately 3200 B.C.

_____ 3. Humans develop the first stone tools – approximately 2,500,000 B.C.

_____ 4. Cities develop along the Tigris and Euphrates rivers – approximately 3500 B.C.

_____ 5. Last ice age ends – approximately 10,000 B.C.

Now answer these questions based on the information above.

6. How much time passed between the development of the first stone tools and the development of agriculture?

____

7. How much time passed between the end of the last ice age and the development of agriculture?

____

8. How much time passed between the time when farming began and when cities developed along the Tigris and Euphrates?

____

Visualizing Time

Visualizing Time

Now try to see these long spans of time by plotting dates on a time line. On this time line, 1 inch = 2,000 years. Because each inch covers so much time, your marks will be approximate. For example, you can mark the current year (Today) and the year A.D. 2000 at the same point on the time line.

Today

Write today's date at the end of the time line.

9. Measure and mark the year 1,000, when the Vikings first explored North America.

10. Measure and mark the year 27 B.C., the year that Octavian became the first emperor of Rome.

11. Measure and mark the approximate date of the beginning of agriculture.

12. Measure and mark the time that Sumerians developed writing—approximately 3200 B.C.

13. Measure and mark the time that cities began to develop along the Tigris and Euphrates rivers.

14. How far would you have to measure back from Today to show when humans developed the first stone tools?

Visualizing Time

Now let's try to "see" the span of history and prehistory. To do so, you'll need a much larger time line.

- Collect a ruler and three pencils or colorful sticks to use as markers.

- Go outside to a large, clear area and place your first marker on the ground. This represents Today.

- Place your next marker a little more than 2.5 inches away from the first. This time span represents the amount of time man has kept a written record of events. This span of time is considered *history*.

- Now, walk 35 **very big** steps in a straight line away from the second marker. Place your third marker on the ground and look back. The distance between the second and third markers represents *prehistory*—the period time before human beings could write. As you can see, prehistory spans a **much** greater length of time than history does!

15. Write a paragraph in your History Journal describing your reaction to what you learned from the second time line.

Student Guide
Lesson 2: Prehistory: Hunter Gatherers and Cave Dwellers

Early humans were hunter-gatherers and cave dwellers. From the beginning, humans distinguished themselves as thinking, inventive beings. They used fire to cook food, warm themselves, and frighten animals away. They crafted stone tools to help them hunt animals and fashion skins into clothing and shelter. Usually, we think of that way of life as belonging to the distant past. But did you know that there are people in the world today who still live very much as people did in the Stone Age?

Lesson Objectives

- Recognize that early humans were nomadic hunter-gatherers and cave dwellers.
- Describe characteristics of hunter-gatherers.
- Identify the period of time when humans made tools from stone.
- List examples of ways early humans used and adapted to their environment.
- Describe the importance of the human discovery of the use of fire.
- Explain the main reasons for human migrations at the end of the Ice Age.

PREPARE

Approximate lesson time is 60 minutes.

Materials

For the Student

The Human Odyssey: Prehistory Through the Middle Ages edited by Klee, Cribb, and Holdren

History Journal

Otzi's Artifacts

Keywords and Pronunciation

history : the period of the past for which written records exist
nomadic : wandering from place to place in search of food
prehistory : the period of time before human beings could write

---

LEARN
Activity 1: In Tune with Nature *(Offline)*

Check Your Reading

- Check your answers to the questions from yesterday's Read On (Chapter 1, beginning to "The Move to Mesopotamia," pages 17-20).
- Then, write a brief definition for each of the following terms in your History Journal. When you have finished, compare your definitions with those in the Keywords section of this lesson.
  history
  nomadic
  prehistory

Activity 2: Prehistory: Hunter Gatherers and Cave Dwellers *(Online)*

In 1991, a group of people hiking in the mountains near the border of Austria and Italy stumbled across something amazing--the body of a man embedded in ice. It turned out that the man had lived and died more than 5,000 years ago. Archaeologists dubbed him "Otzi the Iceman." What did archaeologists learn from Otzi? Use the following website to complete the Otzi's Artifacts sheet:

Museum of Archaeology

Click on the following topics in the website:

The mummy as a World Sensation

The Iceman's Clothing and Equipment

Activity 3: Prehistory: Hunter Gatherers and Cave Dwellers *(Online)*

Open the interactive map of the Bering Land Bridge to see how the migratory patterns of animals caused people to move from place to place.

ASSESS

Lesson Assessment: Prehistory: Hunter Gatherers and Cave Dwellers *(Online)*

You will complete an online assessment covering the main points of this lesson. Your assessment will be scored by the computer.

Name ______________________________ Date ______________________________

Otzi's Artifacts

Using information from the website, complete the table by adding information about Otzi's artifacts.

Artifacts	Ax	Bow, Arrow, and Quiver	Dagger
What materials is it made of?			
What might Otzi have used it for?			

What do these artifacts tell us about the life and times of the person who made them and used them?

____
____
____
____
____
____
____
____

Otzi's Artifacts

What evidence suggests Otzi was a hunter/gatherer?

What evidence tells you Otzi was **not** part of the Stone Age?

Student Guide
Lesson 3: Cave Paintings: What Do We Know About Lascaux?

Hidden away in a cave in southwestern France is a series of 17,000-year-old paintings and engravings on the cave walls. It is unlikely that we will ever know exactly what the artist or artists were trying to say, but this prehistoric artwork does give us some insight into the lives of Stone Age humans.

Lesson Objectives

- Explain the significance of cave art.
- Analyze prehistoric art for information on the lives or beliefs of Stone Age humans.
- Explain how and when farming and herding developed in Mesopotamia.
- Describe the climatic changes that encouraged migration to Mesopotamia.
- Define agricultural revolution, slash-and-burn agriculture, and domestication.
- Identify on a map the Tigris and Euphrates Rivers, the Persian Gulf, and the major physical features of Mesopotamia.

PREPARE

Approximate lesson time is 60 minutes.

Materials

For the Student

Observing Lascaux

The Human Odyssey: Prehistory Through the Middle Ages edited by Klee, Cribb, and Holdren

History Journal

Keywords and Pronunciation

Lascaux (lah-SKOH)

LEARN

Activity 1: Cave Paintings: What Do We Know About Lascaux? *(Online)*

Have you ever been in a cave? You may have found it dark, dank, and kind of creepy. Imagine creating a work of art on the walls of a cave. Quite a challenge, wouldn't you say?

Yet people have discovered paintings and engravings on the walls of caves in countries all over the world--in Spain, France, India, Russia, Brazil, and the United States (to name a few). Some of the artwork dates back to prehistoric times.

Go online and examine some of these Stone Age masterpieces. As you explore some cave art, note the time when the artworks were created. Are they all from prehistoric times? What about the art itself? Do you see any similarities or common themes? How about differences? Why do you think people in so many parts of the world made paintings and engravings in caves?

Activity 2: Cave Paintings: What Do We Know About Lascaux? *(Online)*

Some of the most awesome prehistoric cave paintings in the world are located in France in the cave of Lascaux

Go online to the official
Cave of Lascaux (French Ministry of Culture and Communication)
website and find out how a group of teenagers accidentally stumbled upon this amazing Stone Age art gallery. Take a virtual tour through its chambers and passageways. Be sure to visit the Great Hall of the Bulls and the Shaft of the Dead Man.
Print the Observing Lascaux sheet. As you view the paintings and engravings on the website, complete the sheet.

ASSESS

Lesson Test: Cave Paintings: What Do We Know About Lascaux? (*Online*)

You will complete an online assessment covering the main objectives of this lesson. Your assessment will be scored by the computer.

LEARN

Activity 3: Cave Paintings: What Do We Know About Lascaux? *(Offline)*

- Read Chapter 1, "The Move to Mesopotamia," to "Harnessing the River and Irrigating the Land," pages 21-27.
- As you read, answer the following questions in your History Journal:

1. What are the major physical features of the area that encompassed Mesopotamia?
2. What climatic changes encouraged the development of agriculture in Mesopotamia?
3. How and when did farming develop in Mesopotamia?
4. How and when did herding develop in Mesopotamia?

- Write definitions for the following terms:

agricultural revolution
slash-and-burn agriculture
domestication

Name _______________________________ Date _______________

Observing Lascaux

Using information from the Cave of Lascaux website, complete the table below.

Observe

Make notes about what you see. Use details to describe the images in your notes. (For example, instead of writing “a bull,” you might write “a red bull with its head down.”) You also might want to note some things you don’t see that you might expect to see in a painting.

Animals	Objects/Signs	People	Activities

Analyze

Based on your tour of Lascaux, list at least three things that you can infer or conclude about the lives or beliefs of Stone Age people, and what led you to that conclusion.

1. ____
2. ____
3. ____

Conclude

Based on your observations and reading, why do you think a prehistoric person or people made paintings and engravings in the Cave of Lascaux?

____

Student Guide
Lesson 4: From Nomad to Farmer

Climate changes that took place over thousands of years gradually pushed people to change their ways. Women and men learned to control some aspects of their environment. This control led to a dramatic change in the way people acquired food. Where did the revolution begin? What favorable conditions existed?

Lesson Objectives

- Explain how and when farming and herding developed in Mesopotamia.
- Define *agricultural revolution, slash-and-burn agriculture*, and *domestication.*
- Describe the climatic changes that encouraged migration to Mesopotamia.
- Identify on a map the Tigris and Euphrates Rivers, the Persian Gulf, and the major physical features of Mesopotamia.
- Recognize how the channeling of floodwaters affected the development of civilization.

PREPARE

Approximate lesson time is 60 minutes.

Materials

For the Student

- Identifying Cause and Effect
- Map of Ancient Mesopotamia
- The Human Odyssey: Prehistory Through the Middle Ages edited by Klee, Cribb, and Holdren
- History Journal

Keywords and Pronunciation

agricultural revolution : the giant step forward that humans took when they deliberately planted seeds to grow crops

domestication : the practice of taming wild animals

Euphrates (yoo-FRAY-teez)

Mesopotamia (meh-suh-puh-TAY-mee-uh)

slash-and-burn agriculture : a method of preparing land for farming by slashing the bark of trees to kill them, and then burning the brush and scattering the ashes

Sumer (SOO-mur)

Sumerians (soo-MEHR-ee-uhnz)

Tigris (TIY-gruhs)

Zagros (ZA-gruhs)

LEARN

Activity 1: The Land Between Two Rivers *(Online)*

Check Your Reading

Review Chapter 1, "The Move to Mesopotamia," to "Harnessing the River and Irrigating the Land," pages 21-27.

- Use the Lesson Answer Key to check your answers to the reading questions in your History Journal.
- Then, compare your definitions for *agricultural revolution, domestication,* and *slash-and-burn agriculture* against those in the Keywords section of this lesson.

Use What You Know

Why did people settle the river valley between the Tigris and Euphrates? What sort of events took place that caused nomads to become farmers? Complete the Identifying Cause and Effect sheet to show what happened.

Focus on Geography

View the map of Mesopotamia on page 22 of your textbook and use it to complete the Map of Ancient Mesopotamia sheet. Use this comparison to gain an understanding of physical features and geographic influences in Mesopotamia.

ASSESS

Lesson Assessment: From Nomad to Farmer (*Online*)

You will complete an online assessment covering the main points of this lesson. Your assessment will be scored by the computer.

LEARN

Activity 2: From Nomad to Farmer *(Offline)*

Read Chapter 1, "Harnessing the River and Irrigating the Land," to "Creating a Surplus," pages 28-32.

Activity 3. Optional: From Nomad to Farmer *(Online)*

This activity is OPTIONAL. It's provided for enrichment or extra practice, but not required for completion of this lesson. You may skip this activity.

Explore modern, ancient, physical, and resource maps of
Mesopotamia
at
The British Museum: Maps
.

Name Date

Map of Ancient Mesopotamia

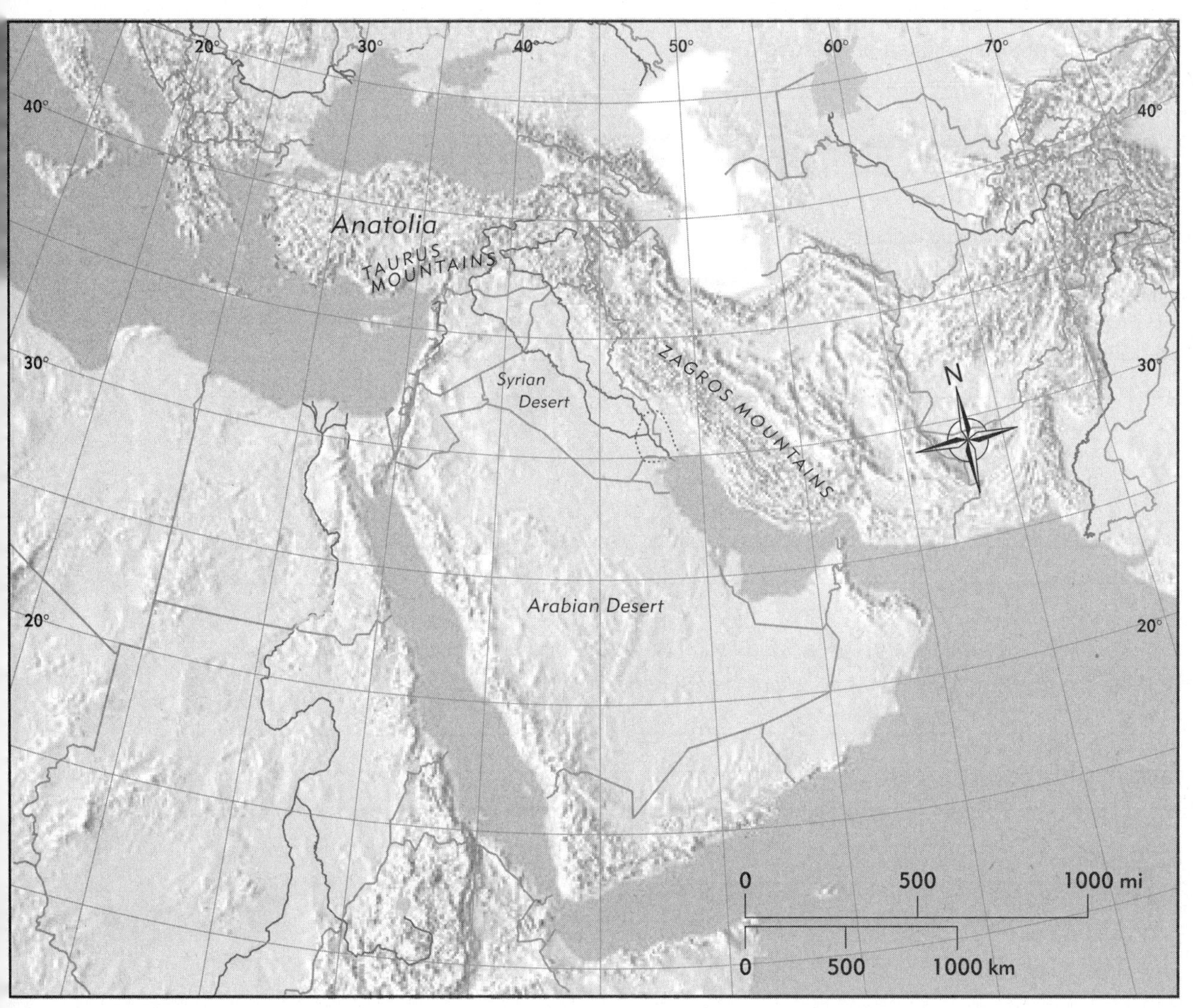

Complete the Map of Ancient Mesopotamia to gain an understanding of physical features and geographic influences in Mesopotamia:

Labeling the Map:

1. Label the Tigris and Euphrates rivers and color them blue.
2. Label the Mediterranean Sea and the Persian Gulf and color them blue.
3. Locate the Zagros Mountains and color them brown.
4. Locate the Syrian and Arabian deserts and color them tan.
5. Label the area called Mesopotamia.

Map of Ancient Mesopotamia

Labeling the Map:

6. Describe the relative location of Mesopotamia.

7. Where in this area would ancient people have likely farmed and why? (Consider the relative location.)

8. From what mountains do the Tigris and Euphrates rivers flow? Into what body of water do they flow?

9. How would you describe the physical features of northern Mesopotamia? How would you describe the physical features of southern Mesopotamia?

10. What was it like to live in ancient Mesopotamia? What was the new land like?

Name _______________________________________ Date ____________________ 

Identifying Cause and Effect

Write each effect in the appropriate space using the Word Bank to help you identify them.

Word Bank

- Villages develop.
- Rising temperatures support agriculture.
- People settle in valleys along the Tigris and Euphrates rivers.
- People develop slash-and-burn agriculture.
- People begin to farm the land.
- People learn to domesticate animals.

Cause	Effect
1. The Ice Age ends.	______________________
2. People discover that they can grow food by scattering seeds.	______________________
3. People need more fertile farmland.	______________________
4. People need a steady supply of meat.	______________________
5. Farmers and herders move from northern Mesopotamia.	______________________
6. Agricultural revolution and domestication of animals gives people a steady supply of food.	______________________

Student Guide
Lesson 5: Leaping Forward

As more people learned to farm, societies changed. Some societies became civilizations. What is a civilization? When the Sumerians harnessed the river and irrigated the land, had they created a civilization? How do historians define a civilization?

Lesson Objectives

- Recognize how the channeling of floodwaters affected the development of civilization.
- Identify the earliest known civilization.
- Identify the criteria used to define a civilization.
- Explain the difference between civilization and other forms of social organization, such as hunting-gathering, agricultural, and herding societies.

PREPARE

Approximate lesson time is 60 minutes.

Materials

For the Student

More Cause and Effect: The Giant Leap Forward

Paragraph Outline

The Human Odyssey: Prehistory Through the Middle Ages edited by Klee, Cribb, and Holdren

History Journal

Keywords and Pronunciation

Sumer (SOO-mur)

Sumerians (soo-MEHR-ee-uhnz)

LEARN
Activity 1: Expansion *(Online)*

Read

- Finish Chapter 1 by reading from "Creating a Surplus'" to the end, pages 32-33.
- Fill out the More Cause & Effect: The Giant Leap Forward sheet to check the reading you did today and at the end of the last lesson.

Use What You Know

What do we mean when we say Sumer is the first known civilization in the world? Write a paragraph that answers the question: How did Sumer meet the criteria to be considered a civilization?

To write the paragraph:

- Print the Paragraph Outline sheet.
- Use your More Cause & Effect: The Giant Leap Forward sheet to help you complete the outline.
- Be sure your outline includes a topic sentence and the three criteria, or requirements that define a civilization.
- Write the paragraph.
- Read the paragraph over and correct any mistakes you find.

ASSESS

Lesson Assessment: Leaping Forward (*Online*)

You will complete an online assessment covering the main points of this lesson. Your assessment will be scored by the computer.

Name ____________________ Date ____________________

More Cause & Effect: The Giant Leap Forward

Directions: Identify the effects and write each one in the appropriate space.

Cause	Effect
1. The people of Sumer built levees along the river and irrigated crops.	____________________
2. Sumerians produced a surplus of food.	____________________
3. Sumerians divided up the labor and developed specialized skills.	____________________

Putting it all Together

4. In the cause and effect exercise above, what did you notice about the effects?

____

____

5. How do we define a civilization?

____

____

____

6. Where was the world's first civilization created?

____

Name Date

Paragraph Outline

Guiding Question: How did Sumer meet the criteria to be considered a civilization?

Your More Cause and Effect sheet has mapped out the main ideas you will need to include in your paragraph. Now organize them in the way you will use them in your paragraph by filling in the outline form below.

- Write your topic sentence.
- Decide which pieces of information you want to use to support your topic sentence and arrange them in the order you will use them.
- If you would like, you can further divide subtopics into specific facts.

Topic Sentence: ____________________

A.
   1.
   2.

B.
   1.
   2.

C.
   1.
   2.

- Use a new sheet of loose-leaf paper to write your paragraph. Keep your outline and More Cause & Effect sheet where you can see them easily.
- Use your topic sentence to introduce your paragraph. Add a sentence of general information or explanation before or after it. For example, you might explain that even though earlier people had customs and art, they still weren't considered a civilization.
- Follow your outline to write the paragraph.

Student Guide
Lesson 6: Unit Review and Assessment

You've finished the unit! Now it's time to review what you've learned and take the Unit Assessment.

Lesson Objectives

- Distinguish between *prehistory* and *history*.
- Describe characteristics of Stone Age hunting-gathering societies.
- Describe the development of agricultural and pastoral societies.
- Identify the geographic features of areas of Southwest Asia where farming communities are believed to have begun.
- Explain the roles of a surplus of food, division of labor, and the building of cities in the development of civilization.
- List examples of ways prehistoric people adapted to and influenced their environments.
- Identify the factors that allowed the development of farming in Southwest Asia.
- Describe how civilization differs from other forms of social organization.
- Explain how geography and climatic conditions combined to encourage humans to migrate.

PREPARE

Approximate lesson time is 60 minutes.

Materials

For the Student

The Human Odyssey: Prehistory Through the Middle Ages edited by Klee, Cribb, and Holdren

History Journal

Question Review Table

LEARN

Activity 1: Offline Review *(Online)*

Start off by reviewing your History Journal. You should:

- Look at activity sheets you completed for this unit.
- Review the Keywords from this unit.
- Read through any writing assignments you completed during the unit.
- Review any offline assessments you took.

When you have finished, go back online to take the assessment.

ASSESS

Unit Assessment: From Gathering to Growing, Part 1 (*Online*)

Complete the computer-scored portion of the Unit Assessment. When you have finished, complete the teacher-scored portion of the assessment and submit it to your teacher.

Unit Assessment: From Gathering to Growing, Part 2 (*Offline*)

Complete the teacher-scored portion of the Unit Assessment and submit it to your teacher.

LEARN

Activity 2: Unit Assessment Review Table *(Online)*

If you earned a score of **less than 80%** on the Unit Assessment, complete the activity.

If you earned a score of **80% or greater**, you may skip this activity.

Let's prepare to retake the Unit Assessment:

- Identify the questions that you answered incorrectly.
- Complete the appropriate review activities listed in the table.

Activity 3: Read On *(Offline)*

Read Chapter 2, from the beginning to "The First Clues: Old Stories," pages 35-36.

Assessment Date

Unit 2: From Gathering to Growing

Before you retake the Unit Assessment, use the table to figure out which activities you should review.

Question Review Table

Circle the numbers of the questions that you missed on the Unit Assessment. Review the activities that correspond with these questions.

Question	Lesson	Review Activity
1,5,11	1: How Long is Long?	Long Ago
2,6,16	2: Prehistory: Hunter Gatherers and Cave Dwellers	In Tune with Nature
3,4,7,8,9,12,14,15,19	4: From Nomad to Farmer	The Land Between Two Rivers
13	2: Prehistory: Hunter Gatherers and Cave Dwellers	In Tune Use What You Know
17,18,19,20	5: Leaping Forward	Expansion

Student Guide

Unit 3: The Mesopotamian Moment
Lesson 1: How Do We Know?

Agriculture, a system of writing, the wheel, and written law all developed in one small area of the world--Mesopotamia. How do we know? We have solid evidence. As archaeologists and historians continue to work in the area between the Tigris and Euphrates Rivers, our knowledge grows and changes. People a century ago knew only a fraction of what you will know about Mesopotamia. Archaeological digs and written records tell us how early people lived and worked.

Prehistoric people did not leave any written records; therefore, archaeologists and historians must piece together information about the past. They study human fossils and artifacts such as tools, jewelry, or pottery. Their investigations aren't easy or exact, but the results are fascinating.

Lesson Objectives

- Distinguish between the work of historians and archaeologists.
- Describe ways in which archaeologists draw conclusions about people of the past.
- Name at least three clues that helped archaeologists and historians document the existence of Sumer.

PREPARE

Approximate lesson time is 60 minutes.

Materials

For the Student

- Historian, Archaeologist, or Both
- Time Capsule
- The Human Odyssey: Prehistory Through the Middle Ages edited by Klee, Cribb, and Holdren
- History Journal

Keywords and Pronunciation

Sumer (SOO-mur)

LEARN

Activity 1: Archaeologists and Historians *(Offline)*

Check Your Reading

Check your reading (Chapter 2, from the beginning to "The First Clues: Old Stories," pages 35-36) by completing the Uncovering the Past activity online.

Use What You Know

One day, archaeologists may learn about you and where you live by examining clues. What will people centuries from now think about you and your life? What will they think you did with a pencil? With a comb? What clues will you leave that tell a lot about how you live? Of course archaeologists in the future won't be 100 percent sure that their detective work is correct, but they'll take great pains to analyze all the evidence. Complete the Historian, Archaeologist, or Both and Time Capsule sheets.

ASSESS

Lesson Assessment: How Do We Know? (*Online*)

You will complete an online assessment covering the main points of this lesson. Your assessment will be scored by the computer.

LEARN

Activity 2: How Do We Know? *(Offline)*

As you read Chapter 2, from "The First Clues: Old Stories" to "The Fourth Clue: A Key to the Strange Writing," pages 37-42, list three clues in your History Journal that helped archaeologists and historians document the existence of Sumer.

Activity 3. Optional: How Do We Know? *(Online)*

This activity is OPTIONAL. It's provided for enrichment or extra practice, but not required for completion of this lesson. You may skip this activity.

To read more about archaeology go to

Ask Dr. Dig

. Browse through the full list, and then click "General Archaeology" and read "How are artifacts classified?" and "Why is it important to draw artifacts?"

Name Date

Time Capsule

Directions: Create your own collection of artifacts (like a time capsule) by listing at least two objects for each of the seven categories on the chart below. The objects should represent today's young Americans--just like you and your friends--for people 1,000 years from now. You may add an additional category and objects in that category. An example has been included.

Categories	Artifacts to Include	* Material/Power (if applicable)	Conclusion(s) That Might be Drawn From Artifacts
Food	juice box	paper, plastic	1. People sometimes ate in locations other than the central family dining area. 2. People did not reuse containers. 3. People ate artificial substances (from the ingredients listed on the box). 4. People did not usually grow their own food.
Clothing			
Housing			
Daily Life			
Tools			
Art			
Ceremonies			
Other Category			

Name Date

Historian, Archaeologist, or Both

Historians and archaeologists both base their conclusions on hard evidence, but the type of evidence they use isn't always the same. Historians rely mainly on written or oral records to learn about the past. Archaeologists are scientists who learn about the past by sifting through the dirt and studying objects from the past.

Directions: Decide whether each description applies best to a historian, an archaeologist, or both. Write each description in the correct location on the Venn diagram.

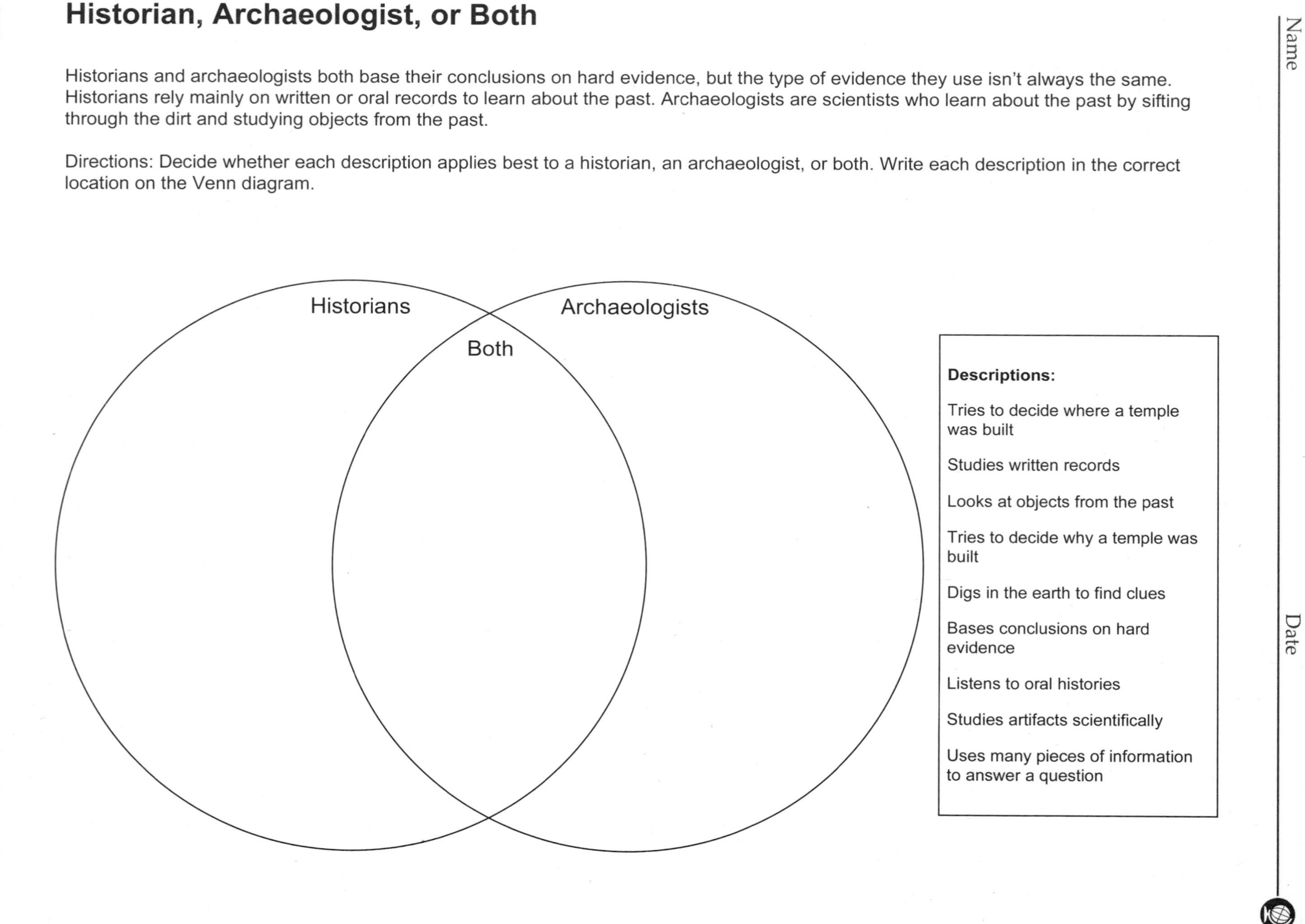

Descriptions:

Tries to decide where a temple was built

Studies written records

Looks at objects from the past

Tries to decide why a temple was built

Digs in the earth to find clues

Bases conclusions on hard evidence

Listens to oral histories

Studies artifacts scientifically

Uses many pieces of information to answer a question

Student Guide
Lesson 2: Finding Sumer

Just when the archaeologists and historians studying the ancient civilizations in Mesopotamia thought they had the answer, another clue would pop up. You've already read about four clues that led to the discovery of Sumer, but there were more.

Lesson Objectives

- Name at least three clues that helped archaeologists and historians document the existence of Sumer.
- Identify methods and work of historians and archaeologists.

PREPARE

Approximate lesson time is 60 minutes.

Materials

For the Student

Who, What, Where

The Human Odyssey: Prehistory Through the Middle Ages edited by Klee, Cribb, and Holdren

History Journal

Keywords and Pronunciation

Mesopotamia (meh-suh-puh-TAY-mee-uh)
Sumer (SOO-mur)

LEARN
Activity 1: Sumer Found *(Online)*

Check Your Reading

While you were reading the previous selection (Chapter 2, from "The First Clues: Old Stories" to "The Fourth Clue: A Key to the Strange Writing," pages 37-42), you were to list at least three things that helped archaeologists and historians document the existence of Sumer. Check your History Journal to see if you listed at least three of the following:

- stories
- writing
- mounds containing the remains of cities
- clay tablets
- cities built upon cities
- various artifacts

Read

Complete Part 1 of the Who, What, Where sheet as you read Chapter 2, from "The Fourth Clue: A Key to the Strange Writing" to the end, pages 42-45. Check your answers against those in the Lesson Answer Key.

Use What You Know

Complete Part 2 of the Who, What, Where sheet. Check your answers against those in the Lesson Answer Key.

ASSESS

Lesson Assessment: Finding Sumer (*Online*)

You will complete an online assessment covering the main points of this lesson. Your assessment will be scored by the computer.

Name Date 

Who, What, Where

Part 1

Directions: Use the Word Bank to answer the questions and identify **who** helped find ancient Sumer, **what** artifacts they found, and **where** they found them. Some of the words in the Word Bank will not be used.

1. I am the great Greek historian who recorded old stories about ancient people. Who am I?

 ____

2. I am the Italian scholar who went to southern Mesopotamia to look for proof that the old stories were true. Who am I? ______________________________

3. I am the strange type of writing found on old bricks in southern Mesopotamia. What am I?

 ____

4. I am the mounds in Mesopotamia that rose up above the flatness of the land. What am I?

 ____

5. I am the place that held the key to unlocking cuneiform writing. Where am I?

 ____

6. I am the king who carved a message in three languages, which eventually helped scholars decipher ancient messages. Who am I? ______________________________

7. I am the pieces of pottery, tablets, helmets and spears found at an ancient site. What am I?

 ____

8. I spent twelve years excavating the Sumerian city of Ur. Who am I?

 ____

9. I am the place that is home to ancient Sumer. Where am I?

 ____

Word Bank
Iran artifacts Persia hieroglyphics
Pietro della Valle Darius Odysseus Herodotus
tels Sir Leonard Woolley Iraq cuneiform

Part 2

1. Imagine you were an archaeologist working with Sir Leonard Woolley in Iraq. Which of the discoveries do you think was the most exciting? Which discovery helped you most in determining what had happened to the people whose remains you found? Explain your answer.

2. Suppose you were a historian studying ancient Sumer. How would your work be different from Woolley's work?

3. Sir Leonard Woolley worked on excavating Ur for twelve years. What years were they?

4. What kinds of changes do you think will occur in the work of archaeologists in the next hundred years?

5. Which work would you prefer, the work of the historian or the archaeologist? Why?

Student Guide
Lesson 3: Cities of Sumer

What is *culture?* Culture includes a people's traditions, language, religion, customs, government, and family structure. It also includes the everyday details of what the people wear and eat and how they work and play--their whole way of life. These characteristics reflect the society's experiences, resources, values, and habits.

Lesson Objectives

- Define *culture, surplus,* and *division of labor.*
- Explain how Sumerians were able to irrigate their crops and grow a surplus of food.
- Describe key physical and governmental features of Sumerian cities.
- Name three characteristics of culture.
- Analyze maps to find information about Sumerian trade.
- Recognize the characteristics of Sumerian trade, including the products traded, the location of trading partners, and the importance of trade in Sumerian life.
- Describe the advantages of using money instead of bartering.
- Identify the invention of the wheel as a major contribution of Mesopotamian civilization.

PREPARE

Approximate lesson time is 60 minutes.

Materials

For the Student

Reading Guide

The Human Odyssey: Prehistory Through the Middle Ages edited by Klee, Cribb, and Holdren

History Journal

Keywords and Pronunciation

culture : The traditions and customs of a people; their way of life and thought.

Sumer (SOO-mur)

Sumerians (soo-MEHR-ee-uhnz)

LEARN

Activity 1: Culture Clues *(Online)*

You will look at many cultures as you study history. To get started thinking about culture, think about the group of people you probably know best--American teens. Click Culture Clues and ask yourself about the whole way of life of this group of people.

Activity 2: Making It Work *(Offline)*

Read

Complete the Reading Guide as you read Chapter 3, from the beginning to *"The Beautiful Bead,"* pages 47-53.

ASSESS

Lesson Assessment: Cities of Sumer (*Online*)

You will complete an online assessment covering the main points of this lesson. Your assessment will be scored by the computer.

LEARN

Activity 3: Cities of Sumer *(Offline)*

As you read Chapter 3, "*The Beautiful Bead*," pages 53-57, look for examples of trade in Sumer.

Name ______________________________ Date ______________________________

Reading Guide

Directions: Complete this sheet as you read today's assignment.

1. Define *culture*. ______________________________

____

2. The Sumerians learned to control the flooding of the Tigris and Euphrates Rivers by building ______________ .

3. They watered their fields in dry weather by ______________________________.

4. What is *division of labor*? ______________________________

____

5. Define *surplus of food*. ______________________________

____

6. How did Sumer's surplus of food lead to the development of cities? ______________

____

____

____

7. Most houses were made of______________ .

8. Major crops included ______________ and ______________ .

9. Why did the Sumerians begin to trade with other peoples? What did they trade?

____

____

____

____

10. What improvements in transportation did the Sumerians make over time? ______________

____

11. The Sumerians first used ______________ for trade, but later switched to ______________ because ______________________________ .

12. The small group who enjoyed the wealth and beauty of Sumer included ______________, ______________ , ______________ , and ______________ .

Document Analysis

Look at the box on page 51. It is a quotation, translated into English, from an actual Sumerian document. It is a primary source, meaning that it was written by someone at that time and in that place. Historians use primary sources to learn about what happened long ago. Historians ask questions about the primary source documents they use.

We don't know exactly who wrote this document. In fact, these words were pieced together from several broken tablets. But a historian would be able to learn quite a bit by analyzing the document and combining it with what she already knows. First, the title tells us something about whom it was written for.

1. Who was the audience, according to the title?

____

Did you say it was written for farmers? That's a reasonable conclusion. But a historian would probably already know that farmers in Sumer could not read. The historian would most likely conclude the document was intended for farm managers and landowners who had access to scribes who could read.

2. A historian would read the document carefully to learn more about Sumerian society. For example, look at Tip 6. A historian might point to part of this tip as evidence that Sumerians had religious beliefs. What part of Tip 6 would support that claim?

____

Did you notice that part of the advice to farmers was to pray to a goddess? That tells us that there was religion in Sumer. It also indicates that there was more than one god/goddess and some or all of them were female.

3. Scan the rest of the document and write one question that you have about Sumerian farming or society.

____

____

Student Guide
Lesson 4: Growing Trade

The Sumerians were among the first to produce enough surplus food to trade with people in far-off places. At first they bartered their extra food for products they did not have, but eventually they developed money and began using it to pay for goods. Trade led to another important innovation. Historians believe the Sumerians invented the wheel and used it on carts to transport goods. The wheel may not seem like complex technology today, but it turned out to be one of the most important inventions of all time.

Lesson Objectives

- Analyze maps to find information about Sumerian trade.
- Recognize the characteristics of Sumerian trade, including the products traded, the location of trading partners, and the importance of trade in Sumerian life.
- Describe the advantages of using money instead of bartering.
- Identify the invention of the wheel as a major contribution of Mesopotamian civilization.

PREPARE

Approximate lesson time is 60 minutes.

Materials

For the Student

Sumer's Growing Trade

The Human Odyssey: Prehistory Through the Middle Ages edited by Klee, Cribb, and Holdren

History Journal

Keywords and Pronunciation

Sumerians (soo-MEHR-ee-uhnz)

LEARN
Activity 1: The Trading Sumerians *(Online)*

Check Your Reading

Think back to the reading assignment from the previous lesson (Chapter 3, "*The Beautiful Bead*," pages 53-57) and answer the following questions in your History Journal:

1. What surplus products did Sumer have?
2. What products did Sumerians want that came from other places?
3. What luxuries did upper-class Sumerians have?
4. List three examples of specialization, or division of labor, in Sumer.

When you have finished, use the Lesson Answer Key to check your answers.

Focus on Geography

Division of labor and surplus food had a profound impact on life in Sumer. Sumerians now had products they could trade--wheat and barley. They were soon bartering their surplus grain for items they did not have--timber, metals, and stones.

1. Refer to page 51 of Chapter 3 to identify the regions or areas where the Sumerians traded. What commodities did they get from the people of those regions? List at least three products the Sumerians traded for and the regions those products came from. One example has been completed for you.

Region: Commodity Traded

mountains to the north (present-day Syria and Turkey): stone and wood

2. On the Sumer's Growing Trade map, create a key. In the key, add symbols for each of the commodities you listed in step 1.
3. Use the map in the atlas on pages 626 and 627 to locate mountains and deserts that would have had an impact on trade routes and label them on the Sumer's Growing Trade map.
4. Using the symbols in your key, show where each commodity originated.
5. Locate possible trade routes that the merchants of Sumer might have followed to and from each of the regions you identified in Step 1. If there is water along the way, include both a land route and a water route. Draw the trade routes on the map.
6. Look at the trade routes you have drawn on the map. What are the advantages and disadvantages of using each route? What problems or obstacles might Sumerian merchants have faced trading with each place you listed in Step 1?
7. Why do you think merchants found it more convenient to pay for goods with money instead of bartering?

Go back online and click Invention of the Wheel.

ASSESS

Lesson Assessment: Growing Trade (*Online*)

You will complete an online assessment covering the main points of this lesson. Your assessment will be scored by the computer.

Name ____________________ Date ____________________

Sumer's Growing Trade

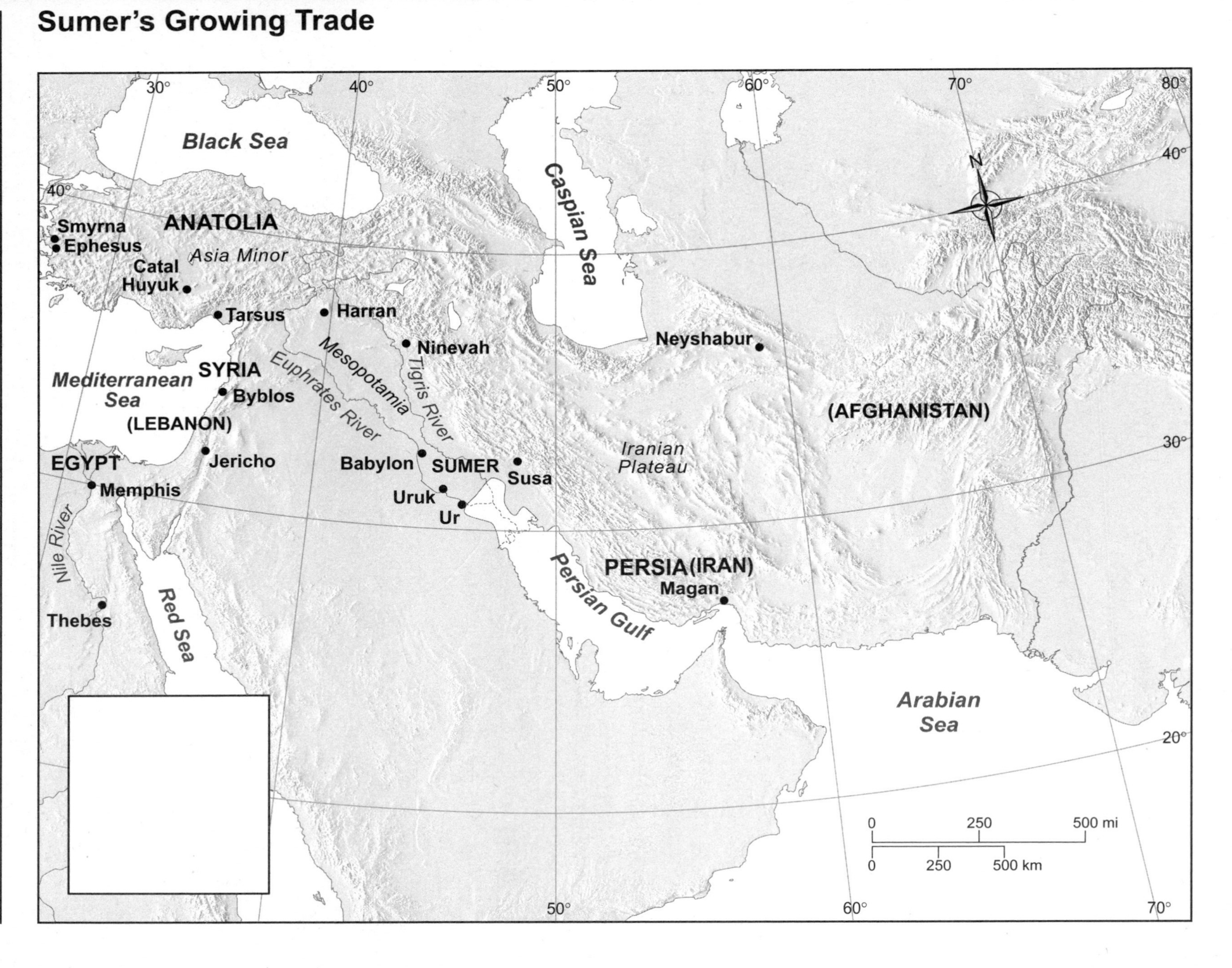

Student Guide
Lesson 5: Ideas About the Gods

The forces of nature are awe-inspiring and sometimes frightening. Throughout the ages people have tried to explain the powerful forces of nature and to make sense of the world around them.

Lesson Objectives

- Identify the major religious beliefs of the Sumerians.
- Describe how religious beliefs helped explain the apparently unpredictable workings of nature.
- Describe what the Sumerians believed were humans' responsibilities to the gods.
- Describe ziggurats.
- Identify the purpose of ziggurats.
- Analyze artifacts to describe human creativity.

PREPARE

Approximate lesson time is 60 minutes.

Materials

For the Student

The Human Odyssey: Prehistory Through the Middle Ages edited by Klee, Cribb, and Holdren

History Journal

Keywords and Pronunciation

Sumerians (soo-MEHR-ee-uhnz)

ziggurat (ZIH-guh-rat) : a stair-stepped temple built by Sumerians

---

LEARN

Activity 1: A Similar Story *(Offline)*

Read

As you read Chapter 4, up to "Ziggurats: Temples to the Gods," pages 59-64, answer these questions in your History Journal. When you have finished, compare your answers with those in the Lesson Answer Key.

1. Use the descriptions on page 64 of your text to identify the Sumerian god who would be responsible for each of these elements in nature:
   a. rain
   b. a long winter
   c. hurricane winds
   d. fertile soil
2. Why did the Sumerians identify the forces of nature with individual gods?
3. How did the Sumerians honor their gods?
4. What did Sumerians believe about human responsibilities to gods?

Use What You Know

Go online to review the Sumerian Gods and Goddesses Flash Cards. Then complete the Think Like an Archaeologist activity by identifying clues in an artifact. Print your results when you have finished.

ASSESS

Lesson Assessment: Ideas About the Gods (*Online*)

You will complete an online assessment covering the main points of this lesson. Your assessment will be scored by the computer.

LEARN

Activity 2: Ideas About the Gods *(Offline)*

As you read Chapter 4, from "Ziggurats: Temples to the Gods" to the end, pages 64-65, consider the following:

1. What role did temples play in Sumerian culture?
2. What was the significance of the placement of the temples?

Prepare to define this term:

ziggurat

Student Guide
Lesson 6: A Ziggurat to the Gods

Art and architecture reflect what a society considers important. In Sumer, people venerated the gods and built imposing stair-stepped temples as homes for the gods of their cities. The Ziggurat of Ur is one of the most famous examples.

Lesson Objectives

- Describe ziggurats.
- Identify the purpose of ziggurats.
- Describe the development of the Sumerian system of writing.
- Identify the earliest known system of writing.

PREPARE

Approximate lesson time is 60 minutes.

Materials

For the Student

The Human Odyssey: Prehistory Through the Middle Ages edited by Klee, Cribb, and Holdren

History Journal

Ziggurat of Ur

Keywords and Pronunciation

ziggurat (ZIH-guh-rat) : a stair-stepped temple built by Sumerians

---

LEARN

Activity 1: The Riches of Ur *(Online)*

Activity 2: A Ziggurat to the Gods *(Online)*

Scholars believe the earliest ziggurats were built around 3000 B.C. Many of the mud-brick towers have disintegrated over the years, but most of the ziggurat in the city of Ur has survived. Archaeologists think it was probably built around 2100 B.C.

- Go to the online activity

  to take a closer look at the ziggurat.
- Print the Ziggurat of Ur sheet and complete it as you explore. You will need to refer to your reading in the textbook to answer some of the questions.

ASSESS

Lesson Assessment: A Ziggurat to the Gods (*Online*)

You will complete an online assessment covering the main points of this lesson. Your assessment will be scored by the computer.

LEARN

Activity 3: A Ziggurat to the Gods *(Offline)*

How do we know about the culture of the Sumerians? How did the people communicate with each other? How did they pass their stories and their history from one generation to the next--and eventually to present-day historians? The Sumerians developed a way to share their ideas in a written form--archaeologists believe it was the first form of written language.
Read Chapter 5, from the beginning to "*The Epic of Gilgamesh*," pages 67-73.

Activity 4. Optional: A Ziggurat to the Gods *(Online)*

This activity is OPTIONAL. It's provided for enrichment or extra practice, but not required for completion of this lesson. You may skip this activity.
At
The British Museum: Ziggurats
you can learn more about The Temple of Ur and the artifacts found there. You can also "build" your own ziggurat by clicking Challenge.

Name ____________________ Date ____________________

Ziggurat of Ur

As you explore the Ziggurat of Ur, answer the following questions.

1. When were the earliest ziggurats built? ____________________

2. When was the Ziggurat of Ur built? ____________________

3. Who was allowed to climb the staircases of ziggurats? ____________________

____

4. What was built on either side of the center staircase to make it stronger? ____________________

____

5. What materials did the people of Ur use to make the ziggurat? ____________________

____

____

6. What two features kept the ziggurat dry? ____________________

____

7. What do archaeologists believe was on the highest terrace of a ziggurat? ____________________

____

Student Guide
Lesson 7: Writing It Down

Writing is so much a part of our lives that most of us take it for granted. But it was actually pretty tough for people to come up with a system of written communication. In fact, it took the Sumerians centuries to develop one, and it was so complex that very few people could read and write it--not even kings and priests. Literacy in Sumer, therefore, was confined to just one social class--a special group known as scribes.
Click Sumerian Writing and type your name to see what it looks like in cuneiform.

Lesson Objectives

- Describe the development of the Sumerian system of writing.
- Identify the earliest known system of writing.
- List examples of the advantages of having a writing system.
- Describe the role of scribes in Sumerian society.

PREPARE

Approximate lesson time is 60 minutes.

Materials

For the Student

The Scribe's Challenge

The Human Odyssey: Prehistory Through the Middle Ages edited by Klee, Cribb, and Holdren

History Journal

Keywords and Pronunciation

cuneiform (kyou-NEE-uh-form) : an ancient Sumerian form of writing that used wedge-shaped marks
scribe : one of an elite class of scholars whose main role in society was reading and writing

---

LEARN

Activity 1: Cuneiform *(Offline)*

Check Your Reading

Review Chapter 5, beginning to "*The Epic of Gilgamesh*," pages 67-73, and write a brief definition for these terms in your History Journal. When you have finished, compare your definitions with those in the Keywords section of this lesson.
cuneiform
scribe

Use What You Know

For every challenge there is usually a solution. Print The Scribe's Challenge and match the challenges of inventing a writing system to the solutions the Sumerians found.

Activity 2: Writing It Down *(Online)*

Find out more about cuneiform at theThe British Museum: Writing. While you're at the museum, test your archaeological skills by piecing together fragments of ancient clay tablets.

When you have finished, write a paragraph in your History Journal summarizing what you learned and questions you still have. See if you can discover the answers to your questions by doing some additional research at the library.

ASSESS

Lesson Assessment: Writing It Down (*Online*)

You will complete an online assessment covering the main points of this lesson. Your assessment will be scored by the computer.

Name Date 

The Scribe's Challenge

Match the Challenges with the Solutions to show how the Sumerians developed a system of writing.

Challenge	Solution
They needed to keep track of numbers and amounts.	They invented pens made of sharpened reeds.
They needed something to write on.	Only wealthy families could afford to send their sons to school for so long.
They needed something to write with.	They used symbols to represent numbers.
They needed to record other kinds of information besides numbers.	Scribe students went to school from sunup to sundown and copied lines of text over and over.
They discovered that pictures and objects sometimes have more than one meaning.	They chose specific marks to represent spoken sounds.
They needed to translate spoken words into written words.	They designed clay tablets that could be dried or baked.
The writing system was complicated and difficult to learn.	They developed cylinder seals to serve as signatures.
Recorders were the only people who learned to write, and therefore they had to write about everything.	They created picture writing.
People who kept records had to know the system very well.	Scribe students had to study math, science, and literature, too.
Schooling was expensive because it took years for someone to learn to write.	They used signs instead of objects to represent some words.
People who couldn't write needed to sign documents.	They developed a school to teach people the system.

Student Guide
Lesson 8: The Epic of Gilgamesh

Do you like good adventure stories with larger-than-life heroes? The Sumerians did. Their most famous epic, or tale, is about a king named Gilgamesh. Generation after generation told the story. Eventually, scribes wrote the epic poem on clay tablets that archaeologists discovered in Mesopotamia thousands of years later. *The Epic of Gilgamesh* is one of the world's earliest pieces of literature, and it's still a good story.

Lesson Objectives

- Recognize *The Epic of Gilgamesh* as a classic of Sumerian literature and the source of information about Sumerian values.
- Identify the first major literary epic in world history.

PREPARE

Approximate lesson time is 60 minutes.

Materials

For the Student

The Hero and Gilgamesh

The Human Odyssey: Prehistory Through the Middle Ages edited by Klee, Cribb, and Holdren

art supplies

History Journal

Keywords and Pronunciation

Enkidu (EN-kee-doo)

Gilgamesh (GIL-guh-mesh)

Utnapishtim (out-nuh-PISH-tim)

LEARN

Activity 1: The Hero *(Offline)*

Read

- Print The Hero and Gilgamesh sheet. Complete the first section, "Before Reading."
- In your textbook, read Chapter 5, "*The Epic of Gilgamesh*," pages 73-77.
- Complete The Hero and Gilgamesh sheet.

Use What You Know

Illustrate a scene or a series of scenes from the story of Gilgamesh. Try to capture an important character interaction or a key scene from the story.

ASSESS

Lesson Assessment: The Epic of Gilgamesh (*Online*)

You will complete an online assessment covering the main points of this lesson. Your assessment will be scored by the computer.

LEARN

Activity 2. Optional: The Epic of Gilgamesh *(Online)*

There is much more to *The Epic of Gilgamesh* than the passage in your textbook. If you would like to read more of the epic:

Check out The Gilgamesh Trilogy retold and illustrated by Ludmila Zeman. The three titles in the series are:

- *Gilgamesh the King*
- *The Revenge of Ishtar*
- *The Last Quest of Gilgamesh*

Name ______________________________ Date ______________________________

The Hero and Gilgamesh

Before Reading

1. We often hear people talk about heroes. But what really makes someone a hero? Brainstorm ideas and write them here.______________________________

____

____

____

After Reading

2. List the three major characters in the story and write a brief description of each character's role:

____

____

____

____

____

The *Epic of Gilgamesh* gives us clues about Sumerian values and the character traits the Sumerians believed were important.

3. List three character traits that the Sumerians valued and a short quotation from the epic that supports your opinion. A couple of examples have been filled in for you.

Valued Character Traits	Clues from *Gilgamesh*
humility	"restless and arrogant…" "Gilgamesh is no shepherd of the city…"
	"Behold Gilgamesh, a man of strength…"

The Hero and Gilgamesh

4. Throughout most of the story, what did Gilgamesh think was important? ________________

5. How did Gilgamesh change his thinking? Cite two examples. ________________

6. What does the change in his thinking say about Sumerian values? ________________

7. Do you consider Gilgamesh a hero? Why? ________________

8. Do you consider Enkidu a hero? Why? ________________

Student Guide
Lesson 9. Optional: Your Choice

You may use today's lesson time to do one or more of the following:

- Complete work in progress.
- Complete the Beyond the Lesson activity in any lesson in this unit.
- Review the Ancient Civilizations Time Line in the Resources section.
- Go on to the next lesson.

Please mark this lesson complete to proceed to the next lesson in the course.

PREPARE

Approximate lesson time is 60 minutes.

Student Guide
Lesson 10: Sumer No More

A thousand years. A millennium. It's hard to imagine. After Sumer reached its height, it continued to thrive for a thousand years. Eventually, however, a complex combination of geographic and physical factors led to the decline of this remarkable civilization.

Lesson Objectives

- Describe the concept of a *millennium.*
- Identify the major geographic and political reasons for Sumer's decline.
- Recognize examples of the interaction between humans and their environments.
- Recognize Sargon's achievements and failings as an empire builder.
- Recognize changes that occurred as a result of Sargon's rule.

PREPARE

Approximate lesson time is 60 minutes.

Materials

For the Student

The Human Odyssey: Prehistory Through the Middle Ages edited by Klee, Cribb, and Holdren

History Journal

Keywords and Pronunciation

Akkad (AK-ad)

Akkadians (uh-KAY-dee-uhnz)

salinization (sa-luh-nuh-ZAY-shun) : a buildup of salts in the soil caused by long periods of irrigation and/or flooding

Sargon (SAHR-gahn)

LEARN

Activity 1: A Millennium Ago *(Online)*

Do you remember what a *millennium* is? It is 1,000 years. To get a sense of how long that really is, do the math problem below.

Activity 2: Focus on Geography *(Online)*

People in Sumer used and changed their environment to produce food for the thousands of residents in the growing city-states. But irrigating the crops eventually affected the soil, and contributed to Sumer's decline. The problem of salinization continues to affect land all over the world today.

To see how irrigation affects the soil in some parts of the world, view the Salinization activity online.

Activity 3: Sumer No More *(Online)*

Complete the Salinization: Then and Now activity using the information you read in your textbook and online.

ASSESS

Lesson Assessment: Sumer No More (*Online*)

You will complete an online assessment covering the main points of this lesson. Your assessment will be scored by the computer.

LEARN

Activity 4: Sumer No More *(Offline)*

A new period in Sumerian history began about 2350 B.C. when Sargon the Akkadian brought all of the city-states of Sumer and Akkad under his rule, creating the first empire in history. As you read Chapter 6, from "The Idea of Civilization" to the end of the chapter, pages 81-87, answer the following questions.

1. Who was Sargon of Akkad?
2. What was/were his major strength[s]?
3. Identify two of Sargon of Akkad's achievements and two of his failings as an empire-builder.
4. What important changes occurred as a result of Sargon's rule?

Activity 5. Optional: Sumer No More *(Online)*

This activity is OPTIONAL. It's provided for enrichment or extra practice, but not required for completion of this lesson. You may skip this activity.

Go to the

U. S. Department of Agriculture

and type in "salinization" in the Search box.

Select "Frequently Asked Questions about Salinity" and learn more about this environmental issue created by society.

Student Guide
Lesson 11: Sargon: A Mighty Ruler

As Sumerian civilization flourished for more than a thousand years, civilizations developed in other parts of the world. Over time the people started trading, and ideas and skills spread.
Sargon the Mighty and the Akkadians learned Sumerian ways and grew more powerful as Sumer declined. Eventually, Sargon brought all the Sumerian city-states under his rule. He built one of the first empires in the world by combining Akkad and Sumer and then conquering other lands. Fighting wars and conquering land proved to be easier in some ways than maintaining an empire.

Lesson Objectives

- Analyze maps to assess the size and scope of Sargon's empire over the course of its development.
- Recognize Sargon's achievements and failings as an empire builder.
- Recognize changes that occurred as a result of Sargon's rule.

PREPARE

Approximate lesson time is 60 minutes.

Materials

For the Student

Empire Building

The Human Odyssey: Prehistory Through the Middle Ages edited by Klee, Cribb, and Holdren

History Journal

Keywords and Pronunciation

Akkad (AK-ad)

Akkadians (uh-KAY-dee-uhnz)

LEARN
Activity 1: Sargon the Great *(Offline)*

Check Your Reading

Compare your answers from the Read On (Chapter 6, from "The Idea of Civilization Spreads," to the end of the chapter, pages 81-87) to those in the Lesson Answer Key.

Use What You Know

You have read that Sargon conquered and united Sumer and Akkad and then went on to conquer other Mesopotamian lands and create an empire. But what is an empire? Complete the Empire Building sheet to understand what it would take to build an empire.

Focus on Geography

Use the map of The First Empires on page 84 for this activity.

- Find the Empire of Akkad. When Sargon was born, there was no Akkadian Empire. He was born in Akkad, the land north of Sumer. Now find Sumer.
- Answer the following questions in your History Journal. Base your answers on the information given in the maps.
  1. Was the Empire of Akkad part of Mesopotamia or was Mesopotamia part of the Empire of Akkad? Explain your answer.
  2. Why might Sargon have wanted to control the land of Sumer?
  3. About how far was it from the Akkadian Empire's westernmost extent to southernmost Sumer?
  4. What Sumerian city-states did Sargon conquer?
  5. The map on page 84 shows the Empire of Akkad during what time period?

ASSESS

Lesson Assessment: Sargon: A Mighty Ruler (*Online*)

You will complete an online assessment covering the main points of this lesson. Your assessment will be scored by the computer.

LEARN

Activity 2. Optional: Sargon: A Mighty Ruler *(Online)*

This activity is OPTIONAL. It's provided for enrichment or extra practice, but not required for completion of this lesson. You may skip this activity.

You've read that Sargon thought of himself as a mighty ruler. In today's language, we might say that Sargon was conceited.

Name ____________________ Date ____________________

Empire Building

Here is your chance to think like Sargon the Mighty and compare your thinking with his actions. You are a skilled warrior and strong leader. You want to create your own empire. But before you do, you must prepare. Think about what Sargon had to do to create his empire. Then chart the advantages and disadvantages of building an empire before you conquer foreign lands.

1. You have to know what you are building, so what is an empire? (Use a dictionary to help you define empire.) ____________________

2. How is a city-state different from an empire? ____________________

3. You need to be ready to run the empire once you create it. What do you need to govern an empire? (Brainstorm some ideas, and draw some from the reading. For example, think about how you might communicate with people in far-off places, oversee building projects, or deal with conquered peoples.)

Communication: ____________________

Expansion: ____________________

Building: ____________________

People Management: ____________________

Empire Building

4. List two or three things Sargon did that you would also do in your empire. Why?
   a. ______________________________
   ____
   b. ______________________________
   ____
   c. ______________________________
   ____

5. List two or three things Sargon did that you would NOT choose to do in your empire. Why?
   a. ______________________________
   ____
   b. ______________________________
   ____
   c. ______________________________
   ____

6. Now that you have formed your empire, what are some advantages of an empire, and what are some disadvantages? Think about it from your own perspective and from the perspective of the conquered people.

Advantages of an Empire	Disadvantages of an Empire

Student Guide
Lesson 12: Hammurabi's Code

Why do we have laws? Is it to protect us from criminals? To make it clear to everyone what is allowed and what is not? To help the government control the citizens? Hammurabi wasn't the first ruler to have laws written down. But his ideas about the purpose and the organization of law have had a lasting impact on the world.

Lesson Objectives

- Explain why codification of law is important.
- Identify Hammurabi and his most significant accomplishment.
- Explain the historical significance of Hammurabi's principle that "the strong shall not oppress the weak."
- Analyze primary source material to recognize the significance of written law.
- Identify Nebuchadnezzar and his major accomplishments.

PREPARE

Approximate lesson time is 60 minutes.

Materials

For the Student

Extra! Extra! Read All About It!

The Human Odyssey: Prehistory Through the Middle Ages edited by Klee, Cribb, and Holdren

Nebuchadnezzar Reading Guide

Keywords and Pronunciation

Babylon (BA-buh-lahn)

codification (KAH-duh-fuh-kay-shun) : arranged or ordered in a systematic way

Hammurabi (ha-muh-RAH-bee)

LEARN

Activity 1: A Code of Law *(Online)*

Hammurabi is still famous today because he established order by giving his people a code of laws that applied to everybody. He tried to protect the weak from the strong. His legal code was an enormous step forward in civilization's concept of justice.

Activity 2: Analyze the Code *(Offline)*

Use What You Know

You are a citizen of Babylon and Hammurabi's Code has just been "released" to the public.

- Read the sections of the code on the Extra! Extra! Read All About It! sheet.
- Review the sections of the code in your text.
- Answer the questions.
- Then write a short letter to a friend in another city telling him what you think of the code. You may be for it, against it, or simply explain it.
- Consider interviewing several other citizens (your parents, siblings, or friends) and including their ideas about the code as well.

ASSESS

Lesson Assessment: Hammurabi's Code (*Online*)

You will complete an online assessment covering the main points of this lesson. Your assessment will be scored by the computer.

LEARN

Activity 3: Hammurabi's Code *(Offline)*

As you read Chapter 7, from the beginning to "Nebuchadnezzar's Hanging Gardens," pages 89-94, answer the questions on the Reading Guide.

Activity 4. Optional: Hammurabi's Code *(Online)*

This activity is OPTIONAL. It's provided for enrichment or extra practice, but not required for completion of this lesson. You may skip this activity.

Name ______________________________ Date ______________________________ 

Extra! Extra! Read All About It!

Directions: Hammurabi has just released his Code of Laws for Babylon. Read these sections of Hammurabi's Code. As you read, use the Word Bank to identify what aspect of Babylonian life each section or group of sections addressed. Then answer the questions and prepare to write a letter.

Word Bank	
protects the rights of the accused	regulates land ownership
illustrates class differences in terms of punishments	regulates construction
shows how children should treat their parents	regulates physicians
shows a judicial system was in place	regulates marriage

Read the Code

2 If any one bring an accusation against a man, and the accused go to the river and leap into the river, if he sink in the river his accuser shall take possession of his house. But if the river prove that the accused is not guilty, and he escape unhurt, then he who had brought the accusation shall be put to death, while he who leaped into the river shall take possession of the house that had belonged to his accuser.

3 If any one bring an accusation of any crime before the elders, and does not prove what he has charged, he shall, if it be a capital offense charged, be put to death.

Which aspect of life do these sections of the code regulate or illustrate?

____

— ◆ — ◆ — ◆ —

5 If a judge try a case, reach a decision, and present his judgment in writing, if later error shall appear in his decision, and it be through his own fault, then he shall pay twelve times the fine set by him in the case, and he shall be publicly removed from the judge's bench, and never again shall he sit there to render judgment.

Which aspect of life does this section of the code regulate or illustrate?

____

— ◆ — ◆ — ◆ —

Extra, Extra, Read All About It

If a chieftain or a man leave his house, garden, and field and hires it out, and someone else takes possession of his house, garden, and field and uses it for three years: if the first owner return and claims his house, garden, and field, it shall not be given to him, but he who has taken possession of it and used it shall continue to use it.

Which aspect of life does this section of the code regulate or illustrate?

____

— ♦ — ♦ — ♦ —

If a son strike his father, his hands shall be hewn off.

Which aspect of life does this section of the code regulate or illustrate?

____

— ♦ — ♦ — ♦ —

If a man knock out the teeth of his equal, his teeth shall be knocked out. [A tooth for a tooth]

If he knock out the teeth of a freed man, he shall pay one-third of a gold mina.

If anyone strike the body of a man higher in rank than he, he shall receive sixty blows with an ox-whip in public.

If a free-born man strike the body of another free-born man of equal rank, he shall pay one gold mina.

Which aspect of life do these sections of the code regulate or illustrate?

____

— ♦ — ♦ — ♦ —

Extra, Extra, Read All About It

215

If a physician make a large incision with an operating knife and cure it, or if he open a tumor (over the eye) with an operating knife, and saves the eye, he shall receive ten shekels in money.

Which aspect of life does this section of the code regulate or illustrate?

If a builder build a house for someone, and does not construct it properly, and the house which he built falls in and kill its owner, then that builder shall be put to death.

If it kill the son of the owner, the son of that builder shall be put to death.

Which aspect of life do these sections of the code regulate or illustrate?

Think about the Code

1. How does the code differ for citizens of different classes?

2. How will the code affect the empire? Are there benefits?

3. Are the punishments too strict? Use an example from the code to support your answer.

Extra, Extra, Read All About It

4. Does the code regulate the daily life of individual citizens? Use an example from the code to support your answer.

____
____
____

5. The empire has grown a great deal in a short time. Has this made the code more important? Why or why not?

____
____
____

6. Hammurabi described the purpose of the code as "to cause justice to prevail…, to destroy the wicked….that the strong may not oppress the weak." Give two examples from the code that suggest that it accomplished its purpose or that suggest it did not.

____
____
____

— ◆ — ◆ — ◆ —

Write about the Code

Circle the approach you will use in your letter. Then write your letter.

For the Code   Against the Code   Informational Reporting

- Your opening should include a brief description of Hammurabi and his code and state your position, if you have taken one.
- Next you should explain and support your position or describe the code in greater detail.
- Finally, should summarize and conclude your letter.

Name ______________________________ Date ______________________________ 

Nebuchadnezzar Reading Guide

Reading Guide

1. How did Babylon change under Hammurabi's rule?______________________________

Roughly 1,100 or 1,150 years passed between the reign of Hammurabi and that of Nebuchadnezzar. If you were to count back in time from today, what year would that take you back to? Think about how much time that is! You would be back in the time of the Vikings--about A.D.900!

2. What happened to Babylon in the thousand years following Hammurabi's rule?______________________________

3. Where did Babylon's trade routes extend during Nebuchadnezzar's rule? ______________________________

4. Describe the walls Nebuchadnezzar had built. ______________________________

5. Describe three great Babylonian architectural accomplishments that were completed during Nebuchadnezzar's reign. ______________________________

Student Guide
Lesson 13: Nebuchadnezzar Builds

Imagine traveling by boat along the Euphrates River to the city of Babylon. You pass through a dusty plain, a desert. The sun is beating down on you and the heat is intense. Now you see the city in the distance. You begin to distinguish the roofs of buildings and a high wall surrounding them. Then you see something else. Plants seem to float above the city! In the middle of this flat, arid land is a green mountain. A mountain that was not there when you visited as a child. How could that be? Who built it? How? Why?
Go to the Ancient Civilizations Time Line. What happened between the reign of Hammurabi and the reign of Nebuchadnezzar?

Lesson Objectives

- Identify Nebuchadnezzar and his major accomplishments.
- Recognize the importance of the Euphrates River to the success and splendor of Babylon.
- Identify the Hanging Gardens as one of the Seven Wonders of the Ancient World.
- Summarize the legend that explains why Nebuchadnezzar built the Hanging Gardens.
- Describe how the Babylonians overcame great architectural and engineering challenges to build the Hanging Gardens.

PREPARE

Approximate lesson time is 60 minutes.

Materials

For the Student

The Human Odyssey: Prehistory Through the Middle Ages edited by Klee, Cribb, and Holdren

Keywords and Pronunciation

Babylon (BA-buh-lahn)
Babylonians (ba-buh-LOH-nee-uhnz)
Hammurabi (ha-muh-RAH-bee)
Herodotus (hih-RAHD-uh-tuhs)
Nebuchadnezzar (neb-yuh-kud-NEH-zur)

LEARN

Activity 1: Check Your Reading *(Offline)*

Instructions

Check Your Reading

Review Chapter 7, from the beginning to "Nebuchadnezzar's Hanging Gardens," pages 89-94, by comparing your answers to the Reading Guide questions with those in the Lesson Answer Key.

Read

Read Chapter 7, from "Nebuchadnezzar's Hanging Gardens" to the end of the chapter, pages 94-97.

Activity 2: Touring Babylon *(Online)*

Use What You Know

Pretend you are writing a travel guide for the ancient world. The chapter you are writing will describe Babylon. Before you begin, you must tour Babylon.

City Guide: Babylon

As you write a city guide for Babylon, use descriptions from your reading and from Tour Babylon to "paint a picture" in words. Be sure to describe the fortified wall, bridges, moat, Ishtar Gate, and the Processional Way. Will readers want to know about the canals, the Euphrates River, temples, and palaces? And of course--don't forget the Hanging Gardens. Certainly, travelers who see them will have questions. Who built them? Why did they build them? And, of course, how? You might even want to print out pictures or draw some to enhance your city guide.

ASSESS

Lesson Assessment: Nebuchadnezzar Builds (*Online*)

You will complete an online assessment covering the main points of this lesson. Your assessment will be scored by the computer.

LEARN

Activity 3. Optional: Nebuchadnezzar Builds *(Online)*

The next activity is OPTIONAL. It's provided for enrichment or extra practice, but not required for completion of this lesson.

You may skip this activity.

Seven Wonders of the Ancient World

- What other ancient monuments rivaled Nebuchadnezzar's Hanging Gardens of Babylon? Explore the
  Seven Wonders of the Ancient World

Student Guide
Lesson 14: Unit Review

You've finished the unit, and now it's time to review what you've learned. You'll take the Unit Assessment in the next lesson.

Lesson Objectives

- Demonstrate mastery of important knowledge and skills in this unit.

PREPARE

Approximate lesson time is 60 minutes.

Materials

For the Student

Comparing Cultures

The Human Odyssey: Prehistory Through the Middle Ages edited by Klee, Cribb, and Holdren

History Journal

LEARN

Activity 1: Online Review *(Online)*

Begin your online review by revisiting the following:

- Uncovering the Past
- Culture Clues
- Sumerian Gods and Goddesses
- Ur Gallery
- Exploring Ur
- Salinization
- Salinization: Then and Now
- Tour Babylon

Activity 2: Offline Review *(Offline)*

History Journal Review

Review what you learned in this unit by going through your History Journal. You should:

- Look at activity sheets and reading guides you completed for this unit.
- Review unit Keywords.
- Read through any writing assignments you completed during the unit.
- Skim through applicable chapters of *The Human Odyssey, Book 1: From Prehistory Through the Middle Ages.*

Don't rush through. Take your time. Your History Journal is a great resource for a unit review.

A Look Back

Complete the Sumer (Mesopotamia) section of the Comparing Cultures sheet. The questions in each category serve as a guide--you may not be able to answer every question about every culture. If you do not have enough space, complete the category on the back or a separate sheet of paper. Some answers have already been given. You can use the following to help you complete the chart.

- Textbook: Part 1, Chapters 2, 3, 4, 5, 6, and 7
- History Journal
- Activity sheets
- Websites listed in Resources
- Flash Cards

Name Date

Comparing Cultures

Category	Sumer (Mesopotamia)	Egypt	Indus Valley	China	Similarities Differences
Geography What was the land like? How did people use the land?	Between the Tigris and Euphrates Rivers. Annual flooding				
Economy What goods were produced? What did they trade? Did they barter or use money? Who had wealth? Who didn't?		Raised wheat, barley, cattle, sheep, reeds; made jewelry; traded jewels, cotton, gold, chickens, ivory; pharaohs and family had wealth, most people were farmers			

Category	Sumer (Mesopotamia)	Egypt	Indus Valley	China	Similarities Differences
Religion and Philosophy What did they believe? What kind(s) of god(s) did they worship? What was the role of religion in daily life?			Don't Know		
Knowledge and Arts What kind of education system did they have? Did they have a writing system? What literature did they create? What art did they produce?				Arts – silk, calligraphy, bronzework; Writing – picture writing (calligraphy)	

Category	Sumer (Mesopotamia)	Egypt	Indus Valley	China	Similarities Differences
Technology What inventions or innovations did they introduce? Why? What impact did the new technology have?	Flooding controlled by levees; crops watered by canals; The wheel led to carts and wagons Sailboats allowed trade and travel on rivers and sea				
Government and Law What type of government did they have? Who had power? Was power shared? Did they have written laws?		Kings who were believed to be gods – known as pharaohs; power not shared			

					Similarities Differences
Society What was the class structure? What was the family/clan structure?			Don't know		
History How did the civilization change over time?				Grew and flourished; Despite invasions and troubles, China's civilization has been continuous	

Student Guide
Lesson 15: Unit Assessment

Today you will take the assessment for The Mesopotamian Moment unit.

Lesson Objectives

- Describe how archaeologists and historians piece together clues to describe the human past.
- Describe important people, characteristics, and contributions of Mesopotamian civilizations.
- Recognize examples of cultural and physical characteristics of Mesopotamia.
- List examples of the relationship between geography and the rise and fall of civilizations.
- List examples of the ways Sumer met the criteria of a civilization.
- Describe how civilization spreads from one region to another.

PREPARE

Approximate lesson time is 60 minutes.

Materials

For the Student

Question Review Table

The Human Odyssey: Prehistory Through the Middle Ages edited by Klee, Cribb, and Holdren

History Journal

ASSESS

Unit Assessment: The Mesopotamian Moment, Part 1 (*Online*)

Complete the computer-scored portion of the Unit Assessment. When you have finished, complete the teacher-scored portion of the assessment and submit it to your teacher.

Unit Assessment: The Mesopotamian Moment, Part 2 (*Offline*)

Complete the teacher-scored portion of the Unit Assessment and submit it to your teacher.

LEARN

Activity 1: Unit Assessment Review Table *(Online)*

If you earned a score of **less than 80%** on the Unit Assessment, complete the activity.

If you earned a score of **80% or greater**, you may skip this activity.

Let's prepare to retake the Unit Assessment:

- Identify the questions that you answered incorrectly.
- Complete the appropriate review activities listed in the table.

Activity 2: A River Rules *(Offline)*

Read On

Read Chapter 8, from the beginning to "Worshiping Many Gods," pages 99-102.

As you read, write a brief definition for *delta* in your History Journal. Compare your definition with the one in the Keywords section of Resources in the next lesson, A River Rules.

Assessment Date

Unit 3: The Mesopotamian Moment

Before you retake the Unit Assessment, use the table to figure out which activities you should review.

Question Review Table

Circle the numbers of the questions that you missed on the Unit Assessment. Review the activities that correspond with these questions.

Question	Lesson	Review Activity
1,2,3,4,5	1: How Do We Know?	Archaeologists and Historians
6,7,12	3: Cities of Sumer	Making It Work
8,17	13: Nebuchadnezzar Builds	Check Your Reading
9,11,35,36	7: Writing It Down	Cuneiform
10,31,32,33,34	5: Ideas About the Gods	A Similar Story
13	8: The Epic of Gilgamesh	Explore
14,27,28,29,30	Unit 2: From Nomad to Farmer	The Land Between Two Rivers
15	2: Finding Sumer	Sumer Found
16	12: Hammurabi's Code	A Code of Law Analyze the Code
18	11: Sargon: A Mighty Rules	Sargon the Great
19,20,21,22,23,24	10: Sumer No More	A Millenium Ago Focus on Geography Use What You Know Read On
25,26	6: A Ziggurat to the Gods	The Riches of Ur Explore Read On
37	All Lessons	
38	All Lessons	
39	All Lessons	

Student Guide
Unit 4: Civilization Spreads
Lesson 1: A River Rules

What's the recipe for civilization? Start with water and good soil. When you figure out how to grow plenty of crops, divert some attention to other activities. Divide up the work. Start by building villages and places to store your surplus food, and then cities. Spend some time inventing a system of writing, and make laws. All these ingredients first combined in Sumer, but civilizations soon sprang up in three other river valleys. Was it a good recipe? Do any of these civilizations still exist?

If you could fly over Egypt in an airplane, you would see a thin, green ribbon running through a red-brown expanse of desert. It is the Nile River Valley. In this fertile strip of land, ancient Egypt flourished. Herodotus, an early Greek historian, called Egypt "the gift of the Nile."

Lesson Objectives

- Explain ways the ancient Egyptians relied on the Nile and used it to create a civilization.
- Identify the longest river in the world.
- Locate on a map the Nile River and the modern countries through which it flows.
- Analyze maps to assess the importance of the Nile in ancient and modern Egypt.
- Recognize the characteristics of trade in ancient Egypt including the products traded, the location of trading partners, and the importance of trade in Egyptian life.
- Explain the origins and significance of the term *pharaoh*.
- Describe the reasons for building the pyramids, sphinxes, and mummifying bodies.

PREPARE

Approximate lesson time is 60 minutes.

Materials

For the Student

Classical World Time Line

The Human Odyssey: Prehistory Through the Middle Ages edited by Klee, Cribb, and Holdren

History Journal

Keywords and Pronunciation

Anubis (uh-NOO-buhs)
delta : a triangular piece of land at the mouth of a river
Giza (GEE-zuh)
Herodotus (hih-RAHD-uh-tuhs)
Horus (HOR-uhs)
Isis (IY-suhs)
Osiris (oh-SIY-ruhs)
Pharaoh (FAIR-oh) : the title for rulers of ancient Egypt
Pharaoh Menkaure (FAIR-oh men-KOW-ray)
Re (rah)
Saqqara (suh-KAHR-uh)

Thoth (thohth)
Zoser (ZHOH-suhr)

LEARN

Activity 1: The Flooding of the Nile *(Online)*

Activity 2: Life Along the Nile *(Online)*

Activity 3: Egypt's Trading Partners *(Online)*

ASSESS

Lesson Assessment: A River Rules (*Online*)

You will complete an online assessment covering the main points of this lesson. Your assessment will be scored by the computer.

LEARN

Activity 4: A River Rules *(Offline)*

Instructions

As you read Chapter 8, from "Worshiping Many Gods" to "Writing it Down," pages 102-107, answer the following questions in your History Journal.

1. Why did the Egyptians call their king *pharaoh?*
2. What power did the pharaoh exercise?
3. For whom did the Egyptians build the pyramids and why did they build them?
4. Why did the Egyptians mummify bodies?
5. What is a sphinx? What was its purpose?
6. Describe the process of building the pyramids.

Activity 5. Optional: A River Rules *(Online)*

Student Guide
Lesson 2: Building Power and Pyramids

For centuries people have marveled at Egypt's pyramids--the oldest and largest stone structures in the world. It's hard to believe the Egyptians built these giant monuments without modern machinery, metal tools, explosives, or even work horses. But why did the Egyptians go to so much trouble to build the pyramids? Why did they spend precious resources on projects that took thousands of workers 20 or 30 years to complete?

Lesson Objectives

- Identify the major gods of Egypt and their relationship to nature.
- Explain the origins and significance of the term *pharaoh*.
- Describe the Egyptians' fascination with the afterlife.
- Describe the reasons for building the pyramids, sphinxes, and mummifying bodies.
- Identify the system of writing of ancient Egypt.
- Describe the use of hieroglyphics and the way in which the modern world rediscovered them.

PREPARE

Approximate lesson time is 60 minutes.

Materials

For the Student

The Human Odyssey: Prehistory Through the Middle Ages edited by Klee, Cribb, and Holdren

History Journal

Keywords and Pronunciation

Anubis (uh-NOO-buhs)
Giza (GEE-zuh)
hieroglyphics (hiy-ruh-GLIH-fiks) : a form of picture-writing used in ancient Egypt
Horus (HOR-uhs)
Isis (IY-suhs)
Osiris (oh-SIY-ruhs)
papyrus (puh-PIY-ruhs) : a plant used in ancient times to make a paper-like writing material
Pharaoh (FAIR-oh) : the title for rulers of ancient Egypt
Pharaoh Khufu (FAIR-oh KOO-foo)
Pharaoh Menkaure (FAIR-oh men-KOW-ray)
Re (rah)
Saqqara (suh-KAHR-uh)
sarcophagus (sahr-KAH-fuh-guhs)
Thoth (thohth)
ziggurat (ZIH-guh-rat) : a stair-stepped temple built by Sumerians
Zoser (ZHOH-suhr)

LEARN

Activity 1: Worshiping Many Gods *(Online)*

Activity 2: Tombs Fit for Kings *(Online)*

ASSESS

Lesson Assessment: Building Power and Pyramids (*Online*)

You will complete an online assessment covering the main points of this lesson. Your assessment will be scored by the computer.

LEARN

Activity 3: Building Power and Pyramids *(Offline)*

Instructions

As you read Chapter 8, "Writing It Down" to "Enjoying the Here and Now," pages 107-109, answer the following questions in your History Journal:

1. How did the Egyptians use hieroglyphics?
2. Once the Egyptian civilization came to an end, people forgot how to read hieroglyphics. What object did French soldiers discover in 1799 that helped scholars learn how to read hieroglyphics?
3. How many years passed between the time the object was created and the time the French soldiers discovered it?
4. How did the object help the scholars decipher hieroglyphics?

- Write a brief definition for each of these words in your History Journal. When you have finished, compare your definitions with those in the Keywords section of this lesson.

hieroglyphics
papyrus

Activity 4. Optional: Building Power and Pyramids *(Online)*

Student Guide
Lesson 3. Optional: Your Choice

You may use today's lesson time to do one or more of the following:
- Complete work in progress.
- Complete the Beyond the Lesson activity in any lesson in this unit.
- Review the Ancient Civilizations Time Line in the Resources section.
- Go on to the next lesson.

Please mark this lesson complete to proceed to the next lesson in the course.

PREPARE

Approximate lesson time is 60 minutes.

Student Guide
Lesson 4: Something to Write About

Like the Sumerians, the ancient Egyptians developed a writing system. For more than 3,000 years they carved hieroglyphics on temple walls, tombs, and monuments. But the Egyptians didn't write only on stone and clay. They invented a lightweight writing material--papyrus. Egyptian scribes could roll the papyrus into cylinders, and soon they had libraries full of their writings. Over time, however, people forgot how to decipher the mysterious picture symbols. It wasn't until centuries later that a stone unlocked the secrets of the ancient Egyptian writing system.

Lesson Objectives

- Identify the system of writing of ancient Egypt.
- Describe the use of hieroglyphics and the way in which the modern world rediscovered them.
- List examples of everyday life in ancient Egypt.
- Explain how archaeologists and historians have learned about the daily lives of ancient Egyptians.

PREPARE

Approximate lesson time is 60 minutes.

Materials

For the Student

The Human Odyssey: Prehistory Through the Middle Ages edited by Klee, Cribb, and Holdren

Keywords and Pronunciation

Hatshepsut (Hat-SHEP-soot)
hieroglyphics (hiy-ruh-GLIH-fiks) : a form of picture-writing used in ancient Egypt
papyrus (puh-PIY-ruhs) : a plant used in ancient times to make a paper-like writing material
Pharaoh Khufu (FAIR-oh KOO-foo)
Pharaoh Menkaure (FAIR-oh men-KOW-ray)
Senmut (sen-MOOT)

LEARN

Activity 1: Ancient Egyptian Writing *(Online)*

Activity 2: Who or What Am I? *(Online)*

Activity 3: The Phoenician Alphabet *(Online)*

ASSESS

Lesson Assessment: Something to Write About (*Online*)

You will complete an online assessment covering the main points of this lesson. Your assessment will be scored by the computer.

LEARN

Activity 4: Something to Write About *(Offline)*

Instructions

Read Chapter 8, "Enjoying the Here and Now" to the end, pages 109-115. As you read, answer the following questions in your History Journal.

1. List some examples of everyday life in ancient Egypt.
2. How did archaeologists and historians learn about daily life in ancient Egypt?

Student Guide
Lesson 5: Life in Ancient Egypt

Do you like to play board games? Do you enjoy boating or going on picnics? Do you like dressing up for special events? Many ancient Egyptians enjoyed these activities, too. How do we know so much about people who lived thousands of years ago? Because they covered the walls of their temples and tombs with scenes of their daily life.

Lesson Objectives

- List examples of everyday life in ancient Egypt.
- Explain how archaeologists and historians have learned about the daily lives of ancient Egyptians.

PREPARE

Approximate lesson time is 60 minutes.

Materials

For the Student

The Human Odyssey: Prehistory Through the Middle Ages edited by Klee, Cribb, and Holdren

History Journal

Comparing Egyptians

Keywords and Pronunciation

Hatshepsut (Hat-SHEP-soot)
Senmut (sen-MOOT)

LEARN

Activity 1: Daily Living in Ancient Egypt *(Offline)*

Instructions

Check Your Reading

Review your reading (Chapter 8, "Enjoying the Here and Now" to the end, pages 109-115) by comparing your answers to the following questions with the ones in the Lesson Answer Key.

1. List some examples of everyday life among the well-to-do in ancient Egypt.
2. How did archaeologists and historians learn about daily life in ancient Egypt?

Activity 2: Comparing Egyptians *(Online)*

ASSESS

Lesson Assessment: Life in Ancient Egypt (*Online*)

You will complete an online assessment covering the main points of this lesson. Your assessment will be scored by the computer.

Name Date

Comparing Egyptians

Compare the everyday life of a wealthy Egyptian to that of an average Egyptian by adding the appropriate information in the columns.

Everyday Life		
	Wealthy Egyptians	Average Egyptians
Entertainment		
Dress		
Work		
Food		
Other		

Use your Everyday Life sheet to write a diary entry in your History Journal. Pretend you lived back in the days of the ancient Egyptians. From the perspective of an average Egyptian working in the home of a wealthy Egyptian, describe your day and what you observed in the lives of your employers. You might include activities of other family members in your household.

Thinking Cap Question: How do we know about the lives of the Egyptians? Write the answer on the back of this sheet.

Student Guide
Lesson 6: How Many Kingdoms?

Historians divide the Egyptian civilization into three distinct periods: the Old Kingdom, the Middle Kingdom, and the New Kingdom. During these periods, powerful dynasties ruled, strong governments developed, and pharaohs built lasting monuments. Sometimes historians include a fourth period--the Late or Decline Period--when Egypt's power began to ebb.

Lesson Objectives

- Analyze time lines to determine how historians categorize the history of ancient Egypt.
- Recognize key events of the Old, Middle, and New Kingdoms of Egypt and the surrounding world at that time.
- Describe examples of Egypt's scientific and mathematical achievements.
- Describe the ancient Egyptians' religious beliefs before the reign of Akhenaten.
- Describe how and why Akhenaten changed and challenged the traditional religious beliefs of Egyptians.
- Recognize why historians sometimes reach conflicting conclusions
- Describe the significance of Tutankhamen's short reign.
- Explain the significance of Howard Carter's discovery of Tutankhamen's tomb.

PREPARE

Approximate lesson time is 60 minutes.

Materials

For the Student

The Human Odyssey: Prehistory Through the Middle Ages edited by Klee, Cribb, and Holdren

History Journal

Kingdoms of Egypt

Keywords and Pronunciation

Akhenaten (ahk-NAH-tuhn)
Amen (AH-men)
Amenhotep (ahm-uhn-HOH-tep)
Hatshepsut (Hat-SHEP-soot)
Tutankhamen (too-tahng-KAH-muhn)
Tutankhaten (too-tahng-KAHT-uhn)

LEARN

Activity 1: Egypt's Three Kingdoms *(Offline)*

Instructions

Read

As you read Chapter 9, from the beginning to "A Disruptive Pharaoh," page 117, answer the following questions in your History Journal. When you have finished, check the answers in the Lesson Answer Key.

1. What are the three main periods in ancient Egyptian history?
2. What were some of the Egyptians' most important accomplishments during the Old Kingdom?
3. What were some of the Egyptians' most important accomplishments during the Middle Kingdom?
4. In which kingdom did Hatshepsut rule?
5. Name two male pharaohs who ruled during the New Kingdom that are still famous today.

Activity 2: The Kingdoms of Egypt *(Online)*

ASSESS

Lesson Assessment: How Many Kingdoms? (*Online*)

You will complete an online assessment covering the main points of this lesson. Your assessment will be scored by the computer.

LEARN

Activity 3: How Many Kingdoms? *(Offline)*

As you read Chapter 9, "A Disruptive Pharaoh" to "Ramses the Second, Ramses the Great," pages 117-119, and "*Discovering the Tomb of Tutankhamen*," pages 123-127, answer the following questions in your History Journal.

1. What were the Egyptians' religious beliefs before Akhenaten came to power?
2. How did Akhenaten change and challenge the traditional religious beliefs of the Egyptians?
3. What important change did Tutankhamen make during her short reign?
4. What was the significance of Howard Carter's discovery of Tutankhamen's tomb?

Kingdoms of Egypt

Read the events listed in the Word Bank, and then refer to the Time Line of the Ancient World to identify the kingdom in which each event occurred. Write the events in the appropriate columns. Then, at the bottom of each column, briefly describe at least one important event that occurred elsewhere in the world during that time span.

Old Kingdom 2686 B.C.–2181 B.C.	Middle Kingdom 1991 B.C.–1786 B.C.	New Kingdom 1554 B.C.–1070 B.C.
Elsewhere in the world:	Elsewhere in the world:	Elsewhere in the world:

Word Bank	
pharaohs work to strengthen Egypt's empire irrigation techniques improved Tutankhamen displays the wealth of the era embalming process developed Hyksos driven out pharaohs encourage trade Akhenaten attempts to revolutionize religion Ramses II builds monuments and temples	pyramids at Giza built Egyptians control Nubia hieroglyphics first widely used Egypt's first female pharaoh - Hatshepsut - rules Sphinx built first tombs built in the Valley of the Kings papyrus first used as a writing material

Answer the following questions.

1. How long did the Old Kingdom last? The Middle? The New? ______________________________

   ____

2. How many years passed between the uniting of Upper and Lower Egypt (before the Old Kingdom) in about 3100 B.C. to the Persians' takeover of Egypt (after the New Kingdom) in 525 B.C.? ____

3. Let's put these events in perspective. The United States became a nation in 1776. How many years has it existed as a country?____

Student Guide
Lesson 7: Significant Pharaohs

Imagine that a new ruler comes to power and tells you to change your religion. How would you feel? What would you do? In ancient Egypt, one pharaoh did just that. What did the Egyptians do when he took away their ancient traditions? How long did the new religion last?

Lesson Objectives

- Describe the ancient Egyptians' religious beliefs before the reign of Akhenaten.
- Describe how and why Akhenaten changed and challenged the traditional religious beliefs of Egyptians.
- Describe the significance of Tutankhamen's short reign.
- Explain the significance of Howard Carter's discovery of Tutankhamen's tomb.
- Recognize why historians sometimes reach conflicting conclusions
- Identify Ramses II.
- Recognize the geographic extent of the Egyptian empire under Ramses II.

PREPARE

Approximate lesson time is 60 minutes.

Materials

For the Student

The Human Odyssey: Prehistory Through the Middle Ages edited by Klee, Cribb, and Holdren

History Journal

Keywords and Pronunciation

Abu Simbel (ah-boo SIM-bel)
Akhenaten (ahk-NAH-tuhn)
Amenhotep (ahm-uhn-HOH-tep)
Aten (AH-tn)
Hittite (HIH-tiyt)
Horus (HOR-uhs)
Isis (IY-suhs)
Kadesh (KAY-desh)
Osiris (oh-SIY-ruhs)
Pharaoh (FAIR-oh) : the title for rulers of ancient Egypt
Ramses (RAM-seez)
Re (rah)
Thoth (thohth)
Tutankhamen (too-tahng-KAH-muhn)
Tutankhaten (too-tahng-KAHT-uhn)

LEARN

Activity 1: Kingdoms of Egypt *(Online)*

Activity 2: Sift the Evidence *(Online)*

ASSESS

Lesson Assessment: Significant Pharaohs (*Online*)

You will complete an online assessment covering the main points of this lesson. Your assessment will be scored by the computer.

LEARN

Activity 3: Significant Pharaohs *(Offline)*

Instructions

As you read Chapter 9, "Ramses the Second, Ramses the Great" to "*Discovering the Tomb of Tutakhamen*," pages 120-123, answer the following questions in your History Journal:

1. Who was Ramses II?
2. After the battle of Kadesh, where did Egyptian control extend?
3. When and how did Egypt's New Kingdom end?
4. What were some of the Egyptian customs that the foreign conquerors adopted?

Activity 4. Optional: Significant Pharaohs *(Online)*

This activity is OPTIONAL. It's provided for enrichment or extra practice, but not required for completion of this lesson. You may skip this activity.

If you would like to read an eyewitness account of the opening of King Tut's tomb, go online to National Geographic Classics: At the Tomb of Tutankhamen.

Student Guide
Lesson 8: Ramses II: Conqueror and Builder

Ramses II might have been considered a giant of his time. He was a dynamic ruler who enlarged the empire, signed a treaty with his Hittite neighbors to keep a permanent peace, and built more temples and tombs than any pharaoh before him. But Ramses II was something of a giant in another way. He stood 5 feet, 9 inches tall--about four inches taller than the average Egyptian man.

Lesson Objectives

- Identify Ramses II.
- Recognize the geographic extent of the Egyptian empire under Ramses II.
- Describe the decline of the New Kingdom and the ways in which foreign conquerors adopted Egyptian culture.

PREPARE

Approximate lesson time is 60 minutes.

Materials

For the Student

The Human Odyssey: Prehistory Through the Middle Ages edited by Klee, Cribb, and Holdren

The 3A's: Art, Architecture, and Artifacts

Mapping Egypt

Keywords and Pronunciation

Abu Simbel (ah-boo SIM-bel)
Amun-Ra (ah-muhn-RAH)
Hittite (HIH-tiyt)
Kadesh (KAY-desh)
Osiris (oh-SIY-ruhs)
Ptah (tah)
Ramses (RAM-seez)
Re-Harakhty (rah huh-RAHK-tee)
Tutankhamen (too-tahng-KAH-muhn)

LEARN

Activity 1: Ramses Reigns *(Online)*

Activity 2: Abu Simbel *(Online)*

Activity 3: Focus on Geography *(Online)*

ASSESS

Lesson Assessment: Ramses II: Conqueror and Builder (*Online*)

You will complete an online assessment covering the main points of this lesson. Your assessment will be scored by the computer.

LEARN

Activity 4. Optional: Ramses II: Conqueror and Builder *(Online)*

Name Date

The 3 A's: Art, Architecture, and Artifacts

The temple at Abu Simbel reflects what Ramses II considered important and wanted people to remember. Study the images in the gallery, and then read the observations below. What was Ramses trying to say?

Select a statement from the Word Bank that describes what could be deduced from each feature of the temple and write it in the deduction column. Then, make one deduction of your own about each feature. The first item has been completed for you.

Observation (What do you see in the image?)	Deduction (What do you think Ramses II is saying?)
1. Ramses fighting at the Battle of Kadesh	The battle was an important event. Ramses wanted people to know he was a mighty warrior.
2. large statues of Ptah, Amun-Ra, Re-Harakhty, and Ramses at a prominent spot in the temple, where rays of sunlight hit them twice a year	
3. eight colossal statues of Ramses dressed as the god Osiris	
4. Hapi, god of the Nile, binding up a hieroglyph that means *unite*	
5. two statues of Nefertari in the Temple of Hathor	
6. four huge statues of Ramses at the front of the Great Temple of Abu Simbel	

Word Bank	
The Nile was important to the Egyptians. Ramses II wanted people to know he was a mighty warrior. Ramses II revered the gods.	Ramses II wanted people to honor him and remember him. Ramses II wanted people to recognize his power and divine nature. Ramses II honored his wife.

7. Write a sentence or two about what you noticed in the art and architecture of the Great Temple of Abu Simbel that indicates what Ramses II thought was important or valuable.

Name ______________________________ Date ______________________________

Mapping Egypt

Study the map of Ancient Egypt and then answer questions 1–2. Use the atlas in your textbook to answer questions 3–4.

1. Look at the boundaries of the Old, Middle, and New Kingdoms. Where is the Nile in relation to the three kingdoms? (Hint: Think about the Nile's relative location.)

   ____

2. In what way do the maps imply that the Egyptians made advances in transportation during the New Kingdom? (Hint: Compare the map of Old Kingdom Egypt with the map of New Kingdom Egypt.)

   ____

3. Use the atlas in the textbook to locate the modern nations that lie entirely or partly within the ancient boundaries of the New Kingdom.

   ____

4. You know that Egypt has been called the "Gift of the Nile" and that the ancient Egyptians depended on the Nile. But did you know that the people of modern Egypt still depend on the Nile? Find the city of Aswan on the modern map in your textbook atlas (look in southern Egypt near Lake Nasser–relative location). This is the site of the Aswan High Dam, an enormous feat of engineering. It was built in the 1960s to control floods and provide much of Egypt with electricity.

   The Aswan Dam keeps the Nile from flooding each year. What positive effects do you think the dam has had on Egypt?

   ____

   What negative effects do you think the dam might have had? (Hint: Think about how floods helped the ancient Egyptian farmers.)

   ____

5. Look at the pictures in the technology section of the site. Ramses's monuments were in the way of the dam. Suppose you are Ramses II. Would you approve or disapprove of the building of the dam?

   ____

Student Guide
Lesson 9: Thinking About Egypt

You have looked at the art and architecture of ancient Egypt and Mesopotamia to learn more about those cultures. Historians study art and architecture to understand a society's values and priorities. But artifacts give clues about other aspects of culture as well. They can show, for example, how monuments were constructed, who did the work and what skills they had, and what natural resources were available in a region.

Lesson Objectives

- Analyze Egyptian art and architecture for information on the society's culture.
- Compare and contrast Egypt's culture and civilization to those of Mesopotamia.

PREPARE

Approximate lesson time is 60 minutes.

Materials

For the Student

The Human Odyssey: Prehistory Through the Middle Ages edited by Klee, Cribb, and Holdren

History Journal

Keywords and Pronunciation

Mesopotamia (meh-suh-puh-TAY-mee-uh)
polytheism (PAH-lee-THEE-ih-zuhm) : belief in many gods

LEARN

Activity 1: Art and Architecture *(Online)*

Activity 2: Comparing Cultures *(Online)*

Instructions

A Look Back

Complete the Egypt section of the Comparing Cultures sheet. You should have completed the Sumer/Mesopotamia section of this chart in the last unit, The Mesopotamian Moment. You can use the following to help you complete this chart:

- Textbook: Chapters 8 and 9
- History Journal
- Activity sheets
- Websites on Egypt: Resources
- Flash Cards
- Online Activities

Compare your answers with the ones in the Lesson Answer Key.

ASSESS

Lesson Assessment: Thinking About Egypt (*Online*)

You will complete an online assessment covering the main points of this lesson. Your assessment will be scored by the computer.

Name Date

Comparing Cultures

Category	Sumer (Mesopotamia)	Egypt	Indus Valley	China	Similarities Differences
Geography What was the land like? How did people use the land?	Between the Tigris and Euphrates Rivers. Annual flooding				
Economy What goods were produced? What did they trade? Did they barter or use money? Who had wealth? Who didn't?		Raised wheat, barley, cattle, sheep, reeds; made jewelry; traded jewels, cotton, gold, chickens, ivory; pharaohs and family had wealth, most people were farmers			

Category	Sumer (Mesopotamia)	Egypt	Indus Valley	China	Similarities Differences
Religion and Philosophy What did they believe? What kind(s) of god(s) did they worship? What was the role of religion in daily life?			Don't Know		
Knowledge and Arts What kind of education system did they have? Did they have a writing system? What literature did they create? What art did they produce?				Arts – silk, calligraphy, bronzework; Writing – picture writing (calligraphy)	

Category	Sumer (Mesopotamia)	Egypt	Indus Valley	China	Similarities Differences
Technology What inventions or innovations did they introduce? Why? What impact did the new technology have?	Flooding controlled by levees; crops watered by canals; The wheel led to carts and wagons Sailboats allowed trade and travel on rivers and sea				
Government and Law What type of government did they have? Who had power? Was power shared? Did they have written laws?		Kings who were believed to be gods – known as pharaohs; power not shared			

Category	Sumer (Mesopotamia)	Egypt	Indus Valley	China	Similarities Differences
Society What was the class structure? What was the family/clan structure?			Don't know		
History How did the civilization change over time?				Grew and flourished; Despite invasions and troubles, China's civilization has been continuous	

Student Guide
Lesson 10: By the Banks of the Indus

Geography influenced the development of many civilizations, and the one you are about to study was no exception. Look at a map of Asia. Begin at the point where the Tigris and Euphrates flow into the Persian Gulf and scan eastward. Look for another big river--one that runs near mountains but not through them. In the fertile valley of this river, city-builders were at work by 2500 B.C.

Lesson Objectives

- Identify on a map the Indus River and major physical features of the South Asian subcontinent.
- Identify on a map the modern countries through which the Indus River flows.
- Explain how the people of the Indus River Valley relied on and used the Indus to create a civilization.

PREPARE

Approximate lesson time is 60 minutes.

Materials

For the Student

Reading Guide

The Geography of India

The Human Odyssey: Prehistory Through the Middle Ages edited by Klee, Cribb, and Holdren

Keywords and Pronunciation

Harappa (huh-RA-puh)
Himalaya (hih-muh-LAY-uh)
Mohenjo-Daro (moh-HEN-joh DAHR-oh)

LEARN

Activity 1: India Becomes Civilized *(Offline)*

Instructions

Explore

Complete the Geography of India sheet. Check your answers against those in the Lesson Answer Key.

Read

As you read Chapter 10, from the beginning to "The Cities of the Indus Valley," pages 129-131, complete the Reading Guide.

ASSESS

Lesson Assessment: By the Banks of the Indus *(Online)*

You will complete an online assessment covering the main points of this lesson. Your assessment will be scored by the computer.

LEARN

Activity 2. Optional: By the Banks of the Indus *(Online)*

Name ______________________________ Date ______________________________

Reading Guide

Directions: Complete this sheet as you read today's assignment. You may need two or more words for some of the blanks.

1. The Indus Valley civilization was flourishing by ________ B.C. and had declined by ________ B.C.

2. Today, the Indian subcontinent contains the countries of ____________________, ____________________, ____________________, ____________________, and ____________________.

3. Civilization flourished on the Indian subcontinent because of the ____________ River.

4. Farmers were able to plant ______________, ______________, and ______________ in the fertile soil of the Indus Valley because the Indus ______________ each spring.

5. To increase their crop yields, farmers built __________________________ that extended the reach of the Indus.

6. Just as in Mesopotamia and Egypt, bountiful harvests and these two developments made civilization possible: ________________________ and ________________________.

7. Farmers in the Indus Valley grew ____________ and used its fibers to make ____________.

zebu

Name ______________________________ Date ______________________________

The Geography of India

Directions: Read the following statements to identify the geographic features:

1. These majestic snow-capped mountains on the northeastern border of India separate the Indian subcontinent from the rest of Asia. ______________________________

2. This river flows into the Bay of Bengal. ______________________________

3. This river gave India its name, though only a small segment of it is in modern India.
____

4. This is the sea into which the mighty Indus flows. ______________________________

5. Use the maps on pages 130, 132, and 631 of your text to locate and label these features or cities on the map on the next page: Indian Ocean, Bay of Bengal, the Himalaya, Hindu Kush Mountains, Mohenjo-Daro, Harappa, Thar Desert (now called Great Indian Desert), Deccan Plateau. Color bodies of water blue and mountains brown.

Use the map to complete the following:

6. Describe the three general geographic features of the land around the Indus River:
m __ __ __ __ __ __ __ __, r __ __ __ __ __, and p __ __ __ __ __

7. Which of the physical features named in Question 6 is common to the ancient Egyptian, Mesopotamian, and Indus civilizations? ______________________________

8. What natural barriers might have protected the people living in the Indus River valley from invasion? ______________________________

9. Through which three modern countries does the Indus flow? ____________________, ____________________, and ____________________ Draw the borders of these countries on your map and label them.

10. A *subcontinent* is a large mass of land that is separated by geography from the continent it is part of. Explain why India is often called a subcontinent. ______________________________
____
____

By the Banks of the Indus

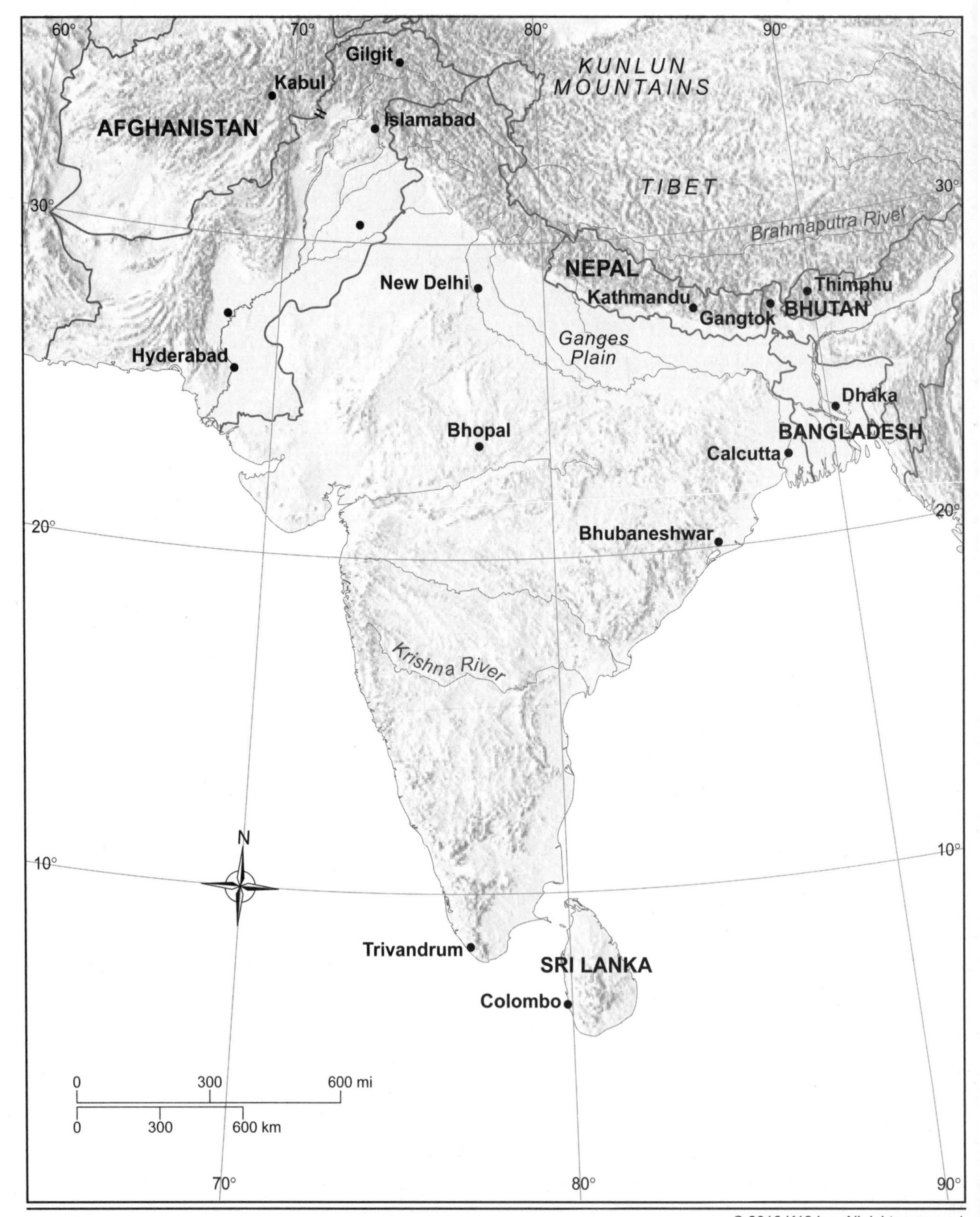

Student Guide
Lesson 11: Remarkable Cities

For nearly a century, historians and archaeologists have been trying to learn more about the early settlers of the Indus Valley. By studying excavations and artifacts, they discovered that members of this ancient society planned orderly cities, built intricate underground plumbing systems, and invented a complex type of writing that still puzzles us today. Until someone cracks the code of the Indus writing system, many of the secrets of this great civilization will remain a mystery.

Lesson Objectives

- Identify major features and innovations of Mohenjo-Daro and other Indus cities.
- Summarize the work of archaeologists in the Indus Valley.
- Explain why archaeologists and historians have limited information about the Indus Valley civilization.
- Recognize current theories on why the Indus Valley civilization declined.

PREPARE

Approximate lesson time is 60 minutes.

Materials

For the Student

Drawing Conclusions

Reading Guide

The Human Odyssey: Prehistory Through the Middle Ages edited by Klee, Cribb, and Holdren

Keywords and Pronunciation

Mohenjo-Daro (moh-HEN-joh DAHR-oh)

LEARN

Activity 1: Cities of the Indus Valley *(Offline)*

Instructions

Read

Complete the Reading Guide as you read Chapter 10, from "The Cities of the Indus Valley" to "In the Valleys of Two Chinese Rivers," pages 131-134.

Use What You Know

These are the steps you take to form conclusions:

- Read to understand the facts.
- "Read between the lines" to gain understanding.
- Ask questions if you need more information.
- Combine all the "evidence" with common sense and what you already know to draw a conclusion.

Historians have drawn several conclusions about the Indus Valley civilization. Complete the Drawing Conclusions sheet by citing evidence that supports each conclusion about the Indus civilization.

Comparing Ancient Civilizations

Add information about the Indus Valley civilization to your Comparing Cultures chart.

ASSESS

Lesson Assessment: Remarkable Cities (*Online*)

You will complete an online assessment covering the main points of this lesson. Your assessment will be scored by the computer.

LEARN

Activity 2. Optional: Remarkable Cities *(Online)*

This activity is OPTIONAL. It's provided for enrichment or extra practice, but not required for completion of this lesson.

You may skip this activity.

While excavating sites in the Indus River Valley, archaeologists have found thousands of square seals inscribed with pictures and symbols. Some experts believe that the symbols are an ancient form of writing.

Name Date

Reading Guide

Directions: Answer these questions as you read today's assignment:

1. What were some of the features and innovations of Mohenjo-Daro and other Indus cities?

2. What do archaeologists believe was the function of the signature, or stamp, seals?

3. What have archaeologists working in the Indus Valley learned about the civilization that once flourished there?

4. Why do archaeologists and historians still have many questions about this ancient civilization?

5. Give two theories that explain the decline of the Indus Valley civilization.

Name Date

Drawing Conclusions

Directions: Read the following three conclusions and think about evidence that has been discovered that seems to support historians' beliefs about the Indus Valley civilization.

Conclusion # 1: The cities of the Indus valley had a strong, centralized government.

Evidence that supports Conclusion # 1:

____

____

____

Conclusion #2: The people of the Indus valley had a highly developed division of labor.

Evidence that supports Conclusion #2:

____

____

____

Conclusion # 3: The people of the Indus valley carried on trade with neighboring civilizations.

Evidence that supports Conclusion # 3:

____

____

____

Evidence that *might* be found elsewhere to support Conclusion #3 (draw your own conclusion):

____

____

Which of the following kinds of evidence do you think is more valuable? Why?

- Written documents from several sources. How valuable? Why?
- Stories passed through generations. How valuable? Why?

____

____

____

____

Student Guide
Lesson 12: Civilization Along the Yellow and Yangtze

Like the ancient civilizations of Sumer, Egypt, and the Indus Valley, early civilization in China developed along rivers, in the valleys of the Huang He or Yellow River in the north and the Yangtze River in central China. The floods of these rivers deposit rich soil for growing crops, but they can also be incredibly destructive.

Lesson Objectives

- Identify on a map the Yellow River, Yangtze River, and major physical features of East Asia.
- Identify on a map the modern countries through which the Yellow and Yangtze Rivers flow.
- Explain why Chinese civilization developed near the Yellow and Yangtze Rivers.
- Recognize examples of the ways people interact with and change the environment.
- Explain that in ancient times the Chinese learned to produce silk from the cocoons of silkworms.

PREPARE

Approximate lesson time is 60 minutes.

Materials

For the Student

Civilization Along the Yellow and Yangtze

The Human Odyssey: Prehistory Through the Middle Ages edited by Klee, Cribb, and Holdren

Keywords and Pronunciation

Chang Jiang (chahng jee-yahng)
Huang He (hwahng hou)
Taklimakan (tah-kluh-muh-KAHN)
Yangtze (YANG-see)

LEARN

Activity 1: Two Mighty Rivers *(Offline)*

Instructions

Read

Read Chapter 10, from "In the Valleys of Two Chinese Rivers" to "Silk People," pages 135-136. As you read, think about how China's ancient civilization is different from the three ancient civilizations you've already studied.

Focus on Geography

Look at the map of ancient China on page 135. Locate the following physical features:

- Himalaya
- Gobi
- East China Sea
- South China Sea
- Yellow River (Huang He)
- Yangtze River

Label the features listed above on the map of China on the Civilization Along the Yellow and Yangtze sheet.
Indicate with symbols where Chinese civilization first developed.

Answer these questions in your History Journal:

1. Describe the relative location of China.
2. Look at a map of the world. Through what modern countries do the Yellow and the Yangtze Rivers flow?
3. Describe the locations of the Yellow and Yangtze in terms of where they rise (begin) and end.
4. What natural barrier would have isolated the ancient Chinese civilizations from the Indus Valley civilization?
5. In what regions did Chinese civilization first develop?

Activity 2: Human-Environment Interaction *(Online)*

Activity 3: The Three Gorges Dam *(Online)*

ASSESS

Lesson Assessment: Civilization Along the Yellow and Yangtze *(Online)*

You will complete an online assessment covering the main points of this lesson. Your assessment will be scored by the computer.

LEARN

Activity 4: Civilization Along the Yellow and Yangtze *(Offline)*

Instructions

Read Chapter 10, "Silk People," pages 136-137. As you read, outline in your History Journal the steps the Chinese used to produce silk cloth. You may illustrate all or some of these steps.

Activity 5. Optional: Civilization Along the Yellow and Yangtze *(Online)*

Name ______________________________ Date ______________________________

Civilization Along the Yellow and Yangtze

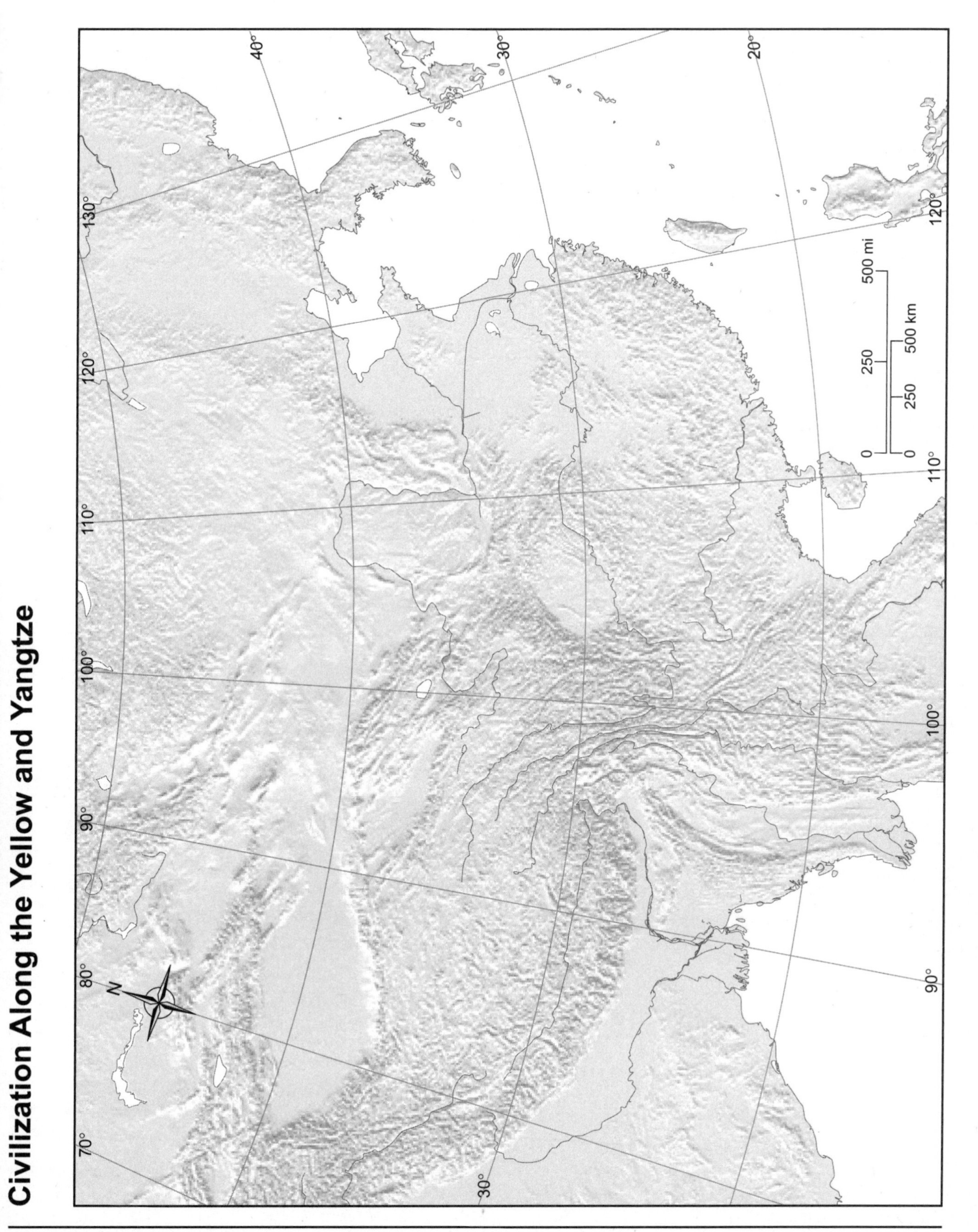

Student Guide
Lesson 13: The Silk People

China's ancient civilization developed differently from the earlier river valley civilizations. China was unique in that silk production started there. Chinese silk is still famous and China continues to be the world's leading silk producer today. Now many countries produce silk, but the silk-production process was once one of the most closely guarded secrets in history. To the Chinese, silk was worth more than gold.

Lesson Objectives

- Demonstrate knowledge gained in previous lessons.
- List three ways China's civilization differed from other river valley civilizations.
- Explain that in ancient times the Chinese learned to produce silk from the cocoons of silkworms.
- Describe the importance of silk and its production to the early Chinese.

PREPARE

Approximate lesson time is 60 minutes.

Materials

For the Student

- Distinguishing Fact from Opinion
- Writing and Religion in Ancient China

The Human Odyssey: Prehistory Through the Middle Ages edited by Klee, Cribb, and Holdren

---

LEARN

Activity 1: Soft as Silk *(Offline)*

Instructions

Check Your Reading

If you haven't already done so, click Check Your Reading to see if you correctly outlined the steps the Chinese used to produce silk cloth.

Use What You Know

Complete the Distinguishing Fact from Opinion sheet.

Lesson Assessment *(Online)*

Read On

- Read the directions on the Writing and Religion in Ancient China sheet before beginning today's reading assignment: Chapter 10, from "Writing and Religion" to the end, pages 137-139.
- Be prepared to define *dynasty.*

ASSESS

Lesson Assessment: The Silk People *(Online)*

You will complete an online assessment covering the main points of this lesson. Your assessment will be scored by the computer.

LEARN

Activity 2. Optional: The Silk People *(Online)*

Name ____________________ Date ____________________

Distinguishing Fact from Opinion

China is the world's oldest continuous civilization. People in China today can trace their language, writing, art, and philosophy further back in time than people in any other modern nation.

Directions: Read each statement. On the blank line, write "Fact" if the statement is a fact or "Opinion" if the statement is an opinion.

_______ 1. Archaeological evidence indicates that silk production may have begun in China as early as 2700 B.C.

_______ 2. Producing silk is a multistep process that involves plants, insects, and humans.

_______ 3. Producing silk was considered women's work in ancient China.

_______ 4. Silkworms are ugly.

_______ 5. Clothing made from silk is very soft.

_______ 6. Clothing made from silk is beautiful.

_______ 7. Silk has been found in royal tombs.

_______ 8. Silk is prettier than gold.

_______ 9. Silk was extremely valuable.

_______ 10. The ancient Chinese were smarter than people in other ancient civilizations.

11. Now think about the facts and form an educated opinion of your own. Write a paragraph expressing your ideas about the Chinese and silk production. Why do you think they so carefully guarded the secret of how to produce silk? Use facts to support your opinion.

____

____

____

____

____

____

____

____

____

Name Date 

Writing and Religion in Ancient China

Directions: Before you read today's selection, fill in the blanks for the first two items of each topic. You'll fill out the third item in each section during the next lesson.

A. Writing in Ancient China

1. This is what I know about this topic:

2. This is one question I'd like answered about this topic:

3. These are two facts I learned from reading about this topic:

B. Religion in Ancient China

1. This is what I know about this topic:

2. This is one question I'd like answered about this topic:

3. These are two facts I learned from reading about this topic:

Student Guide
Lesson 14: Writing and Ruling

The early Chinese were great city-builders. In ancient China, powerful dynasties ruled, populous cities developed, and art and religion flourished. Unlike earlier cultures, however, this one did not fade away.

Lesson Objectives

- Describe Chinese writing and its early relationship to religious ideas.
- Explain the importance of ancestor worship to the Chinese.
- Identify the first Chinese dynasty.
- Describe key advances made under the Shang.
- Recognize characteristics of ancient Chinese culture and ways in which historians and archaeologists have learned about the culture.
- Define *dynasty*.

PREPARE

Approximate lesson time is 60 minutes.

Materials

For the Student

The Human Odyssey: Prehistory Through the Middle Ages edited by Klee, Cribb, and Holdren

Keywords and Pronunciation

calligraphy (kuh-LIH-gruh-fee) : the art of fine or beautiful writing

dynasty : a ruling family that remains in power for many years

---

LEARN

Activity 1: Writing, Religion, and the Mighty Shang *(Online)*

ASSESS

Lesson Assessment: Writing and Ruling (*Online*)

You will complete an online assessment covering the main points of this lesson. Your assessment will be scored by the computer.

Student Guide
Lesson 15: Mapping

Maps can help us understand civilizations. Maps contain information about the land itself--information that may help us understand how people lived long ago and how they live today. You have just studied three important civilizations. Now review the geographic concepts of *place* and *region* as they relate to those civilizations.

Lesson Objectives

- Review geographic concepts of *place* and *region.*
- Use maps to gain information on Asia.

PREPARE

Approximate lesson time is 60 minutes.

Materials

For the Student

The Human Odyssey: Prehistory Through the Middle Ages edited by Klee, Cribb, and Holdren

History Journal

LEARN

Activity 1: Examining Culture *(Online)*

Instructions

The concept of *place* refers to the unique characteristics that distinguish one location from other locations. *Regions* are groups of places that have characteristics in common that set the area apart from the surrounding areas. In this activity you will practice identifying the cultural and physical characteristics of four ancient civilizations: Egypt, Mesopotamia, India, and China. Then you'll answer questions about the characteristics in terms of physical geography.

Activity 2: Focus on Geography *(Offline)*

Instructions

Do you know which two civilizations are parts of the same region? How much do you know about the two continents where civilization began?

Use the atlas in the back of your text to complete the following. Check your answers against those in the Lesson Answer Key when you have finished.

Look at the Climate Zones map on page 640. Match each civilization below with the correct climate. You may use answers more than once or not at all.

Answer Choices: **dry desert** **semiarid steppe** **tropical wet** **humid subtropical**

1. China : ______________________________
2. India : ______________________________
3. Mesopotamia : ______________________
4. Egypt : ______________________________

5. Would you expect much rain to fall in a dry desert climate?

____

6. Which climate do you think would better support trees for wood and food crops such as rice--semiarid steppe or humid subtropical? If you aren't sure, use what you learned from the Climate Zones map and look at the Terrestrial Biomes map to make links between climate and vegetation.

____

7. According to the Terrestrial Biomes map, where would you be more likely to find flocks of sheep grazing on the hillsides--in Egypt or in Mesopotamia?

____

8. Now find the area where you live on the Climate Zones map. What climate zone are you in? Is it the same as any of the early river-valley civilizations?

____

9. a) You have looked at the climates of the river-valley civilizations. Which climate would be likely to support the densest population (lots of people living close together)? Why?

____

____

b) Now look at the Population Distribution map on page 643. Were you correct about which climate could support the densest population?

____

10. Use the same map and look at modern Egypt. Why does a narrow strip of land have a very dense population, while the rest of the country has a sparse population?

____

Go to the map of Eurasia on page 626-627.

11. In what direction would you travel to go from ancient Mesopotamia to the Indus Valley? (To answer this, you'll need to recall where the two civilizations were located and what countries are in those places today. Do you remember the names of the two rivers in Mesopotamia?)

____

12. If you travel by land from Mesopotamia to the Indus Valley, what difficulties will you encounter? What will be the hardest part of the journey in terms of physical geography?

____

13. Now travel on to China. Which is the longer trip--Iraq to Pakistan, or Pakistan to the North China Plain?

____

14. What will be the greatest obstacle on the journey from Pakistan to China?
The Himalaya has the highest mountain in the world. How high is Mount Everest?

__________________________ __________________________

15. You have reached China and plan to be a farmer. Where will you settle to have the best possible farmland--on the North China Plain, in the Gobi, or west of the Mu Us Desert? Why? (Don't forget what you learned from the climates and biomes maps.)

____

____

Turn now to the South Asia map on page 631.

16. India is often called a *subcontinent.* Describe the physical features that isolate India from the rest of Asia.

____

____

17. A look at the Population Distribution map on page 643 will show you that more people live in eastern and southern India today than in the Indus Valley. Use the Terrestrial Biomes maps to explain why this might be.

____

____

____

Finally, turn to the World Physical map on pages 622-623.

18. Use the map scale to determine the distance from the point at which the Yangtze River meets the East China Sea, to the point at which the Nile River meets the Mediterranean Sea. How many miles is it?

____

Student Guide
Lesson 16: Unit Review

You've finished the unit, and now it's time to review what you've learned. You'll take the Unit Assessment in the next lesson.

Lesson Objectives

- Demonstrate mastery of important knowledge and skills in this unit and the previous unit.

PREPARE

Approximate lesson time is 60 minutes.

Keywords and Pronunciation

Assyrians (uh-SIHR-ee-uhnz)
Babylon (BA-buh-lahn)
Hammurabi (ha-muh-RAH-bee)
Hittites (HIH-tiyts)
Minoan (mih-NOH-uhn)
Minoans (mih-NOH-uhns)
Persians (PUHR-zhuhns)

LEARN

Activity 1: A Look Back *(Online)*

Activity 2: History Journal Review *(Offline)*

Instructions

Now, review the unit by going through your History Journal. You should:

- Look at activity sheets and reading guides you completed for the unit.
- Review unit Keywords.
- Read through any writing assignments you completed during the unit.
- Review the offline lesson assessment you took.
- Skim through the chapters of *The Human Odyssey: Prehistory Through the Middle Ages* that you read in this unit.

Student Guide
Lesson 17: Unit Assessment

You've finished this unit! Now take the Unit Assessment.

Lesson Objectives

- List examples of the relationship between geography and the rise and fall of civilizations.
- Describe important people, characteristics, and contributions of the early Egyptian civilization.
- Describe important characteristics and contributions of the ancient Indus Valley civilization and possible explanations for its fall.
- List examples of ways in which the Indus Valley meets the criteria of a civilization.
- Recognize major factors that led to the development of the four river-valley civilizations of Mesopotamia, Egypt, the Indus Valley, and China.
- List examples of ways in which early China meets the criteria of a civilization.
- Recognize the characteristics of trade in ancient Egypt including the products traded, the location of trading partners, and the importance of trade in Egyptian life.
- Compare and contrast the early river-valley civilizations.
- Describe important people, characteristics, and contributions of the early Chinese civilization.
- Recognize examples of human and physical characteristics of place in Egypt, the Indus Valley, and early China.
- List examples of ways in which ancient Egypt meets the criteria of a civilization.

PREPARE

Approximate lesson time is 60 minutes.

Materials

For the Student

Question Review Table

ASSESS

Unit Assessment: Civilization Spreads, Part 1 (*Online*)

Complete the computer-scored portion of the Unit Assessment. When you have finished, complete the teacher-scored portion of the assessment and submit it to your teacher.

Unit Assessment: Civilization Spreads, Part 2 *(Offline)*

Complete the teacher-scored portion of the Unit Assessment and submit it to your teacher.

LEARN

Activity 1: Unit Assessment Review Table *(Online)*

If you earned a score of **less than 80%** on the Unit Assessment, complete the activity.

If you earned a score of **80% or greater**, you may skip this activity.

Let's prepare to retake the Unit Assessment:

- Identify the questions that you answered incorrectly.
- Complete the appropriate review activities listed in the table.

Assessment Date

Unit 4: Civilization Spreads

Before you retake the Unit Assessment, use the table to figure out which activities you should review.

Question Review Table

Circle the numbers of the questions that you missed on the Unit Assessment. Review the activities that correspond with these questions.

Question	Lesson	Review Activity
1 (online)	1: A River Rules	Life Along the Nile
2 (online)	6: How Many Kingdoms?	Egypt's Three Kingdoms
3 (online)	4: Something to Write About	Ancient Egyptian Writing
4 (online); 6 (online); 8 (online)	11: Remarkable Cities	Cities of the Indus Valley
5 (online)	12: Civilization Along the Yellow and Yangtze	Two Mighty Rivers
7 (online); 3 (offline); 6 (offline); 7 (offline)	13: The Silk People	Soft as Silk
9 (online)	11: Remarkable Cities 13: The Silk People	Cities of the Indus Valley Soft as Silk
1 (offline)	7: Significant Pharaohs	Kingdoms of Egypt
2 (offline); 5 (offline)	9: Thinking About Egypt	Comparing Cultures
4 (offline)	8: Ramses II: Conqueror and Builder	Ramses Reigns
8 (offline)	11: Remarkable Cities 5: Life in Ancient Egypt 14: Writing and Ruling	Cities of the Indus Valley Daily Living in Ancient Egypt Writing, Ruling, and Mighty Shang

Student Guide
Unit 5: Writing About the Past

Lesson 1: Think Before You Write
It's time to use what you have learned. Historians often compare and contrast new information with what they already know. You will do the same. How were the early river-valley civilizations alike? How were they different? Write an essay to express your thoughts.

You've trekked through time and visited the early civilizations that developed in Mesopotamia, Egypt, the Indus Valley, and China. It's time to take a quick look back and write about what you've learned. To get ready to write an essay comparing and contrasting the early river valley civilizations, you will analyze the topics and brainstorm with knowledge gained in previous lessons.

Lesson Objectives

- Review information from earlier lessons and units.
- Compare and contrast the early river civilizations.

PREPARE

Approximate lesson time is 60 minutes.

Materials

For the Student

Planning a Compare and Contrast Essay

Reading Guide

The Human Odyssey: Prehistory Through the Middle Ages edited by Klee, Cribb, and Holdren

History Journal

LEARN
Activity 1: Remember and Reflect *(Offline)*

Instructions

Read

Read the Conclusion, "A Look Back and a Leap Forward," pages 141-147.

Complete the Reading Guide as you read.

Use What You Know

The river-valley civilizations that developed in Mesopotamia, Egypt, the Indus Valley, and China shared some important characteristics, but they also differed in many ways.

Sometimes the best way to understand a place is to compare and contrast it with other places. When you compare places, you describe how they are alike. When you contrast places, you point out how they are different.

Today you will get ready to write an essay comparing and contrasting the ancient river valley civilizations you have studied. To prepare:

- Print the Planning a Compare and Contrast Essay sheet.
- Complete the five steps described on the sheet.

ASSESS

Lesson Assessment: Think Before You Write (*Offline*)

You will complete an offline assessment covering some of the main points of this lesson. Your assessment will be scored by the teacher.

Name ______________________ Date ______________________

Reading Guide

1. What do we mean by *civilization*? What would you look for in a society to figure out if it was a civilization or not? ______________________

2. In what four regions did civilization emerge? In what order? ______________________

3. What supported the growth of civilization in all four regions? ______________________

4. What is *division of labor*? How did it lead to the emergence of civilization? ______________________

Name _______________ Date _______________

Planning a Compare and Contrast Essay

Essay: River-valley civilizations developed in Mesopotamia, Egypt, China, and the Indus River Valley. Write an essay comparing and contrasting them.

Step 1: Read and analyze the assignment.

- Read the assignment.
- Highlight important words in each part of the assignment.
- Circle on the list below what the assignment is asking you to do. You may circle more than one item. Does the assignment ask you to:
  1. compare and contrast?
  2. explain?
  3. describe?
  4. agree or disagree with a statement?
  5. prove something?
- Write a sentence explaining what the assignment is asking you to do. Start with "I will _____."

  ____

  ____

  ____
- Show your sentence to an adult and discuss your understanding of the assignment.

Step 2: Record what you know.

- Look at the Comparing Cultures chart that you began in Unit 3, Lesson 14. If you didn't complete the chart, add the information now. For example, did you include that it was easier to farm along the Nile River than in some other areas because it was easier to predict the Nile floods than the floods of the other rivers?

Planning a Compare and Contrast Essay

Step 3: Organize what you know.

- Use the Comparing Cultures chart you completed to help you write the essay. Your chart shows the characteristics of each civilization and should reveal the similarities and differences among the ancient river-valley civilizations. (You might want to jot down notes in the Similarities and Differences column.)
- Study the chart carefully.
- Highlight the most important similarities in one color. Highlight significant differences in another color.
- Look carefully for similarities and differences among the civilizations.

Step 4: Write a thesis statement.

- Now it is time to write a thesis statement. Go back and read the assignment and your sentence of understanding again.
- What is your thesis? You will include it in the introduction to your essay.
    1. Write your thesis in one or two clear sentences.
    2. Use third person–don't use the words "I," "we," or "you."
    3. Do not use any specific pieces of information in this short statement. You will add specifics later.

Sample: The ancient civilizations of Mesopotamia, Egypt, India, and China relied on rivers for their existence, but they developed very different…

Thesis:____

____

____

____

____

Planning a Compare and Contrast Essay

Step 5: Outline

- Your Comparing Cultures chart has helped you organize your information. Now you will create an outline to organize the information the way you will use it in your essay in the form of an outline.

- The body of your essay must contain two main topics. Your topics are how the civilizations are alike and how they are different. (The main topics of an outline follow roman numerals and periods (I., II.) See outline below.

- Write a topic sentence for the first part of the body of your essay on the outline below. Be sure that it tells the reader what this section will be about and how it relates to your thesis statement. Your topic sentence might say something like, "The people of Mesopotamia, Egypt, the Indus Valley, and China all relied on rivers to develop a civilization, and all practiced polytheistic religions closely related to nature."

- Decide which pieces of information you will use to support your topic sentence. In an outline, these are called subtopics. Subtopics follow capital letters and periods (A., B., C.). See outline below.

- Decide what order the information, or subtopics should be in. Add this information beneath your topic sentence on the outline below. Remember to write each subtopic after a capital letter. (You may not need all the capital letters on the outline, and you may add more capital letters if you need them.)

- You can further divide subtopics into specific facts. In an outline, specific facts follow arabic numerals and periods (1., 2., 3., 4.). Each subtopic or specific fact must contain at least two parts (A. and B., or 1. and 2.) See outline below. Add this information beneath your subtopics on the outline below. (You may add more Arabic numerals if you need them.)

- Follow the same procedure for the other section of the body of your essay.

- Check your Comparing Cultures chart. You will not use all of the information, but be sure you have not left out anything that you think is important in completing the assignment.

- Remember, your outline and your essay should match each other exactly.

Planning a Compare and Contrast Essay

I. First Main Topic: Comparing early river valley civilizations

Topic sentence:____

____

____

A.
1.
2.

B.
1.
2.

C.
1.
2.

D.
1.
2.

II. Second Main Topic: Contrasting early river-valley civilizations

Topic sentence:____

____

____

A.
1.
2.

B.
1.
2.

C.
1.
2.

D.
1.
2.

Student Guide
Lesson 2: Writing

Write an essay comparing and contrasting the early civilizations that developed in Mesopotamia, Egypt, the Indus Valley, and China.

Lesson Objectives

- Compare and contrast the river-valley civilizations in a well-constructed essay.
- Compare and contrast the early river civilizations.

PREPARE

Approximate lesson time is 60 minutes.

Materials

For the Student

Writing a Compare and Contrast Essay

The Human Odyssey: Prehistory Through the Middle Ages edited by Klee, Cribb, and Holdren

History Journal

LEARN

Activity 1: Write About It *(Offline)*

Instructions

Use What You Know

In the last lesson, you organized your essay. Now it is time to write the essay.

1. Keep your outline and charts where you can see them easily.
2. Follow the steps on the Writing a Compare and Contrast Essay sheet to write your essay.
3. Share your essay with an adult.

ASSESS

Lesson Assessment: Writing (*Online*)

You will complete an offline assessment covering some of the main points of this lesson.
Your assessment will be scored by the teacher.

LEARN

Activity 2: Writing *(Offline)*

Instructions

Read Part 2, Introduction, pages 149-157.

Name Date

Writing a Compare and Contrast Essay

Step 1: Write the introduction

- Your thesis statement will form the core of your introduction, but you may want to add some other general information to grab the reader's attention. Remember that the main purpose of an introduction in a compare and contrast essay is to identify what you will be comparing and contrasting and preview the main points of comparison in the order you will discuss them.
- You may want to double-space your essay so you have room to make revisions later.

Step 2: Write the body of the essay

- Follow your outline to write the main body of your essay.
- Begin each paragraph with the topic sentence you wrote on your outline. It should state the main point of the paragraph. The other sentences in the paragraph should support that main point. Finish each paragraph with a concluding sentence that reinforces the main point and connects back to the thesis statement.

Step 3: Write the conclusion

- Write a concluding paragraph that summarizes the similarities and differences in broad terms and restates your thesis statement in some way. Write no more than three or four sentences.

Step 4: Revise and refine

- Now go back and make your essay as good as it can be. Read back through the whole essay. Are all your ideas clearly written? Does each paragraph have a topic sentence? Is each paragraph focused? Do all sentences in the paragraph relate to the topic sentence? It not, make any changes now.
- Make sure your essay follows this format:
  Paragraph 1 – Introduction that includes the thesis statement
  Paragraph 2 – Compare the four early river-valley civilizations
  Paragraph 3 – Contrast the four early river-valley civilizations
  Paragraph 4 – Conclusion that summarizes the major ideas and restates the thesis
- Correct any spelling, grammar, or punctuation mistakes you see. (Reading the essay aloud is a good strategy.)
- Save your changes or copy your essay.

Name Date

Planning a Compare and Contrast Essay

Essay: River-valley civilizations developed in Mesopotamia, Egypt, China, and the Indus River Valley. Write an essay comparing and contrasting them.

Step 1: Read and analyze the assignment.

- Read the assignment.
- Highlight important words in each part of the assignment.
- Circle on the list below what the assignment is asking you to do. You may circle more than one item. Does the assignment ask you to:
    1. compare and contrast?
    2. explain?
    3. describe?
    4. agree or disagree with a statement?
    5. prove something?
- Write a sentence explaining what the assignment is asking you to do. Start with "I will _____."

  ____

  ____

  ____
- Show your sentence to an adult and discuss your understanding of the assignment.

Step 2: Record what you know.

- Look at the Comparing Cultures chart that you began in Unit 3, Lesson 14. If you didn't complete the chart, add the information now. For example, did you include that it was easier to farm along the Nile River than in some other areas because it was easier to predict the Nile floods than the floods of the other rivers?

Planning a Compare and Contrast Essay

Step 3: Organize what you know.

- Use the Comparing Cultures chart you completed to help you write the essay. Your chart shows the characteristics of each civilization and should reveal the similarities and differences among the ancient river-valley civilizations. (You might want to jot down notes in the Similarities and Differences column.)

- Study the chart carefully.

- Highlight the most important similarities in one color. Highlight significant differences in another color.

- Look carefully for similarities and differences among the civilizations.

Step 4: Write a thesis statement.

- Now it is time to write a thesis statement. Go back and read the assignment and your sentence of understanding again.

- What is your thesis? You will include it in the introduction to your essay.
    1. Write your thesis in one or two clear sentences.
    2. Use third person–don't use the words "I," "we," or "you."
    3. Do not use any specific pieces of information in this short statement. You will add specifics later.

Sample: The ancient civilizations of Mesopotamia, Egypt, India, and China relied on rivers for their existence, but they developed very different...

Thesis:____

Planning a Compare and Contrast Essay

Step 5: Outline

- Your Comparing Cultures chart has helped you organize your information. Now you will create an outline to organize the information the way you will use it in your essay in the form of an outline.

- The body of your essay must contain two main topics. Your topics are how the civilizations are alike and how they are different. (The main topics of an outline follow roman numerals and periods (I., II.) See outline below.

- Write a topic sentence for the first part of the body of your essay on the outline below. Be sure that it tells the reader what this section will be about and how it relates to your thesis statement. Your topic sentence might say something like, "The people of Mesopotamia, Egypt, the Indus Valley, and China all relied on rivers to develop a civilization, and all practiced polytheistic religions closely related to nature."

- Decide which pieces of information you will use to support your topic sentence. In an outline, these are called subtopics. Subtopics follow capital letters and periods (A., B., C.). See outline below.

- Decide what order the information, or subtopics should be in. Add this information beneath your topic sentence on the outline below. Remember to write each subtopic after a capital letter. (You may not need all the capital letters on the outline, and you may add more capital letters if you need them.)

- You can further divide subtopics into specific facts. In an outline, specific facts follow arabic numerals and periods (1., 2., 3., 4.). Each subtopic or specific fact must contain at least two parts (A. and B., or 1. and 2.) See outline below. Add this information beneath your subtopics on the outline below. (You may add more Arabic numerals if you need them.)

- Follow the same procedure for the other section of the body of your essay.

- Check your Comparing Cultures chart. You will not use all of the information, but be sure you have not left out anything that you think is important in completing the assignment.

- Remember, your outline and your essay should match each other exactly.

Planning a Compare and Contrast Essay

I. First Main Topic: Comparing early river valley civilizations

Topic sentence:____

____

____

A.
1.
2.

B.
1.
2.

C.
1.
2.

D.
1.
2.

II. Second Main Topic: Contrasting early river-valley civilizations

Topic sentence:____

____

____

A.
1.
2.

B.
1.
2.

C.
1.
2.

D.
1.
2.

Student Guide
Lesson 3. Optional: Your Choice

Lesson Objectives

- Explore knowledge and skills taught in this course.

PREPARE

Approximate lesson time is 60 minutes.

Student Guide

Unit 6: Some Lasting Ideas
Lesson 1: A Wise Teacher

People have always wondered how the world came to be and how it works. Their wonderful curiosity led to ideas and insights that have survived through the ages. Almost a billion people practice Hinduism today. Another half billion follow the teachings of Buddha. Confucianism endures in East Asia and elsewhere. How did people form these belief systems? Why have they lasted so long?

How much difference can one person make? When Confucius first began to teach, China was in trouble. Peace and unity had given way to warring among small provinces. Government was corrupt. The rich lived in great houses while the poor lacked even the basics of life--like food. Confucius was honest, fair, and loved learning. He gave China a philosophy that eventually transformed society.

Lesson Objectives

- Identify the most influential philosopher in Chinese history.
- Explain the state of political unrest in China during the time that Confucius lived and taught.
- Describe the Confucian notion of an enlightened ruler.
- Explain why Confucius thought the family provided a good model for Chinese society.

PREPARE

Approximate lesson time is 60 minutes.

Materials

For the Student

Reading Guide

The Human Odyssey: Prehistory Through the Middle Ages edited by Klee, Cribb, and Holdren

History Journal

Keywords and Pronunciation

Confucius (kuhn-FYOO-shuhs)

Zhou (djoh)

LEARN

Activity 1: The Great Teacher *(Offline)*

Instructions

Check Your Reading

Society's traditional values and ideas influence people. You can see that in Ren Li's actions in the story "The Paper Maker's Son" (Part 2, Introduction, pages 149-157).

What Chinese values or ideas influenced Ren Li when she did each of the following? Write your responses in your History Journal.

1. Ren Li stopped to listen in on the calligraphy lesson.
2. Instead of making excuses, she told her father the truth when she returned to the shop with the cold food.

3. Ren Li worked harder than ever--he even did things without being asked.
4. Ren Li stood up for her father when the scholar asked if Ren Li wanted to become something better than a paper maker.

Read

Even the Chinese sage Confucius, whose sayings Ren Li knew by heart, was influenced by the values and ideas of her society. Complete the Reading Guide as you read Part 2, Chapter 1, from the beginning to "The Five Relationships," pages 159-163.

Activity 2: A Time of Turmoil *(Online)*

Instructions

Follow the directions to take the Lesson Assessment online.

ASSESS

Lesson Assessment: A Wise Teacher (*Online*)

You will complete an online assessment covering the main points of this lesson. Your assessment will be scored by the computer.

Name ______________________________ Date ______________________________ 

Reading Guide

Directions: Complete this Reading Guide as you read Part 2, Chapter 1, from the beginning to "The Five Relationships," pages 159-163.

I. From Unity to Warring States

A. The ______________ dynasty was China's first dynasty.

1. It ruled for more than ________________ years.
2. The rulers ______________ the early Chinese people.
3. Under this dynasty, Chinese civilization _____________ and ________________ .

B. The ________________ dynasty came to power around _________________ .

1. China disintegrated into a collection of ________________ _________________.
2. Rich _________________ kept their own armies.
3. Rulers cared little about the ________________ people.

II. Confucius: The Great Teacher

A. Confucius was born around_________________ and at a very early age he decided to become a _________________ .

1. He _____________ ancient writings.
2. He ________________ China's history.
3. He _________________ from state to state.

B. Confucius became a _____________________ and ______________________ teacher.

1. He welcomed all_________________ .
2. He did not like ____________________ pupils.
3. He passed on important ______________ to others.

   a. The secret to a peaceful land and good life was ________________ ______________ .
   b. To live well, a person must be a _________________ .
   c. Right behavior led to a ___________________ ______________________ .

III. In Search of an Enlightened Ruler

A. Confucius wanted to do something about the ________________ and________________ .

1. He wanted to bring back the days of the early ___________________ kings.

2. Those rulers acted with ________________.
3. The common people treated each other ________________.

B. To try out his reforms, Confucius wanted to take a role in ________________.

1. From time to time he took ________________ in the government.
2. He became an excellent ________________ ________________.
3. He was too ________________ for most rulers.

C. He urged rulers to work hard to bring good government to the people.

1. He told rulers to________________ themselves if they wanted their kingdom to change.
2. ________________ officials feared Confucius's ideas of ________________ leadership.
3. Nobles and lords ________________ Confucius's advice.

D. The right opportunity to play an important role in government never came along.

1. Confucius spent most of his life as a ________________.
2. He wanted his students to learn how to live ________________ lives.
3. Confucius wanted them to learn the right ways to ________________ and ________________.
4. He taught as many students as possible so that one day some of his students might become ________________.
5. He taught his students to be the kind of people he wanted to ________________China.

In your own words, describe Confucius's idea of an enlightened ruler.

____

____

____

IV. The Family and Good Government

A. Confucius used the ________________ as a model for good government.

1. From the early years of Chinese civilization, families worshiped their ________________.
2. Young people respected ________________ relatives.

B. Confucius placed great importance on family ________________.

1. He said that within the family, people learn ________________, ________________, and ________________.

2. He urged young people to obey and honor their ____________________ .
3. He taught that older generations should give young people ________________ and ____________________ .

C. Confucius viewed ____________ ___________ as being more important in society than ______________ .

1. He believed that ____________ for others was the key to ___________ government.
2. He thought good conduct _______________ others to be good.
3. He said society would grow more harmonious when people treated others _______________ and with ________________ .

Why did Confucius think the family was a good model for Chinese society?

____

____

____

Student Guide
Lesson 2: Relationships and Rulers

Historians know that economic and political conditions influence people and events. Confucius lived in a time of chaos. Although the Zhou dynasty officially ruled China, the real power belonged to individual feudal lords who fought among themselves and with neighboring peoples for territory and wealth. Confucius was one of the scholars who tried to help restore order and return to enlightened rulers. His teachings became the basis of a great philosophy--Confucianism--and still exert great influence today.

Lesson Objectives

- Describe the five relationships described in Confucian philosophy and explain their importance to a good society.
- Identify the Golden Rule and its earliest known teacher.
- Explain why Confucianism is a philosophy and not a religion.
- Identify the *Analects of Confucius.*

PREPARE

Approximate lesson time is 60 minutes.

Materials

For the Student

- Comparing Religions and Philosophies
- Relationships and Rulers

The Human Odyssey: Prehistory Through the Middle Ages edited by Klee, Cribb, and Holdren

Keywords and Pronunciation

Confucius (kuhn-FYOO-shuhs)
Maya (MIY-uh)
Zhou (djoh)

LEARN

Activity 1: More on Confucius *(Offline)*

Instructions

Read

What were the "five relationships" and why did Confucius believe they were important to a good society? As you read Chapter 1, from "The Five Relationships" to the end, pages 164-167, complete Part 1 of the Relationships and Rulers sheet.

Use What You Know

Finish the Relationships and Rulers sheet by completing Part 2.

Comparing Religions and Philosophies

In earlier units, you completed a chart with information about several early civilizations, or cultures. The chart helped organize the information you needed to write an essay comparing and contrasting those early cultures.

You'll be doing something similar in this unit and upcoming units. This time, you'll be gathering information about early religions and philosophies.

To start, complete the column for Confucianism on the Comparing Religions and Philosophies sheet. You may need to review the previous lesson to complete some of the categories. Since Confucianism is a philosophy and not a religion, it's possible to practice any religion and still strive to uphold the ideals of Confucianism. Therefore, the last two categories in the chart are filled in for you.

ASSESS

Lesson Assessment: Relationships and Rulers (*Online*)

You will complete an online assessment covering the main points of this lesson. Your assessment will be scored by the computer.

Name Date

Comparing Religions and Philosophies

Category	Who founded it?	When was it founded?	What are the principal beliefs?	What are the principal sacred texts?
Confucianism				
Hinduism				
Buddhism				
Judaism				
Christianity				
Islam				

Comparing Religions and Philosophies

Category	Confucianism	Hinduism	Buddhism	Judaism	Christianity	Islam
In which geographic regions does it predominate today?	Confucianism continues to influence millions of people in East Asia, but it is a philosophy and not a religion. Therefore, it's possible to practice any religion and still strive to uphold the ideals of Confucianism.					
Roughly how many followers are there in the world today?	see above					

Name Date

Relationships and Rulers

Complete Part 1 as you read Chapter 1, from "The Five Relationships" to the end, pages 164-167.

Part 1

1. Confucius noted five different kinds of relationships among people. He said there was a proper way to behave in each. Label each box with the name of one of the relationships. In Part 2 you will fill in the rest of the box.

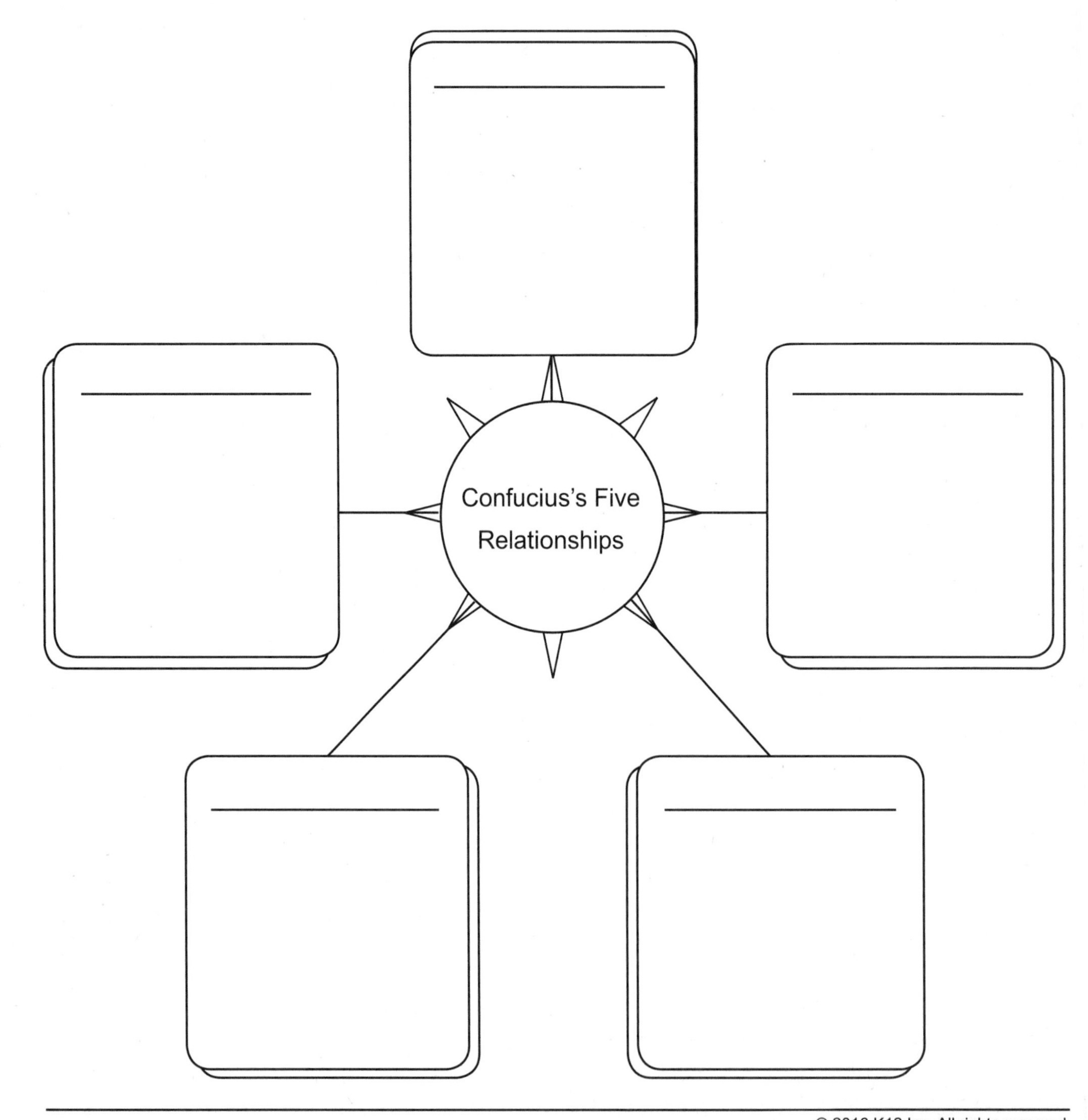

Relationships and Rulers

2. What was Confucius's Golden Rule? ____________________

3. How did Confucius describe a wise man? ____________________

____

How did he describe a good man? ____________________

4. How do Confucian teachings differ from religious ideas? ____________________

____

5. What did Confucius think the Way of Heaven was? ____________________

____

6. What is the *Analects of Confucius*? ____________________

____

7. Who wrote the *Analects of Confucius*? ____________________

8. Describe why Confucius believed the five relationships were important to a good society.

____

____

____

9. Choose three of Confucius's sayings from the *Analects of Confucius* and write them below. Choose the ones that have some kind of meaning or are relevant to you. (Do not translate them yet.)

a. ____________________

Translation: ____________________

b. ____________________

Translation: ____________________

c. ____________________

Translation: ____________________

Relationships and Rulers

Part 2

1. Think about your own relationships with your family and friends. Think about national and local government and the people who are your leaders. What are the relationships in your life like?

____

____

____

In the boxes in Part 1, describe each of the relationships as it exists in your life or how the relationship influences your daily life or the lives of the people around you.

2. On the lines labeled "translation" in question 9, rewrite each of the three sayings in your own words.

Thinking Cap Question

3. Does the Confucian idea of five relationships apply to us today? Why or why not?

____

____

____

Student Guide
Lesson 3: Who Made a Difference?

Can one person make a difference? History tells us that the answer to this question is yes, but you need to think about it yourself.

Lesson Objectives

- Recognize that individuals have exerted great influence in history.
- Summarize the work and influence of Confucius.

PREPARE

Approximate lesson time is 60 minutes.

Materials

For the Student

Personality Profile: Confucius

The Human Odyssey: Prehistory Through the Middle Ages edited by Klee, Cribb, and Holdren

History Journal

LEARN
Activity 1: Personality Profile: Confucius *(Offline)*
Instructions

Who Made a Difference?

Can one person make a difference? Consider some famous people from the past. You've probably heard of Socrates, Jesus, and Muhammad. What about Homer and Shakespeare? Galileo? Isaac Newton? Marie Curie? Albert Einstein? Perhaps you know something about Charlemagne, William the Conqueror, or Attila the Hun. Can you name the country that had Elizabeth I as queen or Catherine the Great as empress? Do you know the works of Michelangelo and Beethoven? What reaction do you have when you hear the name Adolf Hitler? And what about the influence of modern individuals like Martin Luther King, Jr., or Mother Teresa?

Billions of people have lived on Earth over the course of time. Some had a quiet influence that historians will never know about. Others changed the world for better or for worse in ways that made them famous even hundreds or thousands of years later. They might have been philosophers or religious figures. They might have been political or military leaders. Some changed the world through their art or scientific studies. A few committed or promoted evil. And some saw the problems of the world and set out to fix them.

Why do some people rise to fame or infamy? (Look up the word *infamy* if you don't know the meaning--it's a good word.) What factors play a part in making a person influential in some way? Would that person stand out in another time or place or circumstance?

We will never know the answers to all those questions. But historians often look at the power of the individual in history. As you learn about more and more individuals, consider their influence and why they had such an impact on the world. Will you have a notable impact on history? Only time will tell.

Discuss

Discuss with an adult what you have just read.

- Explain what makes an individual influential.
- Describe the characteristics you believe a person who can make a difference should have.
- Does an influential person with such characteristics have a moral obligation to use her or her influence for good?
- Think of someone (other than Confucius) who you believe has made a difference in the world. How did that person influence society? Would the future have been different if the person had used her or her influence in another way?

Personality Profiles

In certain lessons throughout the rest of this course you will take a closer look at some important figures in world history. Most historians agree that these people made a difference. It will be your task to dig into the personalities of these historical figures to understand the following aspects of their lives:

- What influenced them
- What they believed in and taught
- How they influenced and affected society after their death
- How they are remembered today

For each of these people you will complete a Personality Profile sheet. You will need to do a little research on each person using your textbook, Grolier's online encyclopedia, and other sources of information. The first Personality Profile you'll complete is on Confucius.

Personality Profile: Confucius

Most historians consider Confucius to be one of the most influential people in history. He lived two and a half millennia ago, but the world still feels his influence. Confucius was born into humble conditions and lived when Chinese warlords ruled with little concern for high moral principles or common values. Despite his situation, or perhaps because of it, Confucius had a goal of bringing peace and order to China. How much of a difference in history did Confucius make?

Complete the Personality Profile: Confucius sheet by using information from your textbook and Grolier's online encyclopedia.

1. Draw (or cut out and paste) a picture of Confucius in the center oval.
2. Fill in the year he was born and the year he died.
3. On the line below that, write the title he came to be known by and its meaning.
4. In the thought bubble, write something that Confucius might have said to her pupils about the key to good behavior and good government.
5. In the picture frame, draw a picture that illustrates the most important relationship of the Five Relationships.
6. In the first square, identify the influences on Confucius.
7. In the second square, write Confucius's main beliefs.
8. In the third square, explain how Confucius influenced others and his society.
9. In the fourth square, tell how Confucius is remembered today.

In your History Journal, use the information from the Personality Profile: Confucius sheet, your textbook, and Grolier's online encyclopedia to write a summary of the life of Confucius. Include facts about his desire to restore order and good government in China. Begin your paragraph by explaining that individuals influence history. Write a conclusion explaining how Confucius influenced history and answering the questions "Can one person make a difference?" and "Did Confucius make a difference?"

ASSESS

Lesson Assessment: Who Made a Difference? (*Online*)

You will complete an online assessment covering the main points of this lesson. Your assessment will be scored by the computer.

Name Date

Personality Profile: Confucius

Student Guide
Lesson 4: Qin Shi Huangdi Unites China

Qin Shi Huangdi, known as the "Tiger of China," was the first emperor of a united China. He wanted direct control of a centralized government. He got it, but he wasn't a benevolent ruler and he wasn't always wise. Although his reign was short, he left an important legacy and several lasting monuments. Two of the most famous monuments are the Great Wall and his tomb filled with clay warriors.

Lesson Objectives

- Describe at least two steps Qin took to centralize government or standardize procedures in China.
- Describe the purpose of the Tomb of the Underground Warriors.
- Explain why the Great Wall of China was built.
- Identify Qin Shi Huangdi.
- Indicate on a map the extent of the Qin empire and the Great Wall.

PREPARE

Approximate lesson time is 60 minutes.

Materials

For the Student

Qin's Problems

The Human Odyssey: Prehistory Through the Middle Ages edited by Klee, Cribb, and Holdren

History Journal

Keywords and Pronunciation

Qin (chin)

Qin Shi Huangdi (chin shur hwahng-dee)

LEARN

Activity 1: Qin: The Tiger of China *(Offline)*

Instructions

Read

Qin Shi Huangdi seized control of China's warring states in the third century B.C. He was not what Confucius would call an enlightened ruler. Qin believed in the power of might. He unified China under a centralized government and set about solving his empire's problems.

Read Chapter 2, from the beginning to "The Han Dynasty and the Legacy of Confucius," pages 169-173, and complete the Qin's Problems sheet. Check your answers in the Lesson Answer Key.

Focus on Geography

Use the map of The Unification of China on page 174 of your textbook to help you answer the following questions in your History Journal.

1. What was the natural boundary of the Qin empire to the south? To the north?
2. Approximately how many miles did the Qin empire extend from north to south? From east to west?
3. What is the latitude and longitude of the westernmost point of the Great Wall? Of the easternmost point?
4. How does the location of the Great Wall reflect the function of the wall?
5. Now look at the map of modern China in the atlas in your textbook. What has been the most significant change in China's boundaries since the Qin dynasty?

Check your answers with those in the Lesson Answer Key. Then, go back online to complete the lesson.

Activity 2: The Great Wall *(Online)*

ASSESS

Lesson Assessment: Qin Shi Huangdi Unites China (*Online*)

You will complete an online assessment covering the main objectives of this lesson. Your assessment will be scored by the computer.

Name ____________________ Date ____________________

Qin's Problems

Directions: Use the Word Banks to identify Qin's solution to each of the problems and what happened when the solutions were implemented. Some results will be used more than once.

Problem	Solution	Results
1. Loyalty to states rather than empire		
2. Empire very large		
3. Money from one region useless in other regions		
4. Reports from one part of empire couldn't be read in other parts		
5. Villages weigh rice differently		
6. Invaders attack from the north		

Solutions

built Great Wall
standardized system of writing
forced nobles to move to capital and appointed state governors
standardized system of weights and measures
built network of roads and canals
standardized currency

Results

empire unified
made China safer, but many workers died
unified and centralized government made it easier to rule
improved communication among regions

Thinking Cap Question

How might standardization of money, writing, and weights and measures, help unify diverse parts of a large country?

Student Guide
Lesson 5: The Han

Historians look for changes over time in societies. But they also look for continuity--things that stay the same. In China, people welcomed the change from the Qin to the Han dynasty. The Han kept the good features of the Qin dynasty--such as a unified central government--but they instituted many needed reforms. The 400 years of Han rule heralded great advances in technology, commerce, and education. Even today, most Chinese refer to themselves as "the people of Han."

Lesson Objectives

- Describe the main achievements of the Han dynasty.
- Describe the role of Confucian teaching in the Han dynasty.
- Explain the significance of the *Analects of Confucius*.
- Describe the emerging importance of trade on the Silk Road.

PREPARE

Approximate lesson time is 60 minutes.

Materials

For the Student

The Human Odyssey: Prehistory Through the Middle Ages edited by Klee, Cribb, and Holdren

History Journal

Keywords and Pronunciation

Confucius (kuhn-FYOO-shuhs)

Han (hahn)

Qin (chin)

Qin Shi Huangdi (chin shur hwahng-dee)

LEARN

Activity 1: Confucius and the Han I *(Offline)*

Instructions

Read

Read Chapter 2, from "The Han Dynasty and the Legacy of Confucius" to the end, pages 173-177. As you read, list some of the achievements of the Han dynasty in your History Journal. When you've finished, go back online to complete the lesson.

Activity 2: Confucius and the Han II *(Online)*

Activity 3: The Silk Road *(Online)*

ASSESS

Lesson Assessment: The Han (*Online*)

You will complete an online assessment covering the main points of this lesson. Your assessment will be scored by the computer.

Student Guide
Lesson 6: Ideas of the Indus

The Aryans conquered the Indus River Valley people and introduced their own ideas of how society should be organized. Three millennia later their influence can still be seen in the religion and traditions of more than a billion people in the land we know as India.

Lesson Objectives

- Describe the Aryan migration and how it led to the development of Hinduism.
- Explain the origins and key features of the caste system.
- Identify the sacred writings of Hinduism.
- Describe the Hindu belief in reincarnation.

PREPARE

Approximate lesson time is 60 minutes.

Materials

For the Student

A Hindu View of the Four Castes

The Human Odyssey: Prehistory Through the Middle Ages edited by Klee, Cribb, and Holdren

History Journal

Keywords and Pronunciation

Brahmans (BRAH-muhns)
Upanishads (oo-PAH-nih-shahds)
Vedas (VAY-duhz)

LEARN

Activity 1: Aryans, the Caste System, and Hinduism *(Offline)*

Instructions

Read

Read Chapter 3, from the beginning to "Gods on the Ganges," pages 179-183.

Use What You Know

The Aryans differed from the people whose lands they invaded. They thought of themselves as superior to the darker-skinned people of the Indus valley. Over time, a *caste* system developed. It had four distinct classes or castes. There were also people who were "outside" the caste system. These people, who became known as outcastes or untouchables, were considered the bottom level of society.

Complete the Hindu View of the Four Castes sheet. When you've finished, use the Lesson Answer Key to check your work. Place the sheet in your History Journal.

Focus on Geography

The Aryan herders came out of the mountains from central Asia and invaded the Indus River Valley and beyond. Look at the map on page 180 of your textbook and respond to the following in your History Journal.

1. Trace the route of the Aryans as they migrated into the Indian subcontinent. What three modern countries occupy the areas the Aryans traveled through and settled? Use the atlas in the back of your textbook if you need help.
2. What mountain range forced the Aryans to migrate in a southeasterly direction?
3. On what plain did the Aryans settle?
4. In what direction did the Indus river valley people flee from the Aryan conquerors?
5. Give both the absolute and relative location of the easternmost point of the Aryan migration.

ASSESS

Lesson Assessment: Ideas of the Indus (*Online*)

You will complete an online assessment covering the main points of this lesson. Your assessment will be scored by the computer.

LEARN

Activity 2. Optional: Ideas of the Indus *(Online)*

Instructions

This activity is OPTIONAL. It's provided for enrichment or extra practice, but not required for completion of this lesson.

You may skip this activity.

Yoga was developed in India thousands of years ago. Today, most people who practice yoga in the West focus on the physical postures called asanas, breathing exercises called pranayama, and meditation.

Name ______________________________ Date ______________________________

A Hindu View of the Four Castes

Part 1

Read the following English translation of an excerpt from *The Code of Manu*, a Hindu book of sacred law. Then, answer the questions that follow.

For the sake of the preservation of this entire creation, Purusha, the exceedingly resplendent one, assigned separate duties to the classes which had sprung from his mouth, arms, thighs, and feet.

Teaching, studying, performing sacrificial rites, so too making others perform sacrificial rites, and giving away and receiving gifts—these he assigned to the brahmans.

Protection of the people, giving away of wealth, performance of sacrificial rites, study, and nonattachment to sensual pleasures—these are, in short, the duties of a kshatriya.

Tending of cattle, giving away of wealth, performance of sacrificial rites, study, trade and commerce, . . . and agriculture—these are the occupations of a vaishya.

The Lord has prescribed only one occupation . . . for a shudra; namely, service without malice of . . . these other three classes.

1. Which classes of people were allowed to study? ______________________________

   Why? ______________________________

   ____

2. To which caste would a farmer belong? Explain your answer.

   ____

   ____

3. Although people in three classes were allowed to perform sacrificial rites, only those in one class had the authority to preside over others during sacrificial rites. Which class was allowed to preside? Explain your answer.

   ____

   ____

   ____

   ____

A Hindu View of the Four Castes

4. Who belonged to the Kshatriya caste? Explain your answer. ____________________

____

____

5. To which class would someone who washed dishes in a nobleman's house belong?

   Explain your answer. ____________________

____

____

The following questions are not based on the text above. Refer to your textbook if you need help.

6. Who invaded the Indian subcontinent and developed the caste system? ____________________

____

7. Eventually, a large fifth class was added at the bottom of the caste system. What was the name of the class and how did the people in the other classes regard them?

____

____

A Hindu View of the Four Castes

Part 2

1. Label each part of the pyramid below with the names of the five social classes. Put the highest caste at the top of the pyramid and arrange the other castes in descending order below.

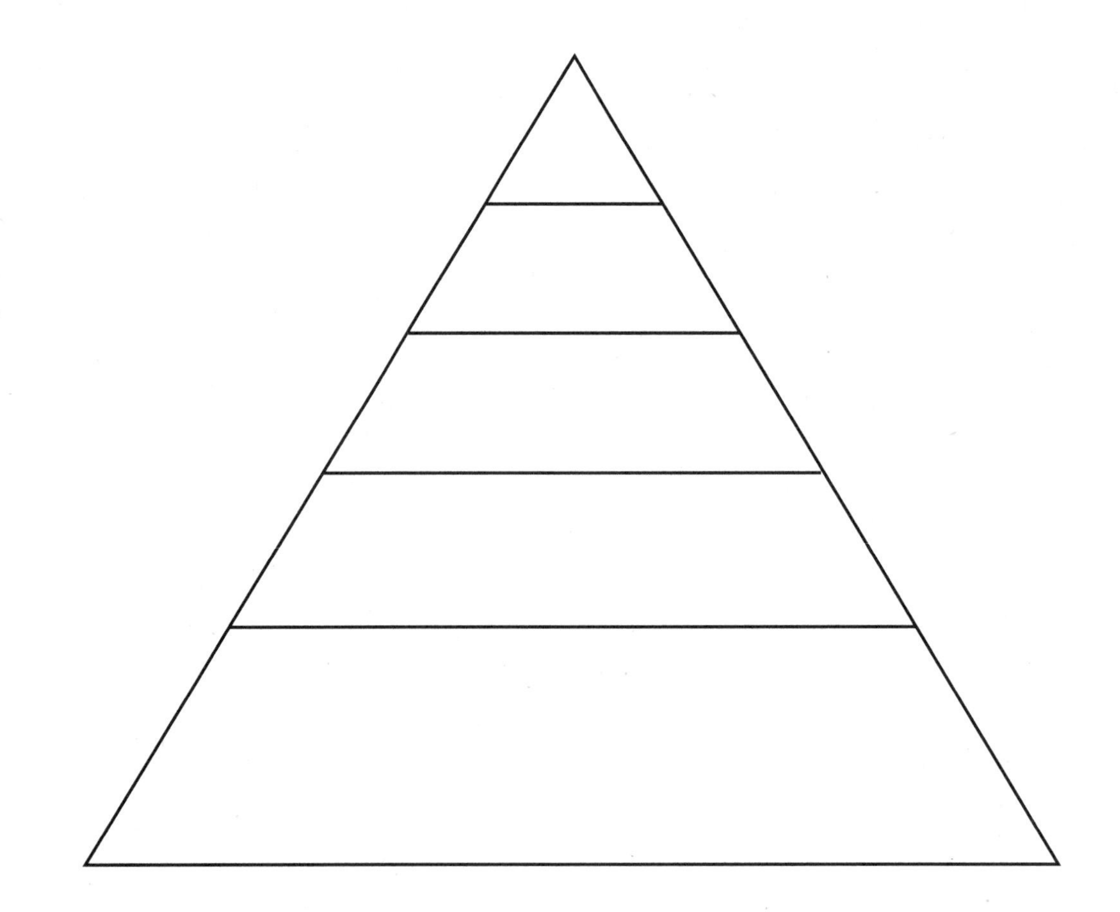

2. Which caste or group made up the largest proportion of the population?________________

____

3. Which caste or group made up the smallest proportion of the population?________________

____

4. The caste system was officially outlawed in India in 1955. How do you think the caste system has affected modern India? What problems might it have caused? ________________

____

____

Student Guide
Lesson 7: The Hindu View

Hinduism blended the beliefs of the Aryans with those of the people of the Indus Valley. Hindus worship many gods as part of one universal essence and believe in the cycle of death and rebirth known as *reincarnation.* In each life, Hindus are supposed to work hard, fulfill the duties of their caste, and work toward betterment in the next life. They believe the self will eventually reach spiritual perfection and unite with the universal spirit. Many Hindu beliefs are spelled out in the *Ramayana*, the epic poem that recounts the heroic adventures of Prince Rama.

Lesson Objectives

- Describe some of the Hindu beliefs regarding the Ganges as a sacred river.
- Identify the three main gods of Hinduism.
- Explain how the *Ramayana* describes the Hindu belief in the importance of duty and honor.

PREPARE

Approximate lesson time is 60 minutes.

Materials

For the Student

Hindu Values

The Human Odyssey: Prehistory Through the Middle Ages edited by Klee, Cribb, and Holdren

Keywords and Pronunciation

Brahma (BRAH-muh)
Ramayana (rah-muh-YAH-nuh)
Shiva (SHIH-vuh)
Upanishads (oo-PAH-nih-shahds)
Vedas (VAY-duhz)
Vishnu (VISH-noo)

LEARN

Activity 1: Hindu Gods and The Ramayana *(Offline)*

Instructions

Read

To many Hindus, the Ganges River is a sacred waterway that can wash away sin. How did that belief develop? Find out by reading Chapter 3, from "Gods on the Ganges" to the end, pages 184-189.
When you've finished reading, answer the following questions.

1. Name the three gods that became very important to Hindus during the first millennium B.C.

____

2. The Ganges River became sacred when _______________________________________.

3. According to Hindu tradition, what is the divine source of the Ganges River?

____

4. Describe, in general terms, the Hindu deities. ______________________________
____
____
____

Use What You Know

Do you remember the *Epic of Gilgamesh*? It was a classic of Sumerian literature and a source of information on Sumerian values. The *Ramayana* is an epic that illustrates Hindu values.

Fill out the Hindu Values sheet to explore the values Hindus admire.

Comparing Religions and Philosophies

Complete the column for Hinduism on the Comparing Religions and Philosophies chart. You may need to review the previous lesson to complete some of the categories. You'll need to research the last two categories. Use the atlas in your textbook and a good Internet search engine to do your research.

ASSESS

Lesson Assessment: The Hindu View (*Online*)

You will complete an online assessment covering the main points of this lesson. Your assessment will be scored by the computer.

Name Date

Hindu Values

Directions: Read the following quotes from *The Ramayana*. Identify characteristics from the Word Bank that the quote exemplifies. Write the characteristic(s) on the lines provided. Each quote may exemplify more than one characteristic and many of the characteristics will be described more than once.

1. "He had protected a holy man from hideous demons…" ______________________
2. "He lifted the bow as if it weighed no more than a toothpick…"

   ____
3. "You know it is our sacred duty to obey our father in all things."

   ____
4. "Rama had no fear." ______________________
5. "Then I will capture it for you." ______________________
6. "But I will never betray my husband." ______________________
7. "Calmly, he raised his bow and aimed the arrow at Ravana's heart."

   ____

Word Bank

fearless obedient devoted loyal
honest clever strong brave

Thinking Cap Question

Duty and honor are important values in Hindu culture. Write several sentences explaining how *The Ramayana* illustrates these and other important personal qualities.

____

____

____

____

____

Student Guide
Lesson 8: The Enlightened One

Born a prince, Siddhartha Gautama abandoned his privileged life at the age of twenty-nine to practice asceticism, or self-denial, with other holy men. But he soon became frustrated with that life too, and began hunting for another way to find the truth. When he was thirty-five, he cleared his mind by meditating and thought he finally understood the truth about life, thereby earning the title of Buddha, or "The Enlightened One." He traveled the countryside, living on charity and persuading others to accept his way of life.

Lesson Objectives

- Summarize Siddhartha Gautama's early life and search for meaning.
- Identify the founder of Buddhism.

PREPARE

Approximate lesson time is 60 minutes.

Materials

For the Student

Personality Profile: Siddhartha Gautama

The Human Odyssey: Prehistory Through the Middle Ages edited by Klee, Cribb, and Holdren

History Journal

Keywords and Pronunciation

asceticism (uh-SEH-tuh-sih-zuhm) : the practice of self-denial for spiritual understanding
ascetics (uh-SEH-tiks)
Buddha (BOO-duh)
Buddhism (BOO-dih-zuhm)
Kasappa (kah-SYAH-pah)
Kisa Gautami (KEE-suh GOW-tah-mee)
Shakyamuni (SHAH-kyah-moo-nee)
Siddhartha Gautama (*sid-DAHR-tuh GOW-tuh-muh*)

LEARN

Activity 1: The Enlightened One *(Offline)*

Instructions

Read

Read Chapter 4, pages 191-199, to learn about the life and teachings of Siddhartha Gautama, the young Indian prince who became the Buddha.

Use What You Know

Begin the Personality Profile: Siddhartha Gautama sheet.

- Draw (or cut out and paste) a picture of Siddhartha Gautama in the center oval.
- Fill in the year she was born and the year she died.
- On the line below that, write the name Siddhartha earned.
- In the thought bubble, write something that Siddhartha might have said to someone right after her enlightenment.
- In the picture frame, illustrate an important event in Siddhartha's life.
- Fill in as much information as you can in the four squares.
- You will add more information in the next lesson.

Write a summary of Siddhartha Gautama's early life and her search for the meaning of life. Use information from the sheet, your textbook, and Grolier's online encyclopedia to help you write the summary. It should consist of three paragraphs:

1. The first paragraph should give some background information about Siddhartha. It should include "the prophecy" and Siddhartha's father's decision.
2. The second paragraph should describe events that occurred between that decision and Siddhartha's commitment to try to eradicate suffering.
3. The third paragraph should cover events from the time Siddhartha left her father's palace to her experience "under the tree."

After writing your summary, check the Lesson Answer Key to see if you included the most important information.

ASSESS

Lesson Assessment: The Enlightened One (*Online*)

You will complete an online assessment covering the main points of this lesson. Your assessment will be scored by the computer.

Name Date

Personality Profile: Siddhartha Gautama

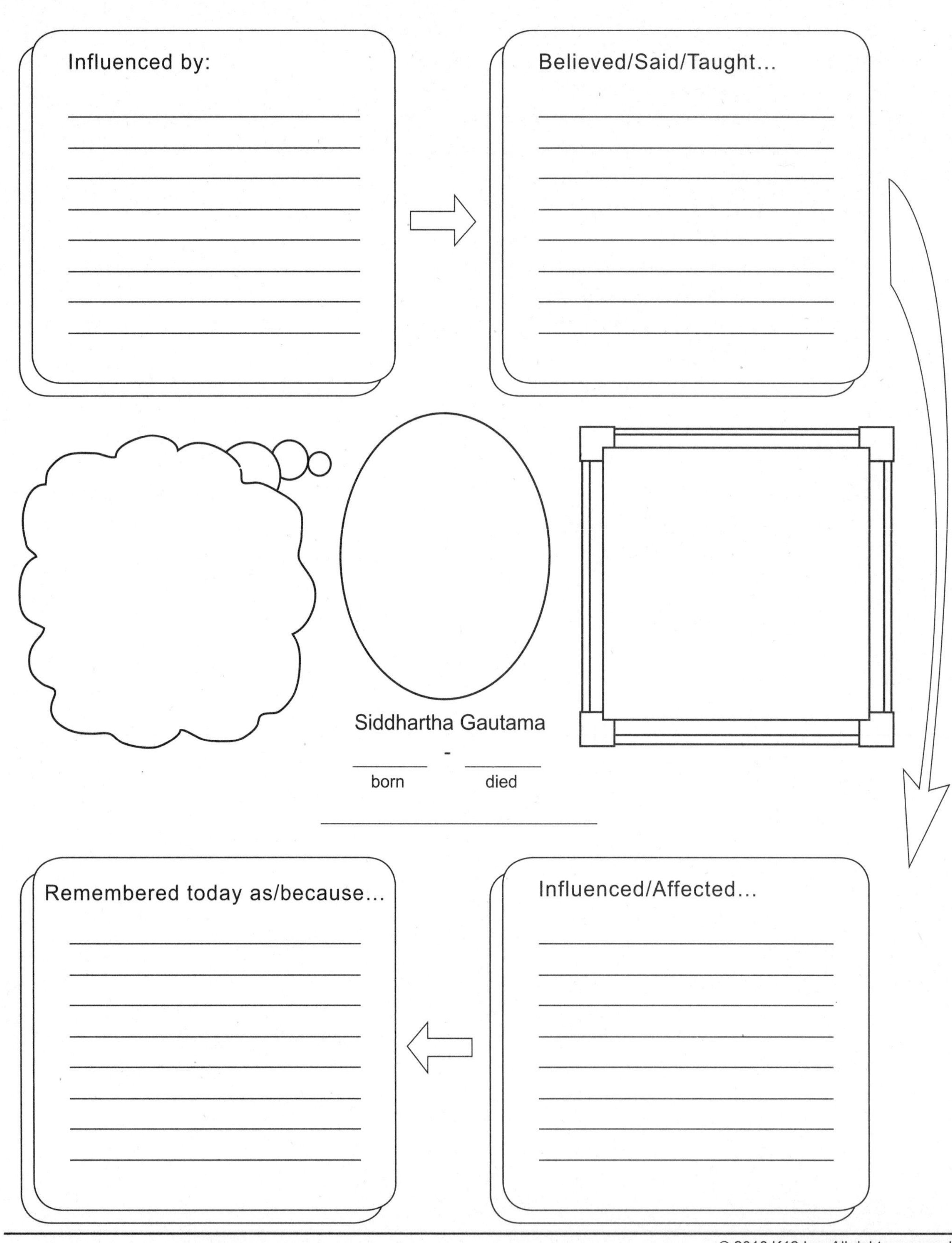

Student Guide
Lesson 9: A Search for Goodness

Siddhartha Gautama emerged from his long period of meditation and began to spread his beliefs. "Speak the truth," he said. "Do not give in to anger. Give generously to those who ask." Buddha explained that suffering was caused by desire, so people have to learn to overcome desire. He urged people to meditate and be compassionate. The reward for living a life filled with good deeds and thoughts? The Buddha called it Nirvana.

Lesson Objectives

- Describe Nirvana.
- Recognize major Buddhist beliefs.
- Describe the split in Buddhism regarding beliefs about Buddha.

PREPARE

Approximate lesson time is 60 minutes.

Materials

For the Student

Wheel of Dhamma

The Human Odyssey: Prehistory Through the Middle Ages edited by Klee, Cribb, and Holdren

History Journal

Keywords and Pronunciation

Buddha (BOO-duh)

dhamma (DHUH-muh)

Nirvana (nir-VAH-nuh)

Siddhartha Gautama (*sid-DAHR-tuh GOW-tuh-muh*)

LEARN

Activity 1: Four Noble Truths and an Eightfold Noble Path *(Offline)*

Instructions

Read

Read Chapter 5, from the beginning to "Asoka Follows the Buddha," pages 200-204.

Use What You Know

Continue adding information to the Personality Profile: Siddhartha Gautama. Use the lesson answer key to check your work.

Analogies help us understand complex ideas or concepts. Let's try to understand the Four Noble Truths by using an analogy. Think about when you are sick.

- You know you don't feel well - The Truth of Suffering.
- You go to the doctor to find out what is wrong - The Truth of the Cause of Suffering.
- You ask the doctor what will make you feel better - The Truth of the End of Suffering.
- You take your medication - The Truth of the Path Leading to the End of Suffering.

Buddhists use a wheel as a symbol. It represents the great wheel of suffering that goes round and round without end. But the Buddha taught that there was an escape to the suffering. Those wishing to escape suffering first needed to understand the Four Noble Truths and the Eightfold Noble Path.
Complete the Wheel of Dhamma sheet to explore the Four Noble Truths and the Eightfold Noble Path. Look back at your reading for help.

Activity 2: Nirvana *(Online)*

Nirvana means "blowing out the flame." Buddha said Nirvana is the highest goal for human beings who seek to end the cycle of birth, death, and rebirth. What exactly is Nirvana and what was Buddha's advice on how to reach it?

ASSESS

Lesson Assessment: A Search for Goodness (*Online*)

You will complete an online assessment covering the main points of this lesson. Your assessment will be scored by the computer.

LEARN

Activity 3. Optional: A Search for Goodness *(Online)*

This activity is OPTIONAL. It's provided for enrichment or extra practice, but not required for completion of this lesson.
You may skip this activity.

Buddhist Chanting

Listen to Buddhist chanting at

Name _______________________________ Date _______________________________

Wheel of Dhamma

On the eight lines outside the wheel, write the names of the eight parts of the Eightfold Noble Path. On the lines inside each section of the wheel, write a short explanation of that Truth as you understand it.

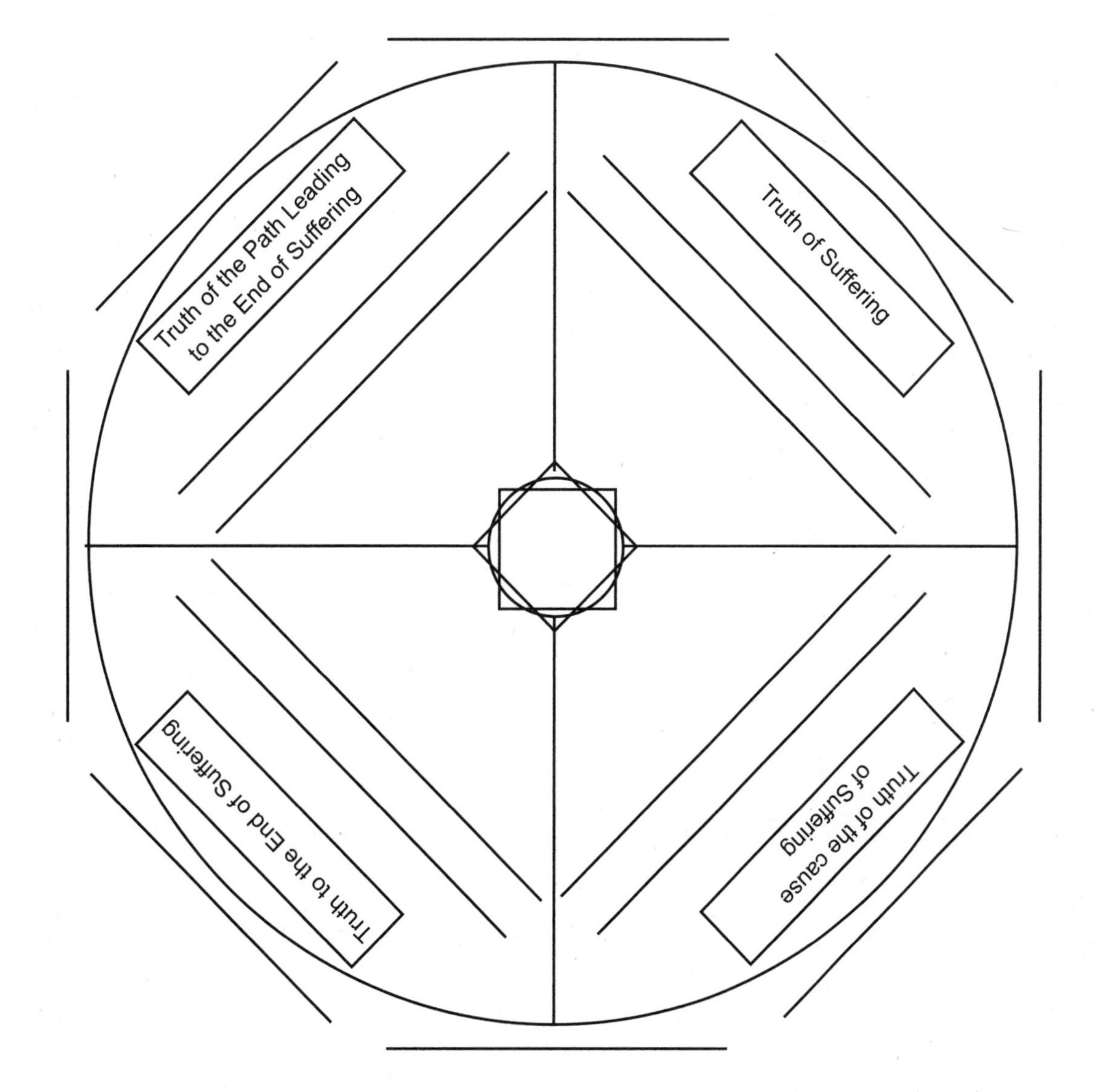

Student Guide
Lesson 10: Diffusion

What could a ruthless warrior king and the peace-loving Buddha have in common? A lot. That is, if the warrior king repents, converts to Buddhism, and then dedicates his life to spreading Buddha's teachings.

Lesson Objectives

- Name the warrior and emperor of ancient India who converted to Buddhism.
- Describe Asoka's achievements and contributions to Buddhism.
- Analyze fiction for the central Buddhist attitude toward human beings and castes or classes.
- Identify on a map the areas of the world where Buddhism is widely practiced today.

PREPARE

Approximate lesson time is 60 minutes.

Materials

For the Student

The Human Odyssey: Prehistory Through the Middle Ages edited by Klee, Cribb, and Holdren

History Journal

Comparing Religions and Philosophies

Keywords and Pronunciation

Asoka (uh-SOH-kuh)
Buddha (BOO-duh)
Buddhism (BOO-dih-zuhm)
Jataka (JAH-tuh-kuh)
Kalinga (kuh-LING-guh)
Mahinda (muh-HEEN-duh)
Maurya (MOWR-ee-uh)
Senerath (say-NAY-ruhth)
Siddhartha Gautama (*sid-DAHR-tuh GOW-tuh-muh*)
Sri Lanka (sree LAHNG-kuh)
stupas (STOO-puhs) : Buddhist places of worship

LEARN

Activity 1: Asoka Follows the Buddha *(Offline)*

Instructions

Read

After reading Chapter 5, from "Asoka Follows the Buddha" to "*The Great Mahinda*," pages 204-207, answer the following questions in your History Journal:

1. Who was the warrior and emperor of ancient India who converted to Buddhism and helped spread Buddha's teachings?
2. What were some of her achievements and contributions to Buddhism?

Then finish the chapter by reading a story, "*The Great Mahinda*," pages 207-211. Answer one more question, and then go back online to continue the lesson.

3. What does this story reveal about the central Buddhist attitude toward human beings and the caste system?

Directions and Data for Focus on Geography activity *(Online)*

You will need the following information when you return online to complete the Focus on Geography activity.

Graphing Data:

Country - Percentage of Total Population That Practices Buddhism

Bhutan - 75%
Brunei - 1%
Cambodia - 95%
China - 1%
India - 1%
Japan - 84%
South Korea - 44%
Laos - 60%
Mongolia - 96%
Myanmar - 89%
Nepal - 8%
Pakistan - 1%
Sri Lanka - 70%
Thailand - 95%

Graphing Directions:

Once you've opened Graph of Buddhism in Asia Today, follow these directions:

1. Click Create to create a data set.
2. Enter a name for the data set (such as Data Set 1) and click Create.
3. If you want, choose another color for the graph bars.
4. In the Y Axis column, enter the percentage number (from the list above) for each country.
5. Click Close.

Activity 2: Focus on Geography *(Online)*

Activity 3: Diffusion *(Online)*

Finish today's lesson by completing the column for Buddhism on the Comparing Religions and Philosophies chart. You may need to review the previous two lessons to complete some of the categories.

ASSESS

Lesson Assessment: Diffusion (*Online*)

You will complete an online assessment covering the main points of this lesson. Your assessment will be scored by the computer.

Name ______________________________ Date ______________________________

Comparing Religions and Philosophies

Category	Who founded it?	When was it founded?	What are the principal beliefs?	What are the principal sacred texts?
Confucianism				
Hinduism				
Buddhism				
Judaism				
Christianity				
Islam				

Comparing Religions and Philosophies

Category	Confucianism	Hinduism	Buddhism	Judaism	Christianity	Islam
In which geographic regions does it predominate today?	Confucianism continues to influence millions of people in East Asia, but it is a philosophy and not a religion. Therefore, it's possible to practice any religion and still strive to uphold the ideals of Confucianism.					
Roughly how many followers are there in the world today?	see above					

Student Guide
Lesson 11: Unit Review

You've finished the unit, and now it's time to review what you've learned. You'll take the Unit Assessment in the next lesson.

Lesson Objectives

- Demonstrate mastery of important knowledge and skills in this unit.

PREPARE

Approximate lesson time is 60 minutes.

Materials

For the Student

The Human Odyssey: Prehistory Through the Middle Ages edited by Klee, Cribb, and Holdren

History Journal

LEARN

Activity 1: A Look Back *(Online)*

Instructions

In this part of the human odyssey, you traveled to India and China and saw the birth of Confucianism, Hinduism, and Buddhism. Think about the religious and philosophical ideas you have read about as you review for the Unit Assessment.

Activity 2: History Journal Review *(Online)*

Now review the unit by going through your History Journal. You should:

- Look at activity sheets and reading guides you completed for the unit.
- Review unit Keywords.
- Read through any writing assignments you completed during the unit.
- Review any offline lesson assessments you took.
- Skim through the chapters of *The Human Odyssey: Prehistory Through the Middle Ages* that you read in this unit.

Student Guide
Lesson 12: Unit Assessment

You've finished the unit! Now it's time to take the Unit Assessment.

Lesson Objectives

- Describe at least two steps Qin took to centralize government or standardize procedures in China.
- Describe the main achievements of the Han dynasty.
- Identify fundamental teachings of Hinduism about many gods, the caste system, and reincarnation.
- Explain the influence of Confucian thought on Chinese society and history.
- Locate on a map the areas of the world where Buddhism is widely followed today.
- Identify Siddhartha Gautama and his historic significance.
- Identify Confucius.
- Identify Asoka.
- Describe the fundamental teachings of Buddhism about the search for Nirvana, the way to live a good life, and reincarnation.
- Identify the fundamental teachings of Confucianism about the role of the individual, the family, and relationships in society.
- Describe the origins of Hinduism.
- Explain how Buddhism and Confucianism spread.

PREPARE

Approximate lesson time is 60 minutes.

Materials

For the Student

Question Review Table

ASSESS

Unit Assessment: Some Lasting Ideas, Part 1 (*Online*)

Complete the computer-scored portion of the Unit Assessment. When you have finished, complete the teacher-scored portion of the assessment and submit it to your teacher.

Unit Assessment: Some Lasting Ideas, Part 2 (*Offline*)

Complete the teacher-scored portion of the Unit Assessment and submit it to your teacher.

LEARN

Activity 1: Unit Assessment Review Table *(Online)*

If you earned a score of **less than 80%** on the Unit Assessment, complete the activity.

If you earned a score of **80% or greater**, you may skip this activity.

Let's prepare to retake the Unit Assessment:

- Identify the questions that you answered incorrectly.
- Complete the appropriate review activities listed in the table.

Assessment Date

Unit 6: Some Lasting Ideas

Before you retake the Unit Assessment, use the table to figure out which activities you should review.

Question Review Table

Circle the numbers of the questions that you missed on the Unit Assessment. Review the activities that correspond with these questions.

Question	Lesson	Review Activity
1 (offline)	8: The Enlightened One	The Enlightened One
2 (offline); 3 (offline)	1: A Wise Teacher	The Great Teacher
4 (offline)	10: Diffusion	Asoka Follows the Buddha
5 (offline); 7 (offline)	9: A Search for Goodness	Nirvana; Four Noble Truths and an Eightfold Noble Path
6 (offline); 9 (offline)	7: The Hindu View	Hindu Gods and the Ramayana
3 (online); 8 (offline); 10 (offline)	2: Relationships and Rulers	More on Confucius
1 (online); 11 (offline)	6: Ideas of the Indus	Aryans, the Caste System, and Hinduism
2 (online); 12 (offline)	10: Diffusion	Focus on Geography

Student Guide

Unit 7: More Lasting Ideas
Lesson 1: Monotheism Takes Hold

Hinduism, Buddhism, and Confucianism have played an enormous role in the development of Asian thought and culture. Western civilization, however, came primarily from the Hebrews and Greeks. The Hebrews introduced enduring ideas about monotheism, justice, law, and morality. The Greeks celebrated people's ability to reason and decipher the mysteries of the world. Where did the Hebrews and the Greeks get their ideas?

Worship just one God? That was a very radical idea in 2000 B.C. Most ancient people worshiped many gods. You have learned that in Egypt, Akhenaten's attempt to introduce the concept of one god failed. But when the Hebrews turned to monotheism, their religion--Judaism--offered a way of thinking that changed the course of world history.

Lesson Objectives

- Define *polytheism*, *monotheism*, *Torah*, and *covenant*.
- Identify the Hebrews as the first people to worship one God and spread that idea.
- Name the religion of the ancient Hebrews.
- Identify Abraham.
- Locate on a map the areas the ancient Hebrews traveled through and settled, and identify the countries that occupy the area today.
- Identify Canaan as the land Jews believed to be "the promised land."

PREPARE

Approximate lesson time is 60 minutes.

Materials

- For the Student
  - Reading Guide
  - The Human Odyssey: Prehistory Through the Middle Ages edited by Klee, Cribb, and Holdren
  - History Journal
  - Hebrews Map
  - art supplies - colored pencils

Keywords and Pronunciation

Akhenaten (ahk-NAH-tuhn)
Canaan (KAY-nuhn) : the ancient name for the land between the Jordan River and the Mediterranean Sea; the Promised Land of the Israelites
covenant : a solemn, binding agreement or promise
Judaism (JOO-duh-ih-zuhm) : the religion of the Jews, who are descendants of the ancient Hebrews; first major religion to teach belief in one God
monotheism (MAH-nuh-THEE-ih-zuhm) : belief in one God
polytheism (PAH-lee-THEE-ih-zuhm) : belief in many gods
Torah (TOHR-uh) : the entire body of wisdom and law contained in Jewish sacred literature and oral tradition; also, the first five books of the Hebrew Bible

---

LEARN

Activity 1: Honoring One God *(Offline)*

Read

Complete the Reading Guide as you read Chapter 6, from the beginning to "*Joseph and His Brothers*," pages 213-219. When you have finished, compare your answers with those in the Lesson Answer Key.
Write a brief definition for each of these words in your History Journal. You can compare your definitions with those in the Keywords section of this lesson.
polytheism
monotheism
Torah
covenant

Activity 2: Looking at the Region *(Online)*

Instructions

Use What You Know

- Complete the Reporting in 2000 B.C. activity.
- Review the Classical World Time Line in the Resources section.

Focus on Geography

- Review the map in the book on page 214. Then, on the Hebrews map:
- Illustrate the travels of the Hebrews.
- Add symbols such as sheep or oxen to show the path from Ur to Palestine.
- Illustrate the highlights of the trip with symbols.
- Make a key to identify all the symbols.

ASSESS

Lesson Assessment: Monotheism Takes Hold (*Online*)

You will complete an online assessment covering the main points of this lesson. Your assessment will be scored by the computer.

Name Date

Reading Guide

1. Who were the Hebrews? What are they best known for?

2. What is Judaism?

3. What is the Torah?

4. In what time period did Judaism develop?

5. Who was Abraham? What is he believed to have done?

6. Explain the agreement, described in the Torah, between God and Abraham.

7. Locate the following areas on a map:
   - The area where the Hebrew civilization originated
   - The area through which the Hebrews traveled after leaving Mesopotamia
   - The area which the Hebrews settled

8. What countries are now in the area that was Canaan in ancient times?

Name Date 

Hebrews Map

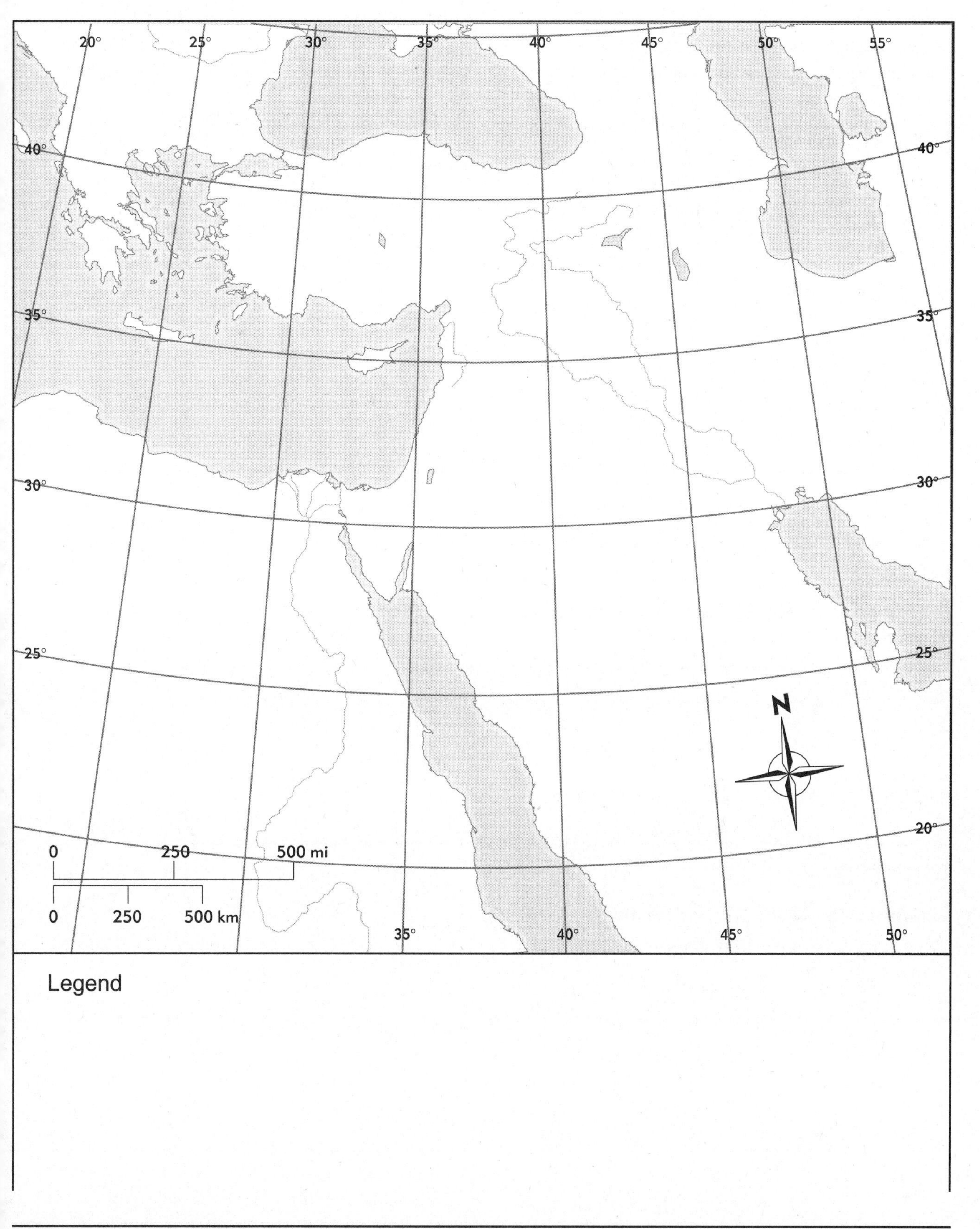

Legend

Student Guide
Lesson 2: Covenants

When you make a promise, do you always keep it? The Hebrews believed that God promised them they would be a mighty nation. But God didn't promise them that life would be easy. The Hebrews endured famine, captivity, persecution, and a grueling journey through the desert. How did these events change their ideas about God and his promise?

Lesson Objectives

- Recognize important beliefs of Judiasm.
- Distinguish between Jewish views of God and the Egyptians' and Sumerians' view.

PREPARE

Approximate lesson time is 60 minutes.

Materials

For the Student

Reading Guide

The Human Odyssey: Prehistory Through the Middle Ages edited by Klee, Cribb, and Holdren

History Journal

LEARN

Activity 1: Honoring the Promise *(Online)*

Read

Read Chapter 6, "*Joseph and His Brothers*" to the end, pages 219-227. As you read, complete the Reading Guide. When you have finished, compare your answers with those in the Lesson Answer Key.

Activity 2: Covenants *(Online)*

ASSESS

Lesson Assessment: Covenants (*Online*)

You will complete an online assessment covering the main points of this lesson. Your assessment will be scored by the computer.

Name Date

Reading Guide

What did the Hebrews learn from the story of Joseph and his brothers?

Making a Family Tree

You've read about many people who helped begin and carry forward the religious ideas of the Hebrews. How will you remember them all? By putting them in a family tree. Here is a list of key names. All but one of these people belong to the same family. Your job is to put them in the correct order, and then write a brief statement that says who each person was and the role he played according to Hebrew literature and beliefs.

Abraham **Joseph** **Moses** **Jacob** **Benjamin** **Isaac**

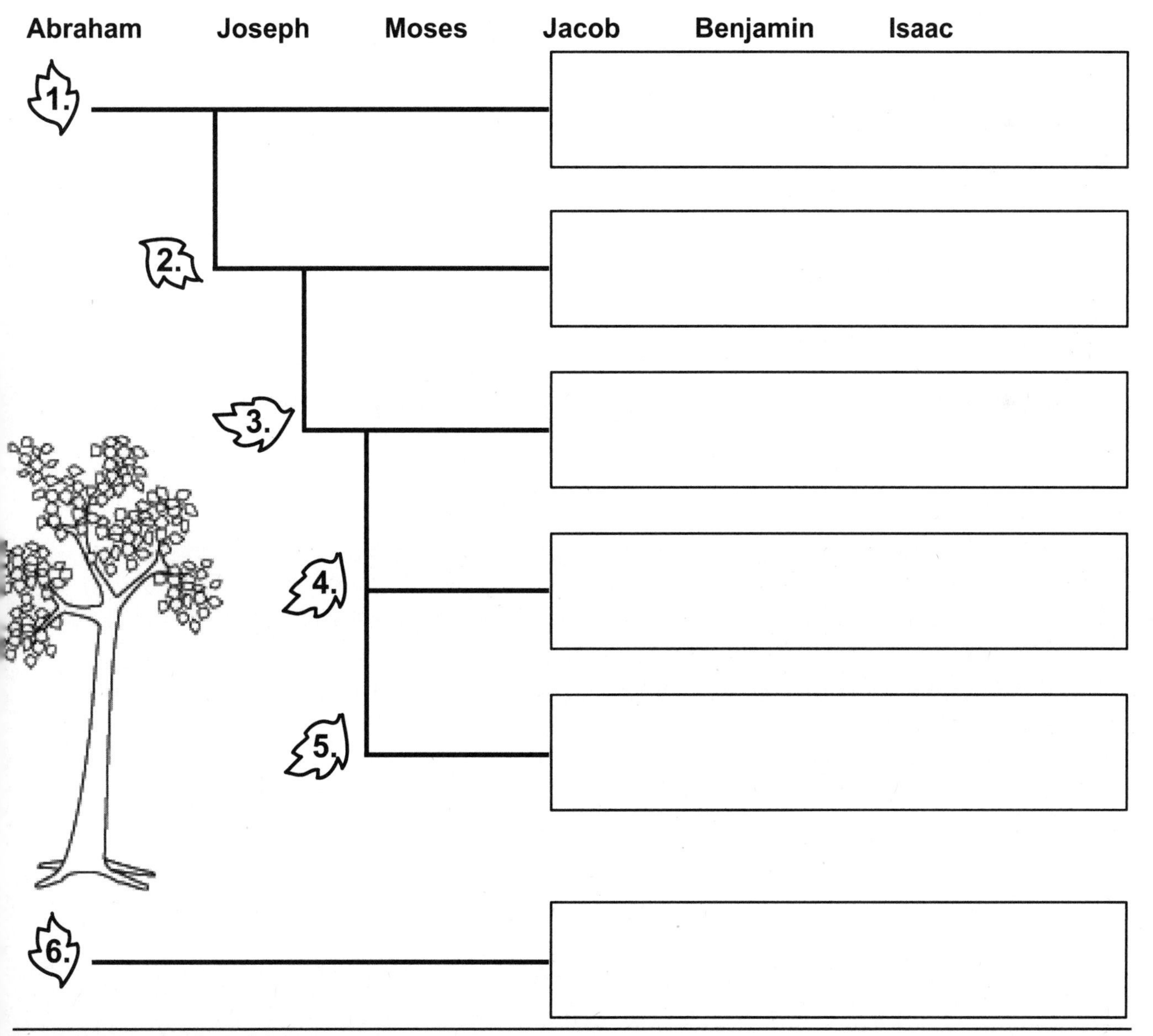

Student Guide
Lesson 3: The Law

Please behave! You've probably heard that many times--but how do you know what that means? You probably know because a parent or some other responsible adult taught you what is expected of you. The Hebrews believed God sent them the Ten Commandments to explain what he expected. The Commandments were God's instructions to all the Hebrew people, not just the leaders.

Lesson Objectives

- Identify Moses.
- Describe the importance of the Ten Commandments to the Hebrews.
- Explain that Hebrew beliefs developed over time.

PREPARE

Approximate lesson time is 60 minutes.

Materials

For the Student

The Human Odyssey: Prehistory Through the Middle Ages edited by Klee, Cribb, and Holdren

History Journal

Comparing Codes and Laws

Keywords and Pronunciation

sabbath (SA-buhth) : the holy day of rest and worship in the Hebrew religion; from Friday at sundown to Saturday at sundown

---

LEARN

Activity 1: The People of the Law *(Offline)*

Read

As you read Chapter 7, from the beginning to "The Land of Milk and Honey," pages 228-232, answer these questions. When you have finished, compare your answers with those in the Lesson Answer Key.

1. Who was Moses and what role did he play in the history of the Hebrew people?
2. How did the story of Moses' struggles help later generations of the Hebrew people?
3. What ideas developed about God's expectations of the Hebrew people?
4. What are the Ten Commandments? Why are the Ten Commandments important to the Hebrews?

Write a brief definition for *sabbath* in your History Journal. When you have finished, compare your definition with the one in the Resources section under the Keywords tab.

Activity 2: The Law *(Online)*

ASSESS

Lesson Assessment: The Law (*Online*)

You will complete an online assessment covering the main points of this lesson. Your assessment will be scored by the computer.

LEARN

Activity 3: The Law *(Offline)*

In this activity you will compare the moral and ethical ideas of the Confucian Codes of Behavior with those of the Ten Commandments.

Print the Comparing Codes and Laws sheet and continue with the lesson.

Name Date

Comparing Codes and Laws

Identify similarities in the moral and ethical ideas of Confucius and the Hebrews by drawing lines to connect similar beliefs.

Confucianism

Confucius's Five Relationships

- Between parent and child
- Between elder brother and younger brother (sisters too)
- Between husband and wife
- Between ruler and subject
- Between friends

Important Beliefs

- The secret to a good life is a good personal character.
- To live well, a person must be a gentleman.
- An enlightened ruler sets high standards for his own behavior.
- An enlightened ruler acts with virtue.
- Families should be an example for all of China to follow.
- Family obligations are important.
- The key to good behavior and good government is concern for others.
- Good conduct is the basis for an orderly society.

The Ten Commandments

1. Thou shalt have no other gods before me.
2. Thou shalt not make unto thee any graven image
3. Thou shalt not take the name of the Lord thy God in vain.
4. Remember the Sabbath day, to keep it holy.
5. Honor thy father and thy mother.
6. Thou shalt not kill.
7. Thou shalt not commit adultery.
8. Thou shalt not steal.
9. Thou shalt not bear false witness against thy neighbor.
10. Thou shalt not covet anything that is thy neighbor's.

Source: Condensed and adapted from the King James Bible, Exodus 20: 1-17

1. Describe the similarities in the moral and ethical beliefs of the Hebrews and the followers of Confucius.

____

____

____

2. What is the main ideological difference between Confucianism and Judaism?

____

Student Guide
Lesson 4: Kings

Ideas about government grow and change over time. An outside threat led the Hebrews to abandon their tribal organization and unite under one king. The kingdom would not last for long, but it had a lasting influence on the Hebrews' view of themselves and their faith.

Lesson Objectives

- Identify on a map the area known as Canaan--the "Promised Land"--and the city of Jerusalem.
- Explain the importance of David and how the city of Jerusalem became the capital of the Jewish kingdom.
- Identify important events in the lives of the Hebrew people and nearby groups between 2000 and 900 B.C.
- Recognize the Assyrians and Babylonians as powerful groups who attacked the Hebrews.
- Describe the developments in Jewish beliefs resulting from the Babylonian Captivity.

PREPARE

Approximate lesson time is 60 minutes.

Materials

For the Student

The Human Odyssey: Prehistory Through the Middle Ages edited by Klee, Cribb, and Holdren

History Journal

Keywords and Pronunciation

Canaan (KAY-nuhn) : the ancient name for the land between the Jordan River and the Mediterranean Sea; the Promised Land of the Israelites

Jericho (JER-ih-koh)

Philistines (FIH-luh-steens) : a seafaring people who fought against the Hebrews for control of Jerusalem

---

LEARN

Activity 1: Kings of the Hebrews *(Offline)*

Read

As you read Chapter 7 from "The Land of Milk and Honey" to "The Babylonian Captivity," pages 232-237, answer these questions. When you have finished, compare your answers with those in the Lesson Answer Key.

1. Who was Joshua? Why was he important to the Hebrew people?

2. Where was Canaan?

3. Explain why the Hebrews called Canaan "the Promised Land."

4. Explain the relationships between Hebrews and other nearby groups.

5. Who were Saul, David, and Solomon?

6. Compare Saul, David, and Solomon as rulers of the Hebrews.

	Order of Rule	Reason Chosen to Rule	Strengths or Accomplishments	Problems
Solomon				
Saul				
David				

Write a brief definition for each of these words in your History Journal. When you have finished, compare your definitions with those in the Keywords section of this lesson.
Canaan
Philistines

Use What You Know

As a television news reporter, you have been asked to prepare a series of news features about Jerusalem. Today you will present the first in the series. Your assignment is to explain the importance of the city of Jerusalem. Use any resources available to you to gather information and locate pictures. Present your feature live to some people or videotape it.

Your feature should:

Identify on a map:

- The area known as Canaan
- The city of Jerusalem

Include information about:

- How Jerusalem became the capital of the kingdom
- Hebrew beliefs about Solomon's temple
- The importance of Jerusalem to the Hebrew people
- The interaction between the Hebrews and nearby groups (including the Philistines, Assyrians, and Babylonians) in the region in ancient times

Information resources that may be helpful include:

- Reference books
- Grolier's online encyclopedia
- World History time line

ASSESS

Lesson Assessment: Kings (*Online*)

You will complete an online assessment covering the main points of this lesson. Your assessment will be scored by the computer.

LEARN

Activity 2: Kings *(Offline)*

Read Chapter 7, "The Babylonian Captivity" to the end, pages 237-239. When you have finished, complete the Comparing Religions and Philosophies chart you started in an earlier unit.

Student Guide
Lesson 5: Renewing Their Faith

Seventy years of Babylonian captivity brought more changes to the Hebrews and their religion. But even during this time of terror and turmoil, the Hebrews did not lose heart. They still believed God was with them, and they met regularly to renew their faith. Lacking temples, they began meeting in synagogues, which became places of worship, teaching, and learning. They turned more and more to prayer, coming to believe that each person could talk directly with God.

Lesson Objectives

- Describe the developments in Jewish beliefs resulting from the Babylonian Captivity.
- Identify *synagogues* as Jewish places of worship and teaching.
- Explain that Judaism has influenced human history--especially Western history--and the religions of Christianity and Islam.
- Summarize the basic beliefs of Judaism.

PREPARE

Approximate lesson time is 60 minutes.

Advance Preparation

- Your student may need references from the library on *synagogues*--Jewish places of worship and teaching.

Materials

For the Student

The Human Odyssey: Prehistory Through the Middle Ages edited by Klee, Cribb, and Holdren

History Journal

Keywords and Pronunciation

Judaism (JOO-duh-ih-zuhm) : the religion of the Jews, who are descendants of the ancient Hebrews; first major religion to teach belief in one God

synagogues (SIH-nuh-gahgs)

LEARN

Activity 1: Tradition *(Offline)*

Check Your Reading

Review Chapter 7, "The Babylonian Captivity" to the end, pages 237-239, by checking your entries on the Comparing Religions and Philosophies chart against those in the Lesson Answer Key.

In your History Journal, write a brief definition for *synagogue*. Compare your definition with the one in the Resources section under the Keywords tab.

Use What You Know

Pretend you are a guest speaker for a history class. Your topic is the Babylonian Captivity. Members of the class have some questions for you. How would you answer them? Write your answers in your History Journal.

- How long were the Hebrews held captive in Babylon?
- Did Hebrew ideas about God and worship change as a result of this captivity?
- How could the Hebrews worship God when they were not in the Promised Land?
- How did Hebrew synagogues differ from the Temple in Jerusalem?
- Did the Hebrews learn anything from the Babylonians?

Activity 2: A Place of Learning and Worship *(Online)*

Synagogues are Jewish places of worship and teaching. In this activity you will gather references from the library or on the Internet to locate examples of synagogues in the United States, Europe, and Israel and write down some details on what you've found.

Here are a few links to help you get started:

- International Sites of Jewish Monuments by Country
- Synagogues on Postcards and Stamps

ASSESS

Lesson Assessment: Renewing Their Faith (*Online*)

You will complete an online assessment covering the main points of this lesson. Your assessment will be scored by the computer.

Student Guide
Lesson 6: Another Land

Unlike some of the other early civilizations, the ancient Greeks had no fertile river valleys that helped farmers grow a surplus of grain. Thin, poor soil covers the rugged hills and mountains of the Greek mainland and its far-flung islands. With such a scarcity of fertile land, how did the Greeks manage to build one of the most remarkable civilizations the world has ever known?

Lesson Objectives

- Identify on a map the Peloponnese, Mediterranean Sea, Aegean Sea, Ionian Sea, and Crete.
- Analyze maps to identify the climate and landforms of Greece.
- Explain the geographic reasons for the development of independent city-states in Greece.
- Describe the ways in which the Greeks relied on and used the sea.
- Describe farming in ancient Greece.
- Identify important gods and goddesses of ancient Greece.
- Explain that the Greek view of humanity differed from that of earlier polytheistic civilizations in that the Greeks believed humans could use their minds and reason to understand the world around them.
- Identify some of the religious beliefs and ideas expressed in Greek myths.

PREPARE

Approximate lesson time is 60 minutes.

Materials

For the Student

Reading Guide

The Human Odyssey: Prehistory Through the Middle Ages edited by Klee, Cribb, and Holdren

History Journal

Keywords and Pronunciation

Aegean (ih-JEE-uhn)
Aphrodite (a-fruh-DIY-tee)
Apollo (uh-PAH-loh)
Ares (AIR-eez)
Artemis (AHR-tuh-muhs)
Dionysus (diy-uh-NIY-suhs)
Hellenes (HEL-eenz)
Hephaestus (hih-FES-tuhs)
Hera (HAIR-uh)
Hestia (HES-tee-uh)
Iliad (IL-ee-uhd)
Ionian (iy-OH-nee-uhn)
labyrinth (LA-buh-rinth)
Minoan (mih-NOH-uhn)

Minos (MIY-nuhs)
Mycenean (miy-suh-NEE-uhn)
Odysseus (oh-DIH-see-uhs)
Peloponnese (PEH-luh-puh-neez)
Peloponnesian (peh-luh-puh-NEE-zhuhn)
Poseidon (puh-SIY-dn)
Prometheus (pruh-MEE-thee-uhs)
Zeus (zoos)

LEARN

Activity 1: Focus on Geography *(Online)*

Activity 2: Greek Civilization *(Offline)*

Read

As you read Chapter 8, from the beginning to "Who Were the Gods? Who Was Man?" pages 240-247, complete the Reading Guide. When you have finished, compare your answers with those in the Lesson Answer Key.

Use What You Know

Imagine you are a farmer living in the hills of ancient Greece. Your brother-in-law, a fisherman who lives on the coast, has just come to visit, and the two of you sit down to talk about your lives and work. Write down what you, as a farmer, might talk about, such as your crops and farm animals. Then write what your brother-in-law might tell you about his experiences as a fisherman. Be sure to mention the weather and climate and how they affect your work and his.

Then, talk about the city-states in which you both live. Explain how geography may have influenced the region to develop separate city-states instead of one government that unifies all the people.

ASSESS

Lesson Assessment: Another Land (*Online*)

You will complete an online assessment covering the main points of this lesson. Your assessment will be scored by the computer.

LEARN

Activity 3: Another Land *(Offline)*

As you read Chapter 8, from "Who Were the Gods? Who Was Man?" to "Wondering About Their World," pages 247-250, and "Greek Gods and Goddesses," page 251, answer the following questions:

1. What are some of the religious beliefs or ideas expressed in the Greek myths?
2. Who were some of the major gods and goddesses of ancient Greece?
3. How did the Greek view of humanity differ from the views of earlier polytheistic civilizations?
4. What three important things did the Greeks believe they could understand with their minds?

Reading Guide

Complete this sheet as you read today's assignment

1. The ancient Greeks made some contributions that have influenced the United States and many other nations. What were the contributions?
   a. ______
   b. ______
   c. ______
   d. ______
   e. ______
   f. ______
2. Civilization was flourishing on the island of Crete as early as 3000 B.C. Historians call this civilization ______ after King ______.
3. Why was civilization slow to develop on the Peloponnesian peninsula?
   ______
   ______
4. Describe farming in ancient Greece—the difficulties, major crops, livestock, and climate.
   ______
   ______
   ______
   ______
5. The first civilization to develop on the mainland of Greece is called ______.
   Why did this civilization pass away? ______
   ______
6. Describe the city-states of ancient Greece.
   ______
   ______
   ______
   ______
7. Why was the sea important to the Greeks? ______
   ______

Student Guide
Lesson 7. Optional: Your Choice

You may use today's lesson time to do one or more of the following:

- Complete work in progress.
- Complete the Beyond the Lesson activity in any lesson in this unit.
- Go on to the next lesson.

Please mark this lesson complete to proceed to the next lesson in the course.

PREPARE

Approximate lesson time is 60 minutes.

Student Guide

Lesson 8: Gods in Ancient Greece

The early Greeks believed the gods controlled nature. Through stories and poems about the gods, the Greeks sought to explain the workings of their world. A favorite story was the myth of Prometheus, in which a god gives the gift of fire to humans. The fire in the myth symbolizes something the Greeks believed separates humans from all other creatures. What does the fire symbolize?

Lesson Objectives

- Explain that the Greek view of humanity differed from that of earlier polytheistic civilizations in that the Greeks believed humans could use their minds and reason to understand the world around them.
- Identify important gods and goddesses of ancient Greece and the characteristics of Greek religious myths.
- Identify some of the religious beliefs and ideas expressed in Greek myths.
- Identify important gods and goddesses of ancient Greece.

PREPARE

Approximate lesson time is 60 minutes.

Materials

For the Student

The Human Odyssey: Prehistory Through the Middle Ages edited by Klee, Cribb, and Holdren

History Journal

Keywords and Pronunciation

Aphrodite (a-fruh-DIY-tee)
Apollo (uh-PAH-loh)
Ares (AIR-eez)
Artemis (AHR-tuh-muhs)
Athena (uh-THEE-nuh)
Dionysus (diy-uh-NIY-suhs)
Hephaestus (hih-FES-tuhs)
Hera (HAIR-uh)
Hestia (HES-tee-uh)
Poseidon (puh-SIY-dn)
Prometheus (pruh-MEE-thee-uhs)
Zeus (zoos)

LEARN

Activity 1: The Greeks and Their Gods *(Online)*

Instructions

Check Your Reading

Review your reading (Chapter 8, from "Who Were the Gods? Who Was Man?" to "Wondering About Their World," pages 247-250, and "Greek Gods and Goddesses," page 251) by comparing your answers to the following questions with the ones in the Lesson Answer Key:

1. What are some of the religious beliefs or ideas expressed in the Greek myths?
2. Who were some of the major gods and goddesses of ancient Greece?
3. How did the Greek view of humanity differ from the views of earlier polytheistic civilizations?
4. What three important things did the Greeks believe humans could understand with their minds?

Use What You Know

Complete at least one of these Use What You Know activities:

The Myth of Prometheus

Myths show that the people who wrote them wanted to understand their world and themselves. In your reading you discovered that the Greeks believed there were three important things humans could understand with their minds:

- The workings of nature
- Human nature
- The best way for human beings to live together in communities

Review the myth of Prometheus and write one or two paragraphs explaining how the myth expresses one or more of these beliefs.

Prometheus and the Gift of Fire Illustrated

To the Greeks, heroes and gods were larger than life. Create two or three illustrations for the myth of Prometheus, and write captions that help explain Greek beliefs and show how the Greeks thought it was possible for people to understand the world.

ASSESS

Lesson Assessment: Gods in Ancient Greece (*Online*)

You will complete an online assessment covering the main points of this lesson. Your assessment will be scored by the computer.

LEARN

Activity 2. Optional: Gods in Ancient Greece *(Online)*

Student Guide
Lesson 9. Optional: Your Choice

You may use today's lesson time to do one or more of the following:

- Complete work in progress.
- Complete the Beyond the Lesson activity in any lesson in this unit.
- Go on to the next lesson.

Please mark this lesson complete to proceed to the next lesson in the course.

PREPARE

Approximate lesson time is 60 minutes.

Student Guide
Lesson 10: The Gift of Reason

The ancient Greeks called humans "the only animal who asks questions." The Greeks thought that by asking the right questions, making careful observations, and using their reasoning powers, they could figure out how the universe worked. Did events happen randomly, they wondered, or did nature follow certain rules or laws?

Lesson Objectives

- Identify one of the Greeks' greatest contributions to Western civilization.
- Recognize how human scientific and philosophical thought progressed from the earliest civilizations to the Greeks and then to modern times.
- Identify areas of study whose names have Greek origins.

PREPARE

Approximate lesson time is 60 minutes.

Materials

For the Student

Greeks Learn About Nature

Reading Guide

The Human Odyssey: Prehistory Through the Middle Ages edited by Klee, Cribb, and Holdren

Keywords and Pronunciation

physis (FIY-sis)

LEARN

Activity 1: A Gift from the Greeks *(Online)*

Instructions

Read

As you read Chapter 8, from "Wondering About Their World" to the end, pages 250-253, complete the Reading Guide. When you have finished, compare your answers with those in the Lesson Answer Key.

Use What You Know

Complete the Greeks Learn About Nature sheet and then compare your answers with the ones in the Lesson Answer Key.

ASSESS

Lesson Assessment: The Gift of Reason (*Online*)

You will complete an online assessment covering the main points of this lesson. Your assessment will be scored by the computer.

Name Date

Greeks Learn About Nature

In their desire to understand nature, the Greeks asked many questions. They wondered what caused lightning, earthquakes, and the sun's movement across the sky. Until they could answer these questions scientifically, the Greeks answered them with explanations based on their polytheistic beliefs. Use the text to recall some of those explanations.

1. What is lightning? ______
2. What causes earthquakes? ______
3. How does the sun move across the sky? ______

The more questions the Greeks asked, the less they liked their traditional answers. They wondered if they could come up with better explanations for how the world worked. Soon, the scientific study of nature became a passion for the Greeks.

4. The Greeks' influence is apparent in many of the words we use today to describe scientific studies. Use a dictionary to look up the words in the chart below. You may use the dictionary at Grolier Online (use the Student Dictionary) or your own desk dictionary. On the back of this sheet, you may want to add two or three more words that have their origins in ancient Greece.

Word	Meaning	Greek Origin? (Yes or No)
Archaeology		
Astronomy		
Biology		

Botany		
Ecology		
Etymology		
Geography		
Geology		
Meteorology		
Philosophy		
Physics		

Psychology		
Zoology		

5. Now write a sentence or two summarizing your impression of the Greek influence on modern scientific and philosophical thought.

____

____

____

Reading Guide

Complete this sheet as you read today's assignment.

1. What did the early Greeks call humans? ______________________________

2. How did the early Greeks explain the forces of nature? ______________________________

3. How were their explanations of nature similar to those of earlier peoples? ______________________________

4. How did the Greeks go a step further than other ancient civilizations in trying to understand nature?

5. The Greeks were certain that they could figure out the "why" and "how" by ______________________________

6. The Greeks saw patterns in nature, and believed that understanding ______________________________ could help them explain the patterns, and even the changes in the patterns. What did this new approach to learning assume?

7. Modern-day scientists still follow the Greek example of using the mind to reason, but they go one step further. What additional step do modern scientists take when trying to understand the laws of nature?

8. The Greeks were among history's earliest ______________________________ and ______________________________

9. What great gift did the Greeks give us? ______________________________

Student Guide
Lesson 11: Stories and Games

The Greeks celebrated human potential in many ways. In poems and stories they paid tribute to qualities like bravery, determination, and resourcefulness. They also celebrated the human body, admiring athletes as much as they did philosophers and statesmen. Every four years they held athletic games at the foot of Mount Olympus to test strength, speed, and courage. One of our most important athletic competitions is directly descended from these games. Do you know what the modern-day contest is called?

Lesson Objectives

- Identify Homer.
- Describe the *Iliad* and the *Odyssey.*
- Describe the purpose and events of the original Olympic games.
- Recognize the work of archaeologists in gaining information on ancient Greece.

PREPARE

Approximate lesson time is 60 minutes.

Materials

For the Student

Reading Guide

The Human Odyssey: Prehistory Through the Middle Ages edited by Klee, Cribb, and Holdren

Keywords and Pronunciation

Achilles (uh-KIH-leez)
Heinrich Schliemann (HIYN-rik SHLEE-mahn)
Iliad (IL-ee-uhd)
Menelaus (me-nl-AY-uhs)
Odyssey (AH-duh-see)

LEARN
Activity 1: A Gift from the Greeks *(Offline)*

Instructions

Read

As you read Chapter 9, from the beginning to "The Human Form as Art," pages 255-258, complete the Reading Guide.
Compare your answers with those in the Lesson Answer Key.

Activity 2: Stories and Games *(Online)*

ASSESS

Lesson Assessment: Stories and Games (*Online*)

You will complete an online assessment covering the main points of this lesson. Your assessment will be scored by the computer.

Reading Guide

Complete this sheet as you read today's assignment.

1. Who was Homer? ____________________
2. The *Iliad* and *Odyssey* are ____________________
3. What is the *Iliad* about? ____________________
4. Who did Homer celebrate in the *Iliad?* ____________________
5. What is the *Odyssey* about? ____________________
6. What is the *Odyssey* a celebration of? ____________________
7. The Greeks admired their ____________ as much as their statesmen or philosophers.
8. How did the Olympic contests celebrate humans? ____________________
9. What were some of the Olympic events? ____________________
10. What evidence indicates that the ancient Greeks participated in the Olympic games?

Student Guide
Lesson 12. Optional: Your Choice

You may use today's lesson time to do one or more of the following:

- Complete work in progress.
- Complete the Beyond the Lesson activity in any lesson in this unit.
- Go on to the next lesson.

Please mark this lesson complete to proceed to the next lesson in the course.

PREPARE

Approximate lesson time is 60 minutes.

Student Guide
Lesson 13: Arts and Histories

Do you take time to appreciate the things you see around you? The ancient Greeks did. They saw beauty in everyday objects and the tasks of ordinary life. Drawings of simple events like picking olives and meeting friends appear on Greek vases. Majestic Greek statues celebrate the human form. The Greeks were also fascinated by the past and by the lessons it could teach them. They became the first to undertake an organized study of history.

Lesson Objectives

- Analyze Greek vessels for information on the form and purpose of art in ancient Greece.
- Identify the Greeks as the first civilization to study history in an organized manner.
- Identify Herodutus as "the father of history."
- Describe the differences between the historical writings of Herodotus and Thucydides.

PREPARE

Approximate lesson time is 60 minutes.

Materials

For the Student

The Human Odyssey: Prehistory Through the Middle Ages edited by Klee, Cribb, and Holdren

History Journal

Artifact Analysis

Keywords and Pronunciation

Herodotus (hih-RAHD-uh-tuhs)

Thucydides (thyoo-SID-uh-deez)

LEARN

Activity 1: Greek Art and Historical Writing *(Online)*

Instructions

Read

As you read Chapter 9, from "The Human Form as Art" to "The Greek 'Citizen-States,'" pages 258-260, answer the following questions:

1. Describe Greek vessels, including what they were used for and the materials they were made of.
2. What were some of the materials Greek artists used?
3. What civilization is credited as the first to study history in an organized manner?
4. Who is known as "the father of history"?
5. What are the main differences between the historical writings of Herodotus and Thucydides?

Activity 2: Analyzing Greek Art *(Online)*

ASSESS

Lesson Assessment: Arts and Histories (*Online*)

You will complete an online assessment covering the main points of this lesson. Your assessment will be scored by the computer.

Artifact Analysis

Answer the following questions about the artifact you chose from the online gallery of Greek vessels:

1. DESCRIPTION OF THE VESSEL:

   Describe how it looks: the material it is made of, shape, color, texture, size, decorations (is anything printed, stamped, written, drawn, or painted on it?).

   ____

   ____

   ____

   ____

2. WHAT THE ARTIFACT TELLS US:

   A. What does it tell us about the technology of the time in which it was made and used?

   ____

   B. What does it tell us about the life and times of the people who made it and used it?

   ____

   C. What does it tell us about what people of the time valued or enjoyed? Answer for both the object itself and its decoration.

   ____

   ____

   D. Can you name a similar item that exists today? ______________

   ____

   E. Would a similar item that exists today be decorated in the same way? Could someone learn the same kinds of information from the modern item? Explain.

   ____

   ____

   ____

   ____

Student Guide
Lesson 14: The Polis

Annapolis, Indianapolis, Metropolis. What do these place names have in common? Where does the suffix *polis* come from, and what does it mean?

Lesson Objectives

- Define *polis*.
- Describe the Greek view of the role and limits of government as seen in the polis.
- Summarize the role and duties of citizens in the polis.
- Recognize that the Greeks did not grant citizenshp to women, foreigners, and slaves.
- Compare the Greek view of good government with other ancient views.

PREPARE

Approximate lesson time is 60 minutes.

Materials

For the Student

Reading Guide

History Journal

Keywords and Pronunciation

democracy : rule by the people, originating in the city-states of ancient Greece
polis (PAH-luhs) : a city-state of ancient Greece

LEARN

Activity 1: The Greek Citizen-States *(Offline)*

Instructions

Read

- As you read Chapter 9, from "The Greek 'Citizen-States'" to "A Tale from the *Odyssey*," pages 260-265, complete the Reading Guide. When you have finished, compare your answers with those in the Lesson Answer Key.
- Write a brief definition for each of these words in your History Journal. When you have finished, compare your definitions with the ones in the Keywords section.

polis
democracy

Use What You Know

Calling all citizens! Think about what the Greek polis required of its citizens. Then review the Athenian Oath on page 263 in your textbook to help you recall as much as possible about the duties of citizenship in one Greek polis.

Write a magazine article that describes what it means to be a Greek citizen. Be sure to list all the qualities of a good citizen, the privileges of citizenship, and the responsibilities of citizens. Don't forget to explain that Greek democracy was limited, however, because the polis did not admit women, slaves, and foreigners as citizens. Illustrate your article if you wish. For additional information and images to add to your article, visit the website in the Beyond the Lesson activity.

ASSESS

Lesson Assessment: The Polis (*Online*)

You will complete an online assessment covering the main points of this lesson. Your assessment will be scored by the computer.

LEARN

Activity 2. Optional: The Polis *(Online)*

This activity is OPTIONAL. It's provided for enrichment or extra practice, but not required for completion of this lesson. You may skip this activity.

Visit these websites to view images of artifacts, read translations of Greek writings, listen to audio, and hear some interesting stories about life in Ancient Greece.

Reading Guide

Complete this sheet as you read today's assignment.

1. The ancient Greeks lived in ______________ such as Athens, Sparta, Corinth, and Thebes.
2. What landforms created natural barriers between the city-states?

   ____

3. What is a *polis?* Why did the Greeks prefer to live there?

   ____

   ____

4. Describe the Greek view of the role of government in the polis.

   ____

   ____

   ____

   ____

5. Summarize the role and duties of citizens in the polis.

   ____

   ____

   ____

   ____

   ____

6. Which groups of people in the polis were not allowed citizenship?______________

   ____

7. How did the Greek view of government differ from the views of other ancient civilizations?

   ____

   ____

   ____

   ____

   ____

8. The Greeks believed people should use their______________ and______________ to choose the kind of government that would work best.

Student Guide

Lesson 15: Telling Tales

Stories like the *Iliad* and the *Odyssey* give us insights into what the ancient Greeks believed and valued. At one point in the *Odyssey*, the hero and his crew are captured by a one-eyed giant--a Cyclops named Polyphemus. Polyphemus is powerful and cruel, and Odysseus must use his wits to escape. See if you can tell what values or beliefs this story illustrates.

Lesson Objectives

- Identify some Greek values and beliefs illustrated in a story.

PREPARE

Approximate lesson time is 60 minutes.

Materials

For the Student

The Human Odyssey: Prehistory Through the Middle Ages edited by Klee, Cribb, and Holdren

History Journal

Keywords and Pronunciation

Cyclopes (siy-KLOH-peez)
Cyclops (SIY-klahps)
Iliad (IL-ee-uhd)
Odysseus (oh-DIH-see-uhs)
Odyssey (AH-duh-see)
Phaeacians (fee-AY-shuhns)
Polyphemus (pah-luh-FEE-muhs)
Telemachus (tuh-LEM-uh-kuhs)

LEARN

Activity 1: Greek Literature *(Offline)*

Instructions

Read

As you read Chapter 9, from "A Tale from the *Odyssey*" to the end, pages 265-269, see if you can find examples of how the story illustrates some of the ancient Greeks' values and beliefs.

Use What You Know

The Greeks admired bravery and resourcefulness. What other human qualities did they admire? The Greeks also thought people should act honorably. What other kinds of behavior did they value? Reread the story of Odysseus and the Cyclops. In your History Journal, list at least three Greek values or beliefs you think the story illustrates, and prove your case with quotations from your reading. Below is an example to get you started:

Belief or value: People should treat strangers with kindness.

Passages in the story that illustrate this belief:

"I will find out what manner of people live there, and whether they will treat us kindly and give us gifts that are due to strangers--gifts of provisions for our voyage."

"My men wanted me to take some of the cheeses and drive off some of the lambs and kids and come away. But this I would not do, for I would rather that he who owned the stores would give us of his own free will the offerings due to strangers."

"I begged again that he would deal with us as just men deal with strangers and suppliants."

ASSESS

Lesson Assessment: Telling Tales (*Online*)

You will complete an online assessment covering the main points of this lesson. Your assessment will be scored by the computer.

LEARN

Activity 2: Telling Tales *(Online)*

Student Guide
Lesson 16: Unit Review

You've finished the unit, and now it's time to review what you've learned. You'll take the Unit Assessment in the next lesson.

Lesson Objectives

- Demonstrate mastery of important knowledge and skills in this unit.

PREPARE

Approximate lesson time is 60 minutes.

LEARN
Activity 1: Online Review *(Online)*

Activity 2: History Journal Review *(Offline)*
Instructions

Review what you've learned in this unit by going through your History Journal. You should:

- Look at activity sheets and reading guides you have completed for the unit.
- Review unit keywords.
- Read through any writing assignments you have completed during the unit.
- Review any offline lesson assessments you have taken.
- Skim through the chapters in The Human Odyssey that you have read in this unit.

Student Guide
Lesson 17: Unit Assessment

You've finished this unit! Now take the Unit Assessment.

Lesson Objectives

- Identify important accomplishments, beliefs, people, and events of the Hebrew people.
- Recognize important cultural achievements of the early Greeks and their emphasis on human achievement.
- Recognize the values, government, and way of life in Greece.
- Compare and contrast the beliefs of early polytheistic civilizations with those of the Hebrews.
- Identify important gods and goddesses of ancient Greece and the characteristics of Greek religious myths.
- Identify on ancient and modern maps the region where Judaism developed.
- Identify on ancient and modern maps the major features of the Greek peninsula.
- Analyze early Greek art for information on values and daily life.
- Analyze maps to assess the reasons for the development of independent city-states in Greece.
- Distinguish between polytheism and monotheism.
- Recognize the lasting influence of Judaism on western civilization.

PREPARE

Approximate lesson time is 60 minutes.

Materials

For the Student

Question Review Table

ASSESS

Unit Assessment: More Lasting Ideas, Part 1 (*Online*)

Complete the computer-scored portion of the Unit Assessment. When you have finished, complete the teacher-scored portion of the assessment and submit it to your teacher.

Unit Assessment: More Lasting Ideas, Part 2 (*Offline*)

Complete the teacher-scored portion of the Unit Assessment and submit it to your teacher.

LEARN

Activity 1: Unit Assessment Review Table *(Online)*

If you earned a score of **less than 80%** on the Unit Assessment, complete the activity.

If you earned a score of **80% or greater**, you may skip this activity.

Let's prepare to retake the Unit Assessment:

- Identify the questions that you answered incorrectly.
- Complete the appropriate review activities listed in the table.

Assessment Date

Unit 7: More Lasting Ideas

Before you retake the Unit Assessment, use the table to figure out which activities you should review.

Question Review Table

Circle the numbers of the questions that you missed on the Unit Assessment. Review the activities that correspond with these questions.

Question	Lesson	Review Activity
1,2,3,27,28,29	1: Monotheism Takes Hold	Honoring One God
4	3: The Law	Use What You Know
5	5: Renewing Their Faith	A Place of Learning and Worship
6	11: Stories and Games	A Gift from the Greeks
7	13: Arts and Histories	Greek Art and Historical Writing
8,18,19,20	14: The Polis	The Greek Citizen-States
9,10,11,12,13,14,15,16	2: Covenants	Use What You Know
17,26	8: Gods in Ancient Greece	The Greeks and Their Gods
21,22,23,24,25	13: Arts and Histories	Analyzing Greek Art
30,31,32,33,34,35	6: Another Land	Focus on Geography

Student Guide

Unit 8: Write Again
Lesson 1: Preparing to Write

The ancient Greeks were truly amazing. They made lasting contributions to science, mathematics, art, literature, government, philosophy, and more. Do some research on the Greeks and report your findings in a well-written essay.

The ancient Greeks left us many legacies in a wide variety of fields--in everything from the arts and sciences to mathematics and philosophy. A *legacy* is something received or passed on from the past. You've already examined some of those legacies and you will explore more in the next unit. Let's get started today by looking at ancient Greeks whose theories, inventions, or ideas still influence us today in the areas of math and science.

Lesson Objectives

- Identify important scientific and mathematical contributions of the ancient Greeks.

PREPARE

Approximate lesson time is 60 minutes.

Materials

For the Student

Greek Scientists and Mathematicians

LEARN

Activity 1: Greek Scientists and Mathematicians *(Offline)*

Instructions

How do we know that we can determine how much carpet we will need in a room by measuring and multiplying to get its square footage? How do we know that it is germs or allergens and not a curse of some sort that gives us runny noses ? We have the Greeks to thank.

While many peoples in ancient Egypt, India, and China made important scientific and mathematical discoveries, most early peoples relied primarily on superstition and their beliefs in a variety of gods to explain the world and themselves. You can learn a lot about the beliefs of the early Greeks from their mythology. But by the sixth century B.C., the Greeks had begun to turn away from magic and from explaining natural occurrences as the result of the whims of the gods. The Greeks began to celebrate the power of human beings to observe the workings of the world and then to apply reason to explain what they saw.

Today it is easy to take that thought process for granted. We might enjoy stories about Zeus and Athena, but we separate the stories from scientific and mathematical reality. We know that lightning is the product of electricity in the atmosphere, not a bolt thrown down from Mount Olympus. Scientific and mathematical thought enables us to attack a terrible disease or an environmental disaster with research and reason so we can find a logical solution. We can invent computers and send shuttles into outer space. We assume that we will learn more and more about the universe as we continue to study it. The Greeks gave the world that way of thinking. That's quite a gift!

Pythagoras was one of the first people to use logic--and only logic--to argue mathematical points. People after her followed his approach in other fields of study. Democritus reasoned that everything is made of tiny particles--atoms. She didn't convince many people to agree with her in her own time, but she did push them to think about matter in new ways. Her student, Hippocrates, taught doctors to look for natural causes and cures for illnesses. She even told people to eat well in order to be healthy.

The list of Greek achievements in science and mathematics could go on and on. As you read about some of the most important contributors to those fields, think about their influence on the world. Their gifts were not limited to a few key discoveries. They changed the way the world thinks.

On the Lasting Effects: Greek Scientists and Mathematicians sheet you'll see the names of four ancient Greeks. Go to Grolier's online encyclopedia. Click on the New Book of Knowledge. In the search field, type in the name of the Scientist or Mathematician. Read about their main scientific and mathematical contributions. As you read about each of the men, ask yourself the following questions:

- What was her lasting contribution to her field?
- Do I think she is fascinating?
- Do I think her achievements are fascinating?

As you read, also identify the field(s) they contributed to (math, science, etc.) and list one or two of their accomplishments or contributions. Try to identify an important impact each man had on the world. Remember, this is preliminary general research. You will select one individual to focus on in your essay and explore her contributions and her impact in greater detail later.

ASSESS

Lesson Assessment: Preparing to Write (*Online*)

You will complete an online assessment covering the main points of this lesson. Your assessment will be scored by the computer.

Name Date

Lasting Effects: Greek Scientists and Mathematicians

Person	Time Period	Field(s)	Accomplishments/Contributions	Impact
Pythagoras				
Euclid				
Archimedes				
Hippocrates				

It is time to choose the person that you want to write about. Which of these ancient Greeks did you think was the most fascinating? Whose contributions interested you the most? Whose legacy do you want to know more about?

The person I will write about is: ____________________

Student Guide
Lesson 2: Organizing Thoughts

Read and analyze sources to evaluate the legacy of one Greek scientist or mathematician in preparation for writing an essay.

Lesson Objectives

- Research one Greek scientist or mathematician.
- Form a thesis statement about the contributions of a Greek scientist or mathematician.
- Create an outline to prepare for writing the essay.

PREPARE

Approximate lesson time is 60 minutes.

Materials

For the Student

- Expository Essay Plan
- Taking Notes

The Human Odyssey: Prehistory Through the Middle Ages edited by Klee, Cribb, and Holdren

---

LEARN

Activity 1: Research *(Offline)*

Instructions

Begin your research by going back to Grolier's online encyclopedia and rereading the article(s) on the Greek scientist or mathematician you selected. Write down the important information on the Taking Notes sheet.
It's time to find other sources. Go online to find more information about the individual you have chosen. Add the information to the Taking Notes sheet. You can try a search engine such as Yahooligans, or use several of the following suggestions.
For Hippocrates go online to:

- San Jose State University Virtual Museum - Hippocrates (http://www.biologie.uni-hamburg.de/b-online/library/history/hippoc.html) to read a short biography
- Nova Online (http://www.pbs.org/wgbh/nova/doctors/oath_classical.html) to read the Hippocratic Oath and explore its impact today
- Antiqua Medicina: Hippocrates (http://www.hsl.virginia.edu/historical/artifacts/antiqua/hippocrates.cfm) to read more about Hippocrates and to read the Hippocratic Oath
- The Quotations Page (http://www.quotationspage.com/quotes.php3?author=Hippocrates) to read quotations from Hippocrates

For Archimedes go online to:

- Mac Tutor History of Mathematics - Archimedes (http://www-groups.dcs.st-and.ac.uk/%7Ehistory/Mathematicians/Archimedes.html)
- Weber State University (http://physics.weber.edu/carroll/Archimedes/principle.htm) to read about Archimedes' principle
- Drexel University (http://www.mcs.drexel.edu/%7Ecrorres/Archimedes/contents.html) to read quick facts on Archimedes
- Eric Weisstein's World of Biography (http://scienceworld.wolfram.com/biography/Archimedes.html) to read a short biography

For Euclid go online to:

- Mac Tutor History of Mathematics - Euclid (http://www-groups.dcs.st-and.ac.uk/%7Ehistory/Mathematicians/Euclid.html) to read a biography
- Read a biography of Euclid at Math Open Reference (http://www.mathopenref.com/euclid.html)

For Pythagoras go online to:

Mac Tutor History of Mathematics - Pythagoras (http://www-groups.dcs.st-and.ac.uk/%7Ehistory/Mathematicians/Pythagoras.html) to read a biography

After you have completed your research, use the Expository Essay Plan to help you organize your information. You'll begin writing the essay in the next lesson.

Name ______________________________ Date ______________________________

Taking Notes

As you research, remember that you are looking for specific information about the person's accomplishments and legacy. The information needs to support your idea that the ancient Greek scientist or mathematician made significant contributions to society.

You may have to leave some sections of the chart blank because the information is not available, and you may have more information in some sections than in others.

Guiding Questions

What is ______________________'s legacy to his field of study and to the world?

General Information

Born: ______________________

Died: ______________________

Where he lived: ______________________

Where he was educated: ______________________

Other general information: ____

____

____

____

Specific Accomplishment(s) and/or Contribution(s) ______________________________

____

____

____

Taking Notes

Impact of Accomplishments in Ancient Times ______________________________

____

____

____

Impact of Accomplishments in Modern Times ______________________________

____

____

____

Writing the Thesis

Now it is time to answer the Guiding Question. Using your chart, think about two or three main points you want to make, and what details will support each of the points. Why do you think this person is more important than the others? What did the person accomplish? What were the short-term results of his contributions? What has been the long-term impact of his contributions?

- Write your answer in one sentence.
- Use third person—don't use the words "I," "we," or "you."

Thesis: ____________________ was an ancient Greek scientist (or mathematician) who left a great legacy because ______________________________

____

Name Date

Expository Essay Plan

An expository essay instructs, provides information, or explains. In this essay, you are presenting information and explaining why you think the Greek scientist or mathematician you chose left a great legacy. But before you begin writing the essay, you need to organize the information you've gathered by creating an outline.

Directions:

1. Your Taking Notes sheet should have helped you identify and organize the information you found while doing your research. Now it is time to create an outline to organize the information in the way you will present it in your essay. You may decide not to use all the information you gathered, but be sure you do not leave out anything that you believe is important to support your thesis.

2. Your essay should include an introductory paragraph, supporting paragraphs, and a concluding paragraph. Each paragraph should cover one main topic and should correspond to a Roman numeral (I., II., III.) on the outline. The main topics should cover:

   - The person's accomplishment and contributions
   - The impact of his accomplishments or contributions in ancient times
   - The impact of his accomplishments or contributions in modern times

3. Write a topic sentence for each paragraph of your essay. Be sure it tells the reader what the section will be about and how the information relates to your thesis statement. Your topic sentence for the introductory paragraph might say something like "Hippocrates was a Greek scientist who left a great legacy." A topic sentence for the second paragraph—the first main topic—might be something like "Hippocrates left a great legacy by contributing to our understanding of the role of nutrition in good health."

4. Decide which pieces of information you will use to support your topic sentences. (These ideas or groups of facts are called *subtopics*.) Subtopics follow capital letters and periods (A., B., C.) on your outline. Add this information beneath your topic sentence.

5. You can further divide subtopics into specific facts. In an outline, specific facts follow Arabic numerals and periods (1., 2., 3., 4.).

6. End your outline and essay with a concluding paragraph.

Student Guide
Lesson 3: Writing

Write an essay about the Greek scientist or mathematician you selected. Make sure your essay includes an introduction with a thesis statement, supporting paragraphs, and a conclusion that summarizes your ideas.

Lesson Objectives

- Demonstrate knowledge gained in previous lessons in a well-constructed essay with a thesis, supporting paragraphs, and a conclusion.

PREPARE

Approximate lesson time is 60 minutes.

Materials

For the Student

The Human Odyssey: Prehistory Through the Middle Ages edited by Klee, Cribb, and Holdren

---

LEARN

Activity 1: Writing the Essay *(Offline)*

Instructions

1. Place your outline and Taking Notes sheet where you can see them easily as you compose your essay. If you need additional information to support your ideas, find it now. Remember, your outline and essay should match each other exactly.
2. Use your thesis statement from your Taking Notes sheet to introduce your essay. The introduction should get the reader's attention and set the scene, so you may want to add some historical information or an explanation before or after the thesis statement. Be sure your introduction tells the reader what you will be writing about. Don't write more than four or five sentences.
3. Follow your outline as you write the body of your essay. Use the topic sentences you wrote in your outline. Explain or support your topic sentences with information from the corresponding section of your outline. Write a concluding sentence that connects back to the thesis statement. Follow the same procedure to write each of the supporting paragraphs.
4. Write a concluding paragraph that summarizes the main ideas of your essay and restates your thesis statement in some way. Write no more than four or five sentences.

ASSESS

Lesson Assessment: Writing (*Offine*)

You will complete an offline assessment covering some of the main points of this lesson. Your assessment will be scored by the teacher.

Student Guide
Lesson 4. Optional: Your Choice

You may use today's lesson time to do one or more of the following:

- Complete work in progress.
- Complete the Beyond the Lesson activity in any lesson in this unit.
- Go on to the next lesson.

Please mark this lesson complete to proceed to the next lesson in the course.

PREPARE

Approximate lesson time is 60 minutes.

Student Guide
Lesson 5: Semester Review: Units 2, 3, and 4

You've finished the first semester! Now it's time to pull together what you have learned this semester. You've learned a lot, so we'll review it unit by unit. Let's start by looking at the following units:

- From Gathering to Growing
- The Mesopotamian Moment
- Civilization Spreads

Lesson Objectives

- Demonstrate mastery of important knowledge and skills taught in the From Gathering to Growing unit.
- Demonstrate mastery of important knowledge and skills taught in the The Mesopotamian Moment unit.
- Demonstrate mastery of important knowledge and skills taught in the Civilization Spreads unit.

PREPARE

Approximate lesson time is 60 minutes.

LEARN

Activity 1: Online *(Online)*

Activity 2: Offline *(Online)*

Instructions

History Journal Review

Review what you learned this semester by going through your History Journal. Look at:

- Completed activity sheets
- Printouts of online activities
- Maps
- Keywords and definitions
- Offline assessments

Be sure to review your Comparing Cultures sheet, which will be particularly helpful.

The Human Odyssey: Prehistory Through the Middle Ages

Read Part 1, Conclusion: A Look Back and a Leap Forward, pages 140-147, of your textbook. This summary will give you a good overview of the From Gathering to Growing, The Mesopotamian Moment, and Civilization Spreads units.

Student Guide
Lesson 6: Semester Review: Units 1, 6, and 7

Let's continue pulling together what you have learned this semester. You've learned a lot, so we'll review it unit by unit. Let's take a look at the following units:

- History: The Map of Time
- Some Lasting Ideas
- More Lasting Ideas

Lesson Objectives

- Demonstrate mastery of important knowledge and skills taught in the History: The Map of Time unit.
- Demonstrate mastery of important knowledge and skills taught in the Some Lasting Ideas unit.
- Demonstrate mastery of important knowledge and skills taught in the More Lasting Ideas unit.

PREPARE

Approximate lesson time is 60 minutes.

LEARN
Activity 1: Online *(Online)*

Activity 2: Offline *(Online)*
Instructions
History Journal Review

Review what you have learned this semester by going through your History Journal. You should look at:

- Completed activity sheets
- Printouts of online activities
- Maps
- Keywords and definitions
- Offline assessments

A review of your Comparing Religions sheet will be particularly helpful.

The Human Odyssey: Prehistory Through the Middle Ages

Read Part 2, Conclusion: The Power of Ancient Ideas, pages 271-277. This summary will give you a good overview of what was covered in the Some Lasting Ideas and More Lasting Ideas units.

Student Guide
Lesson 7: Semester Assessment, Part 1

You've finished the first semester of MS World History I! Now it's time to take the Semester Assessment. This assessment has two parts. Part 1, which you will take today, covers geography. Part 2, which you will complete in the next lesson, covers history.
If you have time after you complete Part 1 of the assessment, you can study for Part 2.

Lesson Objectives

- Use maps, globes, latitude, and longitude to determine absolute and relative locations.
- Identify on a map the seven continents and four oceans.
- List examples of ways early humans used and adapted to their environment.
- Recognize how the channeling of floodwaters affected the development of civilization.
- List examples of the relationship between geography and the rise and fall of civilizations.
- Locate on a map the Nile River and the modern countries through which it flows.
- Identify on a map the modern countries through which the Indus River flows.
- Recognize current theories on why the Indus Valley civilization declined.
- Identify on a map the Yellow River, Yangtze River, and major physical features of East Asia.
- Recognize examples of the ways people interact with and change the environment.
- Identify on a map the area known as Canaan--the "Promised Land"--and the city of Jerusalem.
- Identify on a map the Peloponnese, Mediterranean Sea, Aegean Sea, Ionian Sea, and Crete.
- Explain the geographic reasons for the development of independent city-states in Greece.
- Identify on a map the Tigris and Euphrates Rivers, the Persian Gulf, and the major physical features of Mesopotamia.

PREPARE

Approximate lesson time is 60 minutes.

ASSESS

Semester Assessment: Semester Assessment, Part 1 *(Online)*

You will complete an online assessment covering the main points of this semester. Your assessment will be scored by the computer.

Student Guide
Lesson 8: Semester Assessment, Part 2

Today you will take Part 2 of the Semester Assessment.

Lesson Objectives

- Identify the invention of the wheel as a major contribution of Mesopotamian civilization.
- Describe ziggurats.
- Recognize *The Epic of Gilgamesh* as a classic of Sumerian literature and the source of information about Sumerian values.
- Recognize examples of cultural and physical characteristics of Mesopotamia.
- Describe the reasons for building the pyramids, sphinxes, and mummifying bodies.
- Explain the significance of Howard Carter's discovery of Tutankhamen's tomb.
- Analyze Egyptian art and architecture for information on the society's culture.
- Explain why archaeologists and historians have limited information about the Indus Valley civilization.
- Recognize current theories on why the Indus Valley civilization declined.
- List three ways China's civilization differed from other river valley civilizations.
- Explain why Confucianism is a philosophy and not a religion.
- Distinguish between polytheism and monotheism.
- Recognize characteristics and examples of Muslim art and architecture.
- Analyze art and technologies of China for information on the culture and values.
- Identify the criteria used to define a civilization.
- Define history and identify reasons for studying it.
- Describe the development of the Sumerian system of writing.
- Identify the earliest known system of writing.
- Describe the role of scribes in Sumerian society.
- Recognize Sargon's achievements and failings as an empire builder.
- Identify Hammurabi and his most significant accomplishment.
- Identify Nebuchadnezzar and his major accomplishments.
- Identify the major gods of Egypt and their relationship to nature.
- Explain the origins and significance of the term *pharaoh*.
- Identify the system of writing of ancient Egypt.
- Identify Ramses II.
- Identify major features and innovations of Mohenjo-Daro and other Indus cities.
- Describe Chinese writing and its early relationship to religious ideas.
- Explain the importance of ancestor worship to the Chinese.
- Describe important characteristics and contributions of the ancient Indus Valley civilization and possible explanations for its fall.
- Compare and contrast the early river-valley civilizations.
- Recognize examples of human and physical characteristics of place in Egypt, the Indus Valley, and early China.

- Identify Siddhartha Gautama and his historic significance.
- Identify Confucius.
- Identify Asoka.
- Describe the fundamental teachings of Buddhism about the search for Nirvana, the way to live a good life, and reincarnation.
- Define *polytheism*, *monotheism*, *Torah*, and *covenant*.
- Identify the Hebrews as the first people to worship one God and spread that idea.
- Name the religion of the ancient Hebrews.
- Identify Abraham.
- Summarize the basic beliefs of Judaism.
- Explain the geographic reasons for the development of independent city-states in Greece.
- Explain that the Greek view of humanity differed from that of earlier polytheistic civilizations in that the Greeks believed humans could use their minds and reason to understand the world around them.
- Identify one of the Greeks' greatest contributions to Western civilization.
- Identify Homer.
- Identify important accomplishments, beliefs, people, and events of the Hebrew people.
- Compare and contrast government and values in Sparta and Athens.

PREPARE

Approximate lesson time is 60 minutes.

ASSESS

Semester Assessment: Semester Assessment, Part 2 *(Offline)*

Complete the teacher-scored portion of the Semester Assessment and submit it to your teacher.

Student Guide

Unit 9: Classical Greece
Lesson 1: Classically Different Ways of Life

The Greeks valued serious thought and individual effort, and the results were remarkable. The Greeks gave us philosophy, art, theater, and the concept of democracy. What made such accomplishments possible? Climate, terrain, war, individuals, and even diseases played a role. If any of these factors had been different, history might have taken another course.

What is a classical civilization? What legacy did classical civilizations leave to the modern world? The Greeks--and the Romans who followed them--built classical civilizations. In ancient Greece, two city-states stand out--Athens and Sparta. Their people shared language, religion, and great pride in being Greek. But in other ways they could not have been more different.

Lesson Objectives

- Explain that Greece and Rome are referred to as "classical civilizations."
- Identify characteristics that pulled the Greek city-states together and those that drove them apart.
- Describe important characteristics of life in Sparta.
- Define *oligarchy.*
- Identify key characteristics of life in Athens.
- Compare and contrast government and values in Sparta and Athens.
- Identify people who could and could not be citizens of Athens.
- Identify democratic reformers and their accomplishments in Athens.
- Define *democracy* and describe why Athenian democracy was groundbreaking.

PREPARE

Approximate lesson time is 60 minutes.

Materials

For the Student

- Reading Guide
- What Is a Spartan Life?

The Human Odyssey: Prehistory Through the Middle Ages edited by Klee, Cribb, and Holdren

Keywords and Pronunciation

Acropolis (uh-KRAH-puh-luhs)
Arc de Triomphe (ahrk duh tree-AWNF)
classical : relating to the civilizations and ideas of ancient Greece and Rome between 500 B.C. and A.D. 500
Democritus (dih-MAHK-ruht-uhs)
Ephesus (EH-fuh-suhs)
Hippocrates (hip-AHK-ruh-teez)
oligarchy (AH-luh-gahr-kee) : a government in which a small group of people holds all the power
Pythagoras (puh-THAG-uh-ruhs)

LEARN

Activity 1: What Does Classical Mean? *(Offline)*

Read

As you read the Introduction to Part 3, "What's So 'Classic' About the Classical World?" pages 279-283, complete the Reading Guide. When you have finished, compare your answers with those in the Lesson Answer Key.

Then continue by reading Part 3, Chapter 1, from the beginning to "*Athena's City*," pages 285-289. As you read, list at least three characteristics or features that pulled the Greek city-states together and three that pulled them apart.

Unifying Characteristics:

1. ______________________________
2. ______________________________
3. ______________________________

Dividing Characteristics:

1. ______________________________
2. ______________________________
3. ______________________________

Use What You Know

A Spartan Life

What was the life of a Spartan like? How is yours different? Do you think you would have survived as a Spartan?

Complete the What Is a Spartan Life? chart and answer the last question based on your experiences and personal characteristics.

ASSESS

Lesson Assessment: Classically Different Ways of Life (*Online*)

You will complete an online assessment covering the main points of this lesson. Your assessment will be scored by the computer.

LEARN

Activity 2: Classically Different Ways of Life *(Offline)*

Read Chapter 1, "*Athena's City*," pages 290-295.

Name ______________________________ Date ______________________________

Reading Guide

Read

Answer the following questions as you read the Introduction to Part 3.

1. How does the text define "classical civilizations"?

____

____

2. In what areas of present-day life can you most easily see influences of Greek and Roman society?

____

____

3. Name two examples of Greek and Roman influence in the ideas surrounding the development of the United States.

____

____

What Is Classical?

Suppose you had to explain why historians and others refer to Greece and Rome as "classical civilizations." How could you explain this quickly and succinctly? A Top 10 list might help.

Consider the information presented in the Introduction to Part 3, and think back to what you learned in Unit 7 as well.

List 10 possible reasons history refers to Greece and Rome as classical civilizations. Try to organize your choices from 10 to 1 in order of importance, with 1 being the most important.

Rank Order	Possible reasons history refers to Greece and Rome as classical civilizations

Name ______________________________ Date ______________________________

What Is a Spartan Life?

1. Complete the chart below to create a picture of life in Sparta and compare it with your life today.

Life Issue	Sparta	Modern American Society	
Age at which most children leave home			
Gender roles (What do men do? What do women do?)			
Food supply			
Family living arrangements			
Citizenship			
Type of government			
Important values			

2. Do you think you would have thrived or even survived as a citizen of Sparta? Explain your reasons.

____

____

____

____

____

____

Student Guide
Lesson 2: Athens

In Sparta, life centered on military battles. In Athens, people loved to argue about ideas. While the Spartans were not afraid to take up arms, the Athenians were not afraid to take up new ideas. Athens boasted of peace, plenty, and wisdom. Over time, men who were lucky enough to be citizens participated in government to a degree never before seen. How did their groundbreaking system of government affect future generations, including your own?

Lesson Objectives

- Identify key characteristics of life in Athens.
- Compare and contrast government and values in Sparta and Athens.
- Identify people who could and could not be citizens of Athens.
- Identify democratic reformers and their accomplishments in Athens.
- Define *democracy* and describe why Athenian democracy was groundbreaking.

PREPARE

Approximate lesson time is 60 minutes.

Materials

For the Student

The Human Odyssey: Prehistory Through the Middle Ages edited by Klee, Cribb, and Holdren

History Journal

Keywords and Pronunciation

Cleisthenes (KLIYS-thuh-neez)

Croesus (KREE-sus)

democracy : rule by the people

Solon (SOH-luhn)

LEARN

Activity 1: Athens *(Online)*

Greek myths about Athena provide insight into the values and beliefs of the people of the great city-state of Athens. Click Athena's City and see what you remember about your reading.

Activity 2: Understanding Athens *(Online)*

Explore

Visit

Ancient Greece: Athens

to learn more about the daily life of Athenians.

Read

Read Part 3, Chapter 1, from "The Athenian Way" to the end, pages 295-297.

Look at What Is a Spartan Life? from the previous lesson, Classically Different Ways of Life. You'll notice that the last column is blank. Write *Athens* as the heading for that column. Then fill in the column with the information you learned today about life in Athens.

Activity 3: Defining Athenian Democracy *(Offline)*

You have been selected to give a speech at a ceremony in which the first honorees are inducted into an Athenian Democracy Hall of Fame. It is a great honor. How would you explain democracy? What would you say about the groundbreaking nature of Athenian democracy? Who would the inductees be?

Here is a list of the candidates:

- Athena
- Cleisthenes
- Croesus
- Poseidon
- Solon
- Tellus

Write your speech in your History Journal. In your speech, answer the questions posed in the first paragraph. Then, select the three best candidates and incorporate their contributions into your speech.

ASSESS

Lesson Assessment: Athens (*Online*)

You will complete an online assessment covering the main points of this lesson. Your assessment will be scored by the computer.

LEARN

Activity 4. Optional: Athens *(Online)*

This activity is OPTIONAL. It's provided for enrichment or extra practice, but not required for completion of this lesson.You may skip this activity.

Read more about the rise of Athenian democracy on two websites.

- Ancient Greece: Solon

  features the changes Solon brought about.
- Learn more about Cleisthenes and his impact at

  Ancient Greece: Cleisthenes

  See if you can pass the quiz.

Student Guide
Lesson 3: An Empire Threatens

The Greek city-states were quite different from each other, but when another civilization threatened some outlying Greek communities, Athens came to their aid. Who threatened the Greeks? It was the Persian Empire, the largest empire the world had yet known. Who were the Persians? How far did their power extend? And how did they organize and control such a vast territory?

Lesson Objectives

- Describe the main accomplishments and characteristics of the Persian Empire and its leaders.
- Locate on a map the borders of the Persian Empire at its height, its capital, and the countries that lie within its ancient borders today.
- Summarize the main events of the First and Second Persian Wars.
- Identify the Oracle of Delphi.
- Explain the importance of the Athenians' victory in the Persian Wars.

PREPARE

Approximate lesson time is 60 minutes.

Materials

For the Student

Documenting the Persian Empire

The Human Odyssey: Prehistory Through the Middle Ages edited by Klee, Cribb, and Holdren

Keywords and Pronunciation

Delphi (DEL-fiy)
Herodotus (hih-RAHD-uh-tuhs)
Miltiades (mil-TIY-uh-deez)
Persepolis (puhr-SEH-puh-lis)
phalanx (FAY-langks)
Pheidippides (fih-DIP-uh-deez)
Salamis (SA-luh-muhs)
satrap (SAY-trap) : the governor of a province in ancient Persia
triremes (TRIY-reems)
Zagros (ZA-gruhs)

LEARN

Activity 1: An Empire Threatens *(Online)*

Use the Classical World time line in the Resources section to learn more about the history and rulers of the mighty Persian Empire. Then, read the information on the Documenting the Persian Empire sheet and record significant events and accomplishments on the chart. When you have finished, compare your answers with those in the Lesson Answer Key.

Activity 2: Focus on Geography *(Offline)*

Use the maps on pages 300-301, 626, and 630 to help you answer these questions.

When you have finished, check your answers against those in the Lesson Answer Key.

1. At what longitude was the westernmost point of the Persian Empire at its peak?
2. What two seas were part of the northern border of the empire?
3. Along what river was the southernmost part of the empire?
4. Along what body of water was the original part of the Persian Empire?
5. At what latitude was the center of the original empire?
6. What natural feature formed the eastern boundary of the empire?
7. Consider what you know about the physical geography of the region shown on the map. You have studied the geography of Egypt and Mesopotamia. What explanation can you give for the fact that Cyrus or Darius did not claim the land between the Red Sea and the Persian Gulf?
8. Rounded to thousands, how many miles are between Cyrene in North Africa and the point where the Indus River meets the 30° N latitude line?
9. You can see that the Persian Empire was big. Very big. What present-day countries lie within its ancient boundaries? Use the map of Eurasia on page 626 in your text to find out. To orient yourself, use the latitude and longitude lines on the empire map as well as physical features like rivers and seas.

ASSESS

Lesson Assessment: An Empire Threatens (*Online*)

You will complete an online assessment covering the main points of this lesson. Your assessment will be scored by the computer.

LEARN

Activity 3: An Empire Threatens *(Offline)*

Between 600 and 400 B.C. the Persian Empire grew at a tremendous rate as the Persian rulers conquered one nearby land after another. It would take determination and brilliant strategy for any group to stand a chance against the Persians. Were the Greeks ready for this challenge? To find out, read Chapter 2, from the beginning to "The Brave Three Hundred," pages 299-306.

As you read, prepare to answer some questions about these topics:

- Darius
- Marathon
- Persian Wars
- The Oracle at Delphi

Name Date

Documenting the Persian Empire

The Persians began to expand their empire in the middle of the sixth century B.C. They joined forces with another group called the Medes and took control of Nebuchadnezzar's Babylon. In a short time, under Cyrus the Great, they had taken control of a huge swath of land extending from the eastern edge of Europe to the western rim of the Indus River valley.

Cyrus was an able warrior and made good use of the fine horses that thrived in the valley pasturelands of the Zagros Mountains. The mountains provided iron for weapons as well. But Cyrus kept control in other ways besides military force.

Cyrus allowed conquered peoples to keep their traditions and cultures. He prayed to the Babylonian god Marduk and began the rebuilding of the Hebrew Temple in Jerusalem. He established provinces throughout the empire and appointed governors to oversee them. The result was peace and prosperity greater than anyone had seen before.

After Cyrus died while fighting a battle east of the Hindu Kush mountains near India, his son came to power. Cyrus's son added Egypt to the growing empire, but died soon afterward. His successor was Darius.

Darius continued the policy of dividing the empire into provinces, and sent a satrap, usually someone of royal or noble blood, to each province. But Darius didn't leave the satraps unsupervised. Inspectors followed them, and secretaries used the official language of Aramaic to communicate with Darius. Using roads that were better than any built before that time, messengers traveled as much as 200 miles in a day.

Darius appreciated the best of what he saw in the cultures he conquered. When he had a new capital built at Persepolis, he used architectural designs and artistic styles from Egypt, Greece, and Babylon. He introduced Indian religious ideas into Persian religion and brought farming techniques from Babylon to Central Asia. By the time of his death, Greeks on the west coast of the Aegean Sea were raising crops of Indian rice.

Name Date

Documenting the Persian Empire

You are a record keeper for your city. In the first column, list some facts that describe the accomplishments of Cyrus I. In the second column, do the same for Darius I. Keep in mind that you are a Persian and are proud of your people, culture, and leaders.

Cyrus I	Darius I

Student Guide
Lesson 4: Free to Flourish

The Persian Empire had grown in size and power and even spread from western Asia into parts of Europe and Africa. How could the Greeks--a group of loosely connected city-states--defend themselves against such a mighty force? Which culture would prevail in Europe over time?

Lesson Objectives

- Summarize the main events of the First and Second Persian Wars.
- Identify the Oracle of Delphi.
- Explain the importance of the Athenians' victory in the Persian Wars.

PREPARE

Approximate lesson time is 60 minutes.

Materials

For the Student

The Human Odyssey: Prehistory Through the Middle Ages edited by Klee, Cribb, and Holdren

---

LEARN

Activity 1: Check Your Reading and Read *(Offline)*

The Battle of Marathon

The Athenians faced great challenges in protecting their homes and land. Summarize the main events of the First Persian War by answering the questions below (based on the Read On for Chapter 2, from the beginning to "The Brave Three Hundred," pages 299-306). When you have finished, check your answers against those in the Lesson Answer Key.

1. How did Darius first approach the Greeks to gain their lands? What was their response?

2. Where did the Persian army enter Greece? What city was most at risk? Why?

3. Although the Athenians were unprepared for war, what three things did they have in their favor?

4. What was the Spartans' role in the Battle of Marathon?

5. When the Athenians discovered silver ore in their lands, what did their citizens decide to do with their new wealth? Why?

6. Explain the role of the oracle at Delphi.

Read

Marathon was a remarkable battle and an important turning point for the Greeks. Yet just 10 years later the Persians threatened again, and the Greeks realized they would have to band together to combat their common enemy.

Read how the Greeks fared in the second attack of the Persians in Chapter 2, "The Brave Three Hundred" to the end, pages 306-309. As you read, answer the questions below. When you have finished, check your answers against those in the Lesson Answer Key.

1. When did the Persian Empire next attempt to conquer Greece? Who led this attack? Why did they think they would be successful?

2. Describe the Persian invasion of Greece.

3. How did the Greek navy fare against the Persian navy?

Activity 2: Free to Flourish *(Online)*

Imagine you are a reporter and your assignment is to write news and feature stories about the Persian Wars for a Greek newspaper. Open War News and follow the directions to complete your assignment.

ASSESS

Lesson Assessment: Free to Flourish (*Online*)

You will complete an online assessment covering the main points of this lesson. Your assessment will be scored by the computer.

LEARN

Activity 3. Optional: Free to Flourish *(Online)*

This activity is OPTIONAL. It's provided for enrichment or extra practice, but not required for completion of this lesson. You may skip this activity.

Option 1

Now that you've written your own headlines and article outlines, what do you think the Greeks themselves had to say? Read all about it in an excerpt from

Herodotus's Persian WarsHerodotus's stories about the Persian Wars

As you read, write at least three questions you would like to ask Herodotus if you could actually meet him.

Student Guide
Lesson 5. Optional: Your Choice

You may use today's lesson time to do one or more of the following:

- Complete work in progress.
- Complete the Beyond the Lesson activity in any lesson in this unit.
- Review the Classical World Time Line in the Resources section.
- Prepare for your state standardized test.
- Go on to the next lesson.

Please mark this lesson complete to proceed to the next lesson in the course.

PREPARE

Approximate lesson time is 60 minutes.

Student Guide
Lesson 6: A Golden Time

When the Persian Wars finally ended, the Athenians looked over their ruined city. How could they rebuild after such devastation?
Pericles, a man of great vision and energy, thought Athens could be even better than before. He pictured a city of magnificent buildings and beautiful artwork. He saw an educated population with more political power than the world had ever seen. He envisioned a society that all the Greek city-states--all the world--would emulate. How did the Athenians respond?

Lesson Objectives

- Identify Pericles.
- Recognize key characteristics of Athenian democracy.
- Analyze a primary source to assess Athenian values.

PREPARE

Approximate lesson time is 60 minutes.

Materials

For the Student

Reading Guide

The Human Odyssey: Prehistory Through the Middle Ages edited by Klee, Cribb, and Holdren

History Journal

Keywords and Pronunciation

Pericles (PEHR-uh-kleez) : the foremost statesman of Athens during its golden age
Piraeus (piy-REE-us)

LEARN

Activity 1: A Golden Time *(Offline)*

Read Chapter 3, from the beginning to "Architecture and Art in the Age of Pericles," pages 311-317, to learn about Pericles, the man who led Athens into a golden age. As you read, complete the Reading Guide. Then compare your answers with those in the Lesson Answer Key.

Activity 2: A Golden Time *(Online)*

Defining Pericles

Pericles called Athens a "school for Greece." What might he have meant by those words?

Complete the Personality Profile: Pericles to explore the life and ideas of this great Greek leader. You will need to look closely at the primary source, Pericles' own words, on pages 316-317 of the text, as well as the other information in today's reading. Print the completed activity and place it in your History Journal.

When you have finished, use the Lesson Answer Key to check your work.

ASSESS

Lesson Assessment: A Golden Time (*Online*)

You will complete an online assessment covering the main points of this lesson. Your assessment will be scored by the computer.

Name ________________________________ Date ________________________________

Reading Guide

Athens

1. Describe Athens:

   immediately following the Persian Wars ________________________________

   ____

   ____

   after rebuilding ________________________________

   ____

   ____

2. What is this period of time called? (two different names)

   ________________________________ and ________________________________

Understanding Athenian Democracy

1. What role did each of the following play in the Athenian system of government?

	Purpose	Who Participated?	How Were They Chosen?
The Assembly			
The Council of Athens			
Polis Jobs			
The Generals			
The Juries			

Name Date 

Reading Guide

2. Who was allowed to participate in Athenian democracy?

3. What groups could not participate in the political process?

4. Do you think the groups that couldn't vote or officially participate influenced politics in Athens? If so, how?

5. Who was eligible to vote in ancient Athens?

Student Guide
Lesson 7: Art and Architecture

The Greeks valued reason and logic and appreciated balance in many aspects of life. More than any people before them, they admired and honored the individual. As you have seen with other civilizations, art and architecture reflects a society's values. Think about the connections between values and art as you look more closely at the artistic achievements of the Greeks during the golden age of
Pericles

.

Lesson Objectives

- Recognize the purposes and characteristics of Athenian architecture.
- Analyze Athenian art and architecture for characteristics of style.

PREPARE

Approximate lesson time is 60 minutes.

Materials

For the Student

Student Guide

Keywords and Pronunciation

Pericles (PEHR-uh-kleez) : the foremost statesman of Athens during its golden age

---

LEARN

Activity 1: Art and Architecture *(Offline)*

Read Chapter 3 from "Architecture and Art in the Age of Pericles" to "Greek Theater: Dramatically Different," pages 317-319, including the sidebar about the Parthenon.

Activity 2: Art and Architecture *(Online)*

Greek art and architecture contained elements that have inspired modern artists and architects. Complete the activity Elements of Greek Design to learn about the form and structure of Greek architecture and to explore modern architecture that relies on Greek design.

Activity 3: Art and Architecture *(Online)*

Open the Photo Tour of Athens and follow the directions to design your brochure. When you have finished, print your brochure and place it in your History Journal.

Remember, there is room for only four photographs on the brochure, so be selective and think carefully about the pictures you choose. Your photos must illustrate the kind of Greek art or architecture that tourists would likely see on the tour. The pieces should be art or architecture created between about 450 B.C. and 420 B.C. You must also explain to the travel-agency owners why you selected those images to represent classical Greek architecture.
When you have finished, print your brochure and place it in your History Journal.

ASSESS

Lesson Assessment: Art and Architecture (*Online*)

You will complete an online assessment covering the main points of this lesson. Your assessment will be scored by the computer.

LEARN

Activity 4. Optional: Art and Architecture *(Offline)*

This activity is OPTIONAL. It's provided for enrichment or extra practice, but not required for completion of this lesson. You may skip this activity.
For further study choose from any of the following activities:

- Sketch a model of the Parthenon.
- Construct or carve a metope from modeling clay.
- Draw or describe a building in the Greek style you might design for your town.

Student Guide
Lesson 8: The Play's the Thing

Have you ever been to a play? Did you laugh at the funny parts or cry at the sad ones? When the play was over, did you thank the Greeks for the good time you had? You probably answered no to the last question, but plays actually have their roots in ancient Greece. The Greeks gave the world a new form of storytelling--drama, or the play. Greek dramas are still considered some of the greatest plays ever written.

Lesson Objectives

- Recognize the main characteristics of Greek theater.
- Describe the development of Greek theater.
- Identify Aeschylus, Sophocles, and Euripides and their contributions to literature.

PREPARE

Approximate lesson time is 60 minutes.

Materials

For the Student

The Human Odyssey: Prehistory Through the Middle Ages edited by Klee, Cribb, and Holdren

Keywords and Pronunciation

Aeschylus (ES-kuh-lus)
Aristophanes (air-uh-STAHF-uh-neez)
comedy : a type of Greek play that poked fun at human flaws or failings
Lysistrata (lih-sih-STRAH-tuh)
Medea (muh-DEE-uh)
Oedipus (ED-uh-puhs)
orchestra : the circular or semicircular area of a Greek theater that held the chorus or actors
Sophocles (SAHF-uh-kleez)
tragedy : a type of Greek play that explored family relationships or relationships between humans and the gods

---

LEARN

Activity 1: The Play's the Thing *(Offline)*

Read Chapter 3, "Greek Theater: Dramatically Different" to the end, pages 319-325.

Activity 2: The Play's the Thing *(Online)*

The annual Tony Awards honor the best plays, writers, actors, and directors on Broadway today. The producers of this year's televised Tony Awards ceremony want to open with a short tribute to the ancient Greeks and their contributions to theater, and they have asked you to create the tribute.

Note: If you would like to include more information than is in your text, do the Web research in the Beyond the Lesson activity first, and then come back to this activity.

ASSESS

Lesson Assessment: The Play's the Thing (*Online*)

You will complete an online assessment covering the main points of this lesson. Your assessment will be scored by the computer.

LEARN

Activity 3. Optional: The Play's the Thing *(Online)*

This activity is OPTIONAL. It's provided for enrichment or extra practice, but not required for completion of this lesson. You may skip this activity.

Greek drama set the stage for today's theatre. How?

Student Guide
Lesson 9: The Decline of Athens

Athens flourished in the years after the defeat of Persia. Athenian art, architecture, drama, and an even more democratic government were examples to all of Greece and beyond. But while most Greek city-states admired the Athenians and looked to them for leadership, some resented them. Eventually, war broke out. Would Athens survive the war? Would Sparta take her place?

Lesson Objectives

- Describe the main cause of the Peloponnesian War.
- Explain the main reasons for Athens' defeat in the Peloponnesian War.
- Recognize the results of the Peloponnesian War.
- Identify the Delian League.

PREPARE

Approximate lesson time is 60 minutes.

Materials

For the Student

Reading Guide

The Human Odyssey: Prehistory Through the Middle Ages edited by Klee, Cribb, and Holdren

History Journal

Keywords and Pronunciation

Delian League (DEL-lee-uhn) : a defensive alliance among the city-states of Greece led by Athens
Delos (DEE-lahs)
Peloponnesian (peh-luh-puh-NEE-zhuhn)
Peloponnesian War : war (431-404 B.C.) between Sparta and Athens, which led to the fall of Athens
plague : an infectious disease of animals and humans caused by a bacterium

---

LEARN
Activity 1: The End of an Era *(Online)*

Read

As you read Chapter 4 from the beginning to "Socrates: The Gadfly of Athens," pages 326-330, complete the Reading Guide. When you have finished, check your answers against those in the Lesson Answer Key.

Use What You Know

Imagine that the Athenian government has established a committee to investigate why Athens was defeated in the Peloponnesian War. You are its chairperson. Now you must deliver your report. You have decided to prepare a one-page summary of your lengthy findings.

Write that summary in your History Journal. It should include a brief summary of the causes of the Peloponnesian War, a discussion of what Athens could have done to avoid the war, and a list of the main reasons for the Athenian defeat.

Check your answers against those in the Lesson Answer Key.

Activity 2: Focus on Geography *(Online)*

Are elements of the Athenian defeat still plaguing you? Plagues are a recurring phenomenon in human history and the one that hit Athens in 430 B.C. was one of the most notable--it helped Sparta defeat Athens. Visit these websites to find out more about the medical disaster that contributed to the fall of Athens:

Thucydides on the Plague

-to learn more about the beginning of the plague, its possible origin, and the symptoms of the disease.

The Plague in Athens During the Peloponnesian War

-This a complicated reading that describes the plague and offers details about what people knew about it at the time.

Then, click The Plague of Athens to see how much you learned about the plague.

ASSESS

Lesson Assessment: The Decline of Athens (*Online*)

You will complete an online assessment covering the main points of this lesson. Your assessment will be scored by the computer.

Name Date

Reading Guide

1. Describe the changes in Athens after the Greeks defeated the Persians.

2. What was the Delian League?

3. Describe some of the problems faced by this alliance.

4. What was Sparta's role during this time?

5. How did the war between Athens and Sparta begin?

Student Guide
Lesson 10: Different Perspectives

Our experiences influence the way we see events. Athenians took enormous pride in their accomplishments and way of life. But many other Greeks thought the Athenians were far too proud, and some even saw Athens as an arrogant bully. When Pericles made a speech honoring those who had died defending Athens, he explained why the entire world should admire Athens. But how would you have reacted if you had been a citizen of Thasos, the island that had tried to withdraw from the Delian League? Would you have seen Athens as a place to be admired?

Lesson Objectives

- Analyze primary sources to discern differing viewpoints about Athens.
- Recognize how other Greek city-states reacted to Athenian dominance.
- Define *philosophy, monarchy, aristocracy, democracy,* and *anarchy.*
- Identify Socrates, Plato, and Aristotle and their key ideas and achievements.

PREPARE

Approximate lesson time is 60 minutes.

Materials

For the Student

Delian League

The Human Odyssey: Prehistory Through the Middle Ages edited by Klee, Cribb, and Holdren

History Journal

Keywords and Pronunciation

Delian League (DEL-lee-uhn) : a defensive alliance among the city-states of Greece led by Athens

---

LEARN

Activity 1: Different Perspectives *(Offline)*

The Delian League was supposed to be an association of Greek city-states, but Athens quickly took control. When some city-states wanted to leave the league, the Athenians prevented them from withdrawing.

Pericles proudly held Athens up as an example for the other city-states to follow, but Thucydides criticized the Delian League and the way Athens controlled it. Explore their two points of view by completing the Delian League sheet.

Don't forget to do the Read On after you take the assessment.

ASSESS

Lesson Assessment: Different Perspectives (*Online*)

You will complete an online assessment covering the main points of this lesson. Your assessment will be scored by the computer.

LEARN

Activity 2: Different Perspectives *(Offline)*

Read Chapter 4 from "Socrates: The Gadfly of Athens" to "Alexander the Great," pages 330-336.

As you read, define these terms:

- anarchy
- aristocracy
- democracy
- monarchy
- philosophy

The Delian League

The Delian League was started as an association of Greek city-states. Each city-state contributed to the defense of all the members. Athens, as the wealthiest and strongest member, quickly took control. When the Persian threat diminished, some city-states wanted to leave the league, but Athens prevented them from withdrawing. Pericles praised Athens as an example for the entire world, but not everyone agreed. Thucydides criticized the Delian League and the way Athens controlled it.

Read each section aloud. Then answer the questions that follow.

Part 1

Pericles:

"When our work is done, we are in a position to enjoy all kinds of recreation for our spirits. There are ceremonies and contests all year. In our homes we find a beauty and good taste which delight us every day and drive away our cares."

Thucydides:

"...the Athenians were very severe and exacting, and made themselves offensive by applying the screw of necessity [applying economic pressure] to men who were not used to and in fact not disposed for any continuous labour."

Questions:

1. Which author describes Athens as a place with time for pleasant relaxation? ____________
2. Which author describes people being forced to do hard work? ____________
3. Circle three words in each quotation that give either a positive or a negative impression of Athens.
   Now look at the words you circled.
   Are the words from Thucydides positive, negative, or some of each? ____________
   Are the words from Pericles positive, negative, or some of each? ____________

Part 2

Thucydides:

"In some other respects the Athenians were not the old popular rulers they had been at first; and ... it was easy for them to reduce [defeat] any that tried to leave the confederacy."

Pericles:

"Ours is a democracy because power is in the hands not of a minority, but of the whole people."

Questions:

4. Pericles says that Athens is a democracy. How does he explain what he means by democracy?
   ____
5. Do you think Thucydides would agree that Athens was a democracy? ____________
   Would he see Athens's role in the Delian League as democratic? Why or why not?____________
   ____

Part 3

Thucydides:

"For this the allies had themselves to blame, the wish to get off service making most of them arrange to pay their share of the expense in money instead of in ships, and so to avoid having to leave their homes. Thus while Athens was increasing her navy with the funds they contributed, a revolt always found them without resources or experience for war."

Question:

6. According to Thucydides, the members of the league were partly to blame for their situation. They could not leave the league because Athens would attack. Athens was able to attack because the members had given Athens money to build a navy, instead of building their own. Was Athens justified in using the resources of the league in this way? Why or why not? ____________________

   ____

   ____

Pericles:

"I could tell you what we gain by defeating our enemies. Instead, I would rather have you gaze on the greatness of Athens every day. Then you would...realize her greatness."

Questions:

7. Pericles asks you to gaze on the greatness of Athens every day in order to judge that greatness. Do you agree with him that looking at the buildings and life of the city of Athens is the best way to judge the city-state? ____

8. Are there other questions you would like to ask about Athens before making a judgment?

   ____

   ____

   ____

Student Guide
Lesson 11: Three Great Thinkers

The Athenians loved to learn. They found all kinds of study worthwhile, and they asked questions about everything--about how the world works, about the nature of right and wrong, and about the value of government. Who were the greatest thinkers of ancient Greece? What questions did they ask and what answers did they find?

Lesson Objectives

- Define *philosophy, monarchy, aristocracy, democracy,* and *anarchy.*
- Identify Socrates, Plato, and Aristotle and their key ideas and achievements.

PREPARE

Approximate lesson time is 60 minutes.

Keywords and Pronunciation

anarchy : absence of any law and order; the failure of democracy
aristocracy : rule by a few
Aristotle (AIR-uh-stah-tl)
democracy : rule by the people
Lyceum (liy-SEE-uhm)
Macedonia (ma-suh-DOH-nee-uh)
Meletus (muh-LEE-tus)
monarchy : rule by one person
philosophy : the study of truth, knowledge, and the things of fundamental importance in life
Plato (PLAY-toh)
Socrates (SAHK-ruh-teez)

LEARN

Activity 1: Three Great Thinkers *(Online)*

Check your definitions from the Read On activity in the last lesson, Different Perspectives, against those in the Keywords section of this lesson.
Then click Three Great Thinkers and identify the key ideas and achievements of Socrates, Plato, and Aristotle.

Activity 2: Three Great Thinkers *(Offline)*

The Athenians asked questions about everything--about how the world works, about the nature of right and wrong, and about the value of government. Some of the questions they asked were:
What is a good life?
How do we live a good life?
What is justice?
What is it possible to know with certainty?
What is the universe made of?
Which of the questions considered by the ancient Greeks do you think are most important today? Identify your choices and/or write your own questions about issues you think are important today.

____
____
____
____
____

What do you think Socrates meant when he said, "The unexamined life is not worth living"?

____
____
____
____
____

Do you agree or disagree with this statement? Why?

____
____
____
____
____

Activity 3: Three Great Thinkers *(Online)*

Socrates was very fond of asking questions. What questions do you still have about him? Write three questions in your History Journal.
Now, learn more about the ancient Greek philosophers by visiting the PBS website
PBS: The Greeks
. Listen to the introduction, enter the site, and explore the information on Socrates. Can you find answers to any of your questions?

ASSESS

Lesson Assessment: Three Great Thinkers (*Online*)

You will complete an online assessment covering the main points of this lesson. Your assessment will be scored by the computer.

Student Guide
Lesson 12. Optional: Your Choice

You may use today's lesson time to do one or more of the following:

- Complete work in progress.
- Complete the Beyond the Lesson activity in any lesson in this unit.
- Review the Classical World Time Line in the Resources section.
- Prepare for your state standardized test.
- Go on to the next lesson.

Please mark this lesson complete to proceed to the next lesson in the course.

PREPARE

Approximate lesson time is 60 minutes.

Student Guide
Lesson 13: Alexander the Great

When someone is called "the great," what does it mean? Would you have given Alexander that epithet? If so, how would you explain that he was great? How did Alexander's personality, policies, and conquests affect his empire and the world? Think about all of this as you create some Alexander the Great trading cards.

Lesson Objectives

- Identify Alexander the Great.
- Locate on a map the areas Alexander conquered.
- Explain how Alexander's actions and conquests changed the world.

PREPARE

Approximate lesson time is 60 minutes.

Materials

For the Student

The Empire of Alexander the Great

The Human Odyssey: Prehistory Through the Middle Ages edited by Klee, Cribb, and Holdren

History Journal

LEARN

Activity 1: Alexander the Great *(Offline)*

Read Chapter 4 from "Alexander the Great" to the end, pages 336-339. Then go back online to complete a map and an online activity.

Activity 2: Focus on Geography *(Online)*

Imagine that a group of scholars is arguing about Alexander's conquests. Historians from your local university have asked you to review maps of his empire. To do your review, complete The Empire of Alexander the Great sheet. Look at the map on page 339 in your text to see the empire. Use the maps in the atlas in the back of your textbook to help you locate modern countries. By the time you have finished, you should be an expert at recognizing key features of Alexander's empire.

Activity 3: Alexander the Great *(Online)*

You have just been challenged with the question "Was Alexander great or not?" Your position is that Alexander was great, but you will have to persuade everyone else. Create your own series of Flash Cards about the Alexander the Great.

ASSESS

Lesson Assessment: Alexander the Great (*Online*)

You will complete an online assessment covering the main points of this lesson. Your assessment will be scored by the computer.

LEARN

Activity 4. Optional: Alexander the Great *(Online)*

This activity is OPTIONAL. It's provided for enrichment or extra practice, but not required for completion of this lesson. You may skip this activity.

Alexander fought many battles during the years of his conquests. Visit the website Alexander of Macedon: Alexander the Great to learn more about when and where he fought.

Name ________________________________ Date ________________

The Empire of Alexander the Great

In your study of Alexander's empire, the local historians would like you to respond to the following questions:

1. According to the map, what large bodies of water help define the borders of Alexander's Empire?

   ________________ ________________
   ________________ ________________
   ________________ ________________

2. Locate and name four main rivers within Alexander's empire.

   ________________ ________________
   ________________ ________________

3. Use the map scale on page 339 to determine approximately how far Alexander's armies had to travel from Sardis to Taxla.

   ____

4. List at least 15 modern countries that lie within the ancient boundaries of Alexander's Empire. You may use the maps in the atlas of your textbook to help you locate modern countries.

   ________________ ________________ ________________
   ________________ ________________ ________________
   ________________ ________________ ________________
   ________________ ________________ ________________
   ________________ ________________ ________________

5. Finally, the professors want you to take another careful look at the map and write a question that you think they should have asked. You will need to give them the answer, too.

   Q: ________________________________

   A: ________________________________

   ____

Student Guide
Lesson 14: Unit Review

You've finished the unit, and now it's time to review what you've learned. You'll take the Unit Assessment in the next lesson.

Lesson Objectives

- Demonstrate mastery of important knowledge and skills in this unit.

PREPARE

Approximate lesson time is 60 minutes.

Materials

For the Student

The Human Odyssey: Prehistory Through the Middle Ages edited by Klee, Cribb, and Holdren

History Journal

Optional

Missing Metadata

LEARN

Activity 1: A Look Back *(Online)*

You've been studying the important ideas and beliefs of the Greeks and of the ancient Greek philosophers, and you've been looking at the development of philosophy, art, theater, and democracy. Think about what you've learned as you review for the Unit Assessment.

Student Guide
Lesson 15: Unit Assessment

You've finished the unit! Now take the Unit Assessment.

Lesson Objectives

- Recognize important Athenian people, ideas, and achievements.
- Recognize important leaders and achievements of the Persian Empire.
- Summarize key events in the rise and fall of Athenian power and culture.
- Compare and contrast characteristics of Sparta and Athens.
- Describe characteristics of Greek art, architecture, and literature.
- Locate on a map the boundaries of the Persian Empire.
- Locate on a map the extent of Alexander's conquests.
- Identify Greece and Rome as classical civilizations.
- List changes that occurred as a result of Alexander the Great's rule.

PREPARE

Approximate lesson time is 60 minutes.

Materials

For the Student

Question Review Table

ASSESS

Unit Assessment: Classical Greece, Part 1 (*Online*)

Complete the computer-scored portion of the Unit Assessment. When you have finished, complete the teacher-scored portion of the assessment and submit it to your teacher.

Unit Assessment: Classical Greece, Part 2 (*Offline*)

Complete the teacher-scored portion of the Unit Assessment and submit it to your teacher.

LEARN

Activity 1: Unit Assessment Review Table *(Online)*

If you earned a score of **less than 80%** on the Unit Assessment, complete the activity.

If you earned a score of **80% or greater**, you may skip this activity.

Let's prepare to retake the Unit Assessment:

- Identify the questions that you answered incorrectly.
- Complete the appropriate review activities listed in the table.

Assessment Date ______________________

Unit 9: Classical Greece

Before you retake the Unit Assessment, use the table to figure out which activities you should review.

Question Review Table

Circle the numbers of the questions that you missed on the Unit Assessment. Review the activities that correspond with these questions.

Question	Lesson	Review Activity
1,40	1: Classically Different Ways	What Does Classical Mean?
2,3,4,24,26	11: Three Great Thinkers	Check Your Reading
5,18,20	3: An Empire Threatens	Explore
6,8,922,26	4: Free to Flourish	Check Your Reading and Read
7,10	9: The Decline of Athens	The End of an Era
11,12,13,14,15,16,17	2: Athens	Understanding Athens
19	2: Athens	Defining Atheian Democracy
21	6: A Golden Time	Read
23,25	8: The Play's the Thing	Use What You Know
28,29,30,31,32	7: Art and Architecture	Explore
33	3: An Empire Threatens	Focus on Geography
34,35,36,37,38,39	13: Alexander the Great	Focus on Geography
41	13: Alexander the Great	Use What You Know

Student Guide

Unit 10: Rome: Republic and Empire
Lesson 1: A Republic Is Born

The Greeks were great innovators, but the Romans built an empire on the ideas of others. We can still see the influence of the ancient Romans. People still walk on Roman roads and get water from Roman aqueducts. Many modern languages have their roots in Latin--the language of Rome. The Roman Republic's form of government--representative democracy--enjoys ever-growing influence. And Christianity, born in a Roman province, has spread to all corners of the world.

Everyone has heard of Rome. It is sometimes called the Eternal City. But when was it actually founded? In the seventh century B.C. a group of people called Etruscans took control of a farming village named Rome and taught the people there new ways of building and using the land. Rome became a wealthy city. What characteristics made Rome a desirable place to build a city? What encouraged its success? What kind of civilization developed there and what did the people of early Rome value?

Lesson Objectives

- Identify characteristics of climate and terrain that made Rome a good site for a city on the Italian peninsula.
- Identify Romulus and Remus and summarize the legend about the foundation of Rome.
- Define *paterfamilias, rex, patrician,* and *republic.*
- Analyze the story of Horatius to find information about Roman values.

PREPARE

Approximate lesson time is 60 minutes.

Materials

For the Student

The Human Odyssey: Prehistory Through the Middle Ages edited by Klee, Cribb, and Holdren

Reading Guide

Keywords and Pronunciation

Amulius (uh-MYOO-lee-us)
Aventine (A-vuhn-tiyn)
Etruscans (ih-TRUHS-kuhns)
Horatius (huh-RAY-shus)
Horatius Cocles (KAWK-leez)
Marcus Agricola (MAHR-kus uh-GRIK-uh-luh)
Palatine (PA-luh-tiyn)
paterfamilias (pa-tuhr-fuh-MIH-lee-us) : the oldest living male in a family and--according to Roman law--the absolute ruler of the household
patricians (puh-TRIH-shuhns) : members of the aristocratic ruling families of early Rome
Porsena (PAWR-suh-nuh)
Remus (REE-mus)
republic : a government in which citizens elect leaders who rule on behalf of the people

res publica (rays POO-blih-kah)
Romulus (RAHM-yuh-lus)
Tarquinius (tahr-KWIN-ee-uhs)

LEARN

Activity 1: Why Rome? *(Offline)*

Instructions

Read

After reviewing the Classical Time Line, read Chapter 5, from the beginning to "Marcus Agricola, a Boy of Early Rome," pages 340-346 and answer the following questions in your History Journal.

1. Why did settlers choose Latium as a good place to live?
2. What advantages did Palatine offer the people who settled there?
3. Summarize the famous legend about how Rome was founded.
4. Who were Romulus and Remus?

When you have finished, compare your answers with the ones in the Lesson Answer Key.

Activity 2: Focus on Geography *(Online)*

Activity 3: A Republic Is Born *(Offline)*

Instructions

Complete the Reading Guide as you read Chapter 5, from "Marcus Agricola, a Boy of Early Rome" to "A Matter of Class: Plebeians vs. Patricians," pages 346-351. Compare your answers with those in the Lesson Answer Key.

ASSESS

Lesson Assessment: A Republic Is Born (*Online*)

You will complete an online assessment covering the main points of this lesson. Your assessment will be scored by the computer.

LEARN

Activity 4. Optional: A Republic Is Born *(Online)*

Name ______________________________ Date ______________________________ 

Reading Guide

Complete this sheet as you read today's assignment.

1. As you read define the following terms.
   a. paterfamilias

   b. fasces

   c. *rex*

   d. patrician

   e. republic

2. Describe Marcus's life as a young boy on a farm.
____
____
____
____

3. Describe Claudia's life as a young girl on a farm.
____
____
____
____

4. What are the two most important values that Marcus and his family must clearly understand?
______________________________ and ______________________________

5. Why were the patricians unhappy with kings?

6. The patricians forced King Tarquinius to flee Rome and they had to form a new government. What form of govenrment did they create?

7. How did the story of "Horatius at the Bridge" show good examples of loyalty and discipline?

Student Guide
Lesson 2: Celebrating Citizenship

You read about the brave soldier Horatius who saved Rome by risking his own life. The Romans told that story for centuries because they admired the values it conveyed. But no matter how loyal or brave or hardworking they were, soldiers and other common people in Rome often had to endure poverty and even slavery. Even the common men who became wealthy did not have a voice in government. How could the common people make life better for themselves and their families? How could they make the republic they loved a better place for all citizens?

Lesson Objectives

- Describe the problems Rome's common people faced and how they responded to them.
- Describe the roles of plebeians, the Twelve Tables, consuls, and senators in Roman society.
- Summarize the most important achievements of the Roman Republic.
- Analyze "The Story of the Cincinnatus" to find information about the Roman ideals of citizenship.

PREPARE

Approximate lesson time is 60 minutes.

Materials

For the Student

- All About the Roman Republic
- Reading Guide

The Human Odyssey: Prehistory Through the Middle Ages edited by Klee, Cribb, and Holdren

Keywords and Pronunciation

Aequi (EE-kwiy)
Horatius (huh-RAY-shus)
Lucius Quinctius Cincinnatus (LOO-shee-us KWINGK-shee-us sin-sih-NAT-us)
Mount Algidus (MOUNT AL-jee-dus)
patricians (puh-TRIH-shuhns) : members of the aristocratic ruling families of early Rome
plebeians (plih-BEE-uns) : the commoners of ancient Rome
Racilia (ruh-SIL-ee-uh)

LEARN

Activity 1: Plebeians vs. Patricians *(Offline)*

Instructions

Read

As you read Chapter 5, from "A Matter of Class: Plebeians vs. Patricians" to "*The Story of Cincinnatus*," pages 352-354, answer questions 1-6 in the Reading Guide. Complete the entire Reading Guide before you compare your answers with those in the Lesson Answer Key.

Use What You Know *(Online)*

Complete the All About the Roman Republic activity to explore Roman society and to recognize the similarities between the republic of ancient Rome and the republican government of the United States.

Read

As you read Chapter 5, from "*The Story of Cincinnatus*," to the end, pages 355-357, answer Questions 7 and 8 in the Reading Guide. Then, compare your answers with those in the Lesson Answer Key.

ASSESS

Lesson Assessment: Celebrating Citizenship (*Online*)

You will complete an online assessment covering the main points of this lesson. Your assessment will be scored by the computer.

Name ______________________ Date ______________________

Reading Guide

Complete this sheet as you read today's assignment.

1. What were some of the problems Rome's common people faced, and how did they respond to them?

2. What did the plebeians accomplish by changing the laws?

3. Describe the role of the consuls.

4. Describe the role of the Senate.

5. Describe the Centuriate and Tribal Assemblies.

6. What were some of the successful features of the republic?

Stop here for now and continue the lesson in the Student Guide.

7. How did Cincinnatus and the Roman people demonstrate citizenship? List some examples from "The Story of Cincinnatus."

8. Describe some of the values Cincinnatus demonstrated.

Name Date 

All About the Roman Republic

Who or What Am I?

Identify people or things in Roman society by entering the appropriate answer for each question.

1. I am one of the two officials responsible for overseeing the government. Who am I?
2. I am the most powerful body in the Roman Republic. What am I?
3. I am the written laws of the Roman Republic. What am I?
4. I am a member of the common people or class. Who am I?
5. My members came from wealthy, landowning families. What am I?
6. I eventually gained a voice in the Roman Republic. Who am I?
7. I am elected to a one-year term. Who am I?

Comparing Republics

Use the Word Bank to help you compare the governments of ancient Rome and the United States. Complete the chart and answer the questions.

Word Bank		
Guarantees that the law is the same for all	Consuls	Legislative branch, which proposes and approves laws

Roman Republic	United States Government	Role
	President	Executive branch, which executes (enforces) laws
Senate and Assemblies	House of Representatives and Senate	
Twelve Tables	Constitution	

Thinking Cap Question: What role did the plebeians eventually play in the government of the Roman Republic?

Did You Know? The Roman Republic allowed a practice that might seem odd today. In times of extreme crisis the consuls could choose—and then the Senate would appoint for six months—a dictator who had absolute power to make laws and command the army. How did this practice contribute to the stability of the Roman Republic?

Thinking Back: Rome had a republic or representative government. Athens had a direct democracy. Can you explain the difference? Which style of government does the United States have?

Student Guide
Lesson 3: Fighting for Power

Over a span of nearly five centuries, the Roman Republic grew in wealth, power, and size. By 264 B.C. Rome dominated the Italian peninsula. But another power across a narrow expanse of sea threatened. Carthage, on the coast of what is now Tunisia, was the wealthiest city in the Mediterranean. As Rome gained control of Italy, Carthage conquered the Spanish coast and Sicily, which posed a more immediate threat just off the toe of the Italian boot. A series of three bloody wars in 120 years settled the question of who would control the Mediterranean. Those wars brought changes the Romans could not have anticipated.

Lesson Objectives

- Recognize the main cause of the Punic Wars and who fought them.
- Describe the main events and leaders of the Punic Wars.
- Describe important changes that took place in Rome after the end of the Punic Wars.

PREPARE

Approximate lesson time is 60 minutes.

Materials

For the Student

The Human Odyssey: Prehistory Through the Middle Ages edited by Klee, Cribb, and Holdren

Keywords and Pronunciation

Aequi (EE-kwiy)
Bacchus (BAH-kuhs)
Carthage (KAHR-thij)
Carthaginians (kahr-thuh-JIN-ee-uhns)
Ceres (SEER-eez)
Hannibal (HAN-uh-buhl)
Minerva (muh-NUR-vuh)
Mount Algidus (MOUNT AL-jee-dus)
Punic (PYOO-nik)
Punicus (PYOO-nih-kus)
Racilia (ruh-SIL-ee-uh)

LEARN

Activity 1: Before and After the Punic Wars *(Online)*

Instructions

Read

As you read Chapter 6, from the beginning to "Hard Times in the Roman Republic," pages 359-369, answer the following questions. Compare your answers with those in the Lesson Answer Key.

1. What was the main cause of the Punic Wars and who fought in them?
2. Describe the main events and leaders of the Punic Wars.

Use What You Know

Before and After

To explore the important changes in Rome after the end of the Punic Wars, go online to complete the Before and After activity.

Roman Changes

Use the information from Before and After to help you complete this activity. You are a newspaper reporter working for the *Roman Times*. Your assignment is to interview a Roman citizen who lived during and after the Third Punic War. The citizen has seen many changes in Rome over the course of her lifetime.

1. In your History Journal or the Online Notebook write at least four interview questions about the following topics:
   - Values of the Roman people (what they thought was important)
   - Economy (how the Romans made a living, who worked and who owned land)
   - Social structure or class system
   - Territory or boundaries

Sample questions: What changes have you seen in the values of the Romans? How did most people make a living before the Third Punic War? After?

1. Write up the interview in your History Journal or the Online Notebook. Then compare your ideas with those in the Lesson Answer Key.

ASSESS

Lesson Assessment: Fighting for Power (*Online*)

You will complete an online assessment covering the main points of this lesson. Your assessment will be scored by the computer.

Student Guide
Lesson 4: Julius Caesar

Rome's rapid growth brought political, economic, and social changes. The government tried to deal with those changes, but by 88 B.C. there was a real crisis. The republic that was a model for representative government was in ruins. Then, as is often the case in times of crisis, one leader emerged. That leader was Julius Caesar.

Lesson Objectives

- Describe the crises in the Roman Republic by 88 B.C.
- Compare Julius Caesar and Cincinnatus and their relationship to societal changes.
- Summarize the achievements of Julius Caesar.
- Recognize the extent of the Roman Empire at its height and the measures emperors took to unify the empire.
- Describe the role of trade between Rome and the East (the Silk Road).
- Define Pax Romana and forum.

PREPARE

Approximate lesson time is 60 minutes.

Materials

For the Student

Reading Guide

The Human Odyssey: Prehistory Through the Middle Ages edited by Klee, Cribb, and Holdren

History Journal

Keywords and Pronunciation

Et tu, Brute? (ay TOO broot-AY)
Forum : the great public meeting place of Rome
Julius Caesar (JOOL-yus SEE-zuhr)
Octavian (ahk-TAY-vee-uhn)
Rubicon (ROO-bih-kahn)
veni, vidi, vici (WAY-nee, WEE-dee, WEE-kee)

LEARN

Activity 1: Julius Caesar *(Offline)*

Instructions

Read

Read Chapter 6, from "Hard Times in the Roman Republic" to the end, pages 369-371; and Chapter 7, from the beginning to "A Murder Foretold," pages 372-375. Complete the Reading Guide as you read. When you have finished, compare your answers with those in the Lesson Answer Key.

Activity 2: Julius Caesar *(Online)*

ASSESS

Lesson Assessment: Julius Caesar (*Online*)

You will complete an online assessment covering the main points of this lesson. Your assessment will be scored by the computer.

LEARN

Activity 3: Julius Caesar *(Offline)*

Instructions

Read Chapter 7, from "A Murder Foretold" to "The Pax Romana," pages 375-377.

Reading Guide

Complete this sheet as you read today's assignment. Some items need two or more words to make a complete answer.

1. Where did farmers like Firmus go? Was it easy for them to find work and housing? How did slave labor affect their chances of finding work?

2. What is the Forum?

3. What does the expression "to cross the Rubicon" mean?

4. Where did the expression "*Veni, vidi, vici*" originate?

5. What title did Caesar give himself, and why did this title make some Romans unhappy?

Student Guide
Lesson 5: From Republic to Empire

For nearly 200 years after the death of Julius Caesar and the rise of Caesar Augustus, the Roman Empire enjoyed a period of affluence and relative calm that extended throughout the Mediterranean. It became known as the *Pax Romana*, or Roman Peace. How did the government of Rome foster peace and prosperity? What unified the vast empire?

Lesson Objectives

- Define *Pax Romana* and *forum.*
- Recognize the extent of the Roman Empire at its height and the measures emperors took to unify the empire.
- Describe the role of trade between Rome and the East (the Silk Road).

PREPARE

Approximate lesson time is 60 minutes.

Materials

For the Student

Reading Guide

The Human Odyssey: Prehistory Through the Middle Ages edited by Klee, Cribb, and Holdren

Keywords and Pronunciation

Appian (A-pee-uhn)
Appiaus Claudius Caecus (AP-ee-uhs KLAWD-ee-uhs SEE-kuhs)
Brindisi (BREEN-dee-zee)
Brundisium (bruhn-DIH-zee-uhm)
Cicero (SIS-uh-roh)
Circus Maximus (SUHR-kus MAK-suh-mus)
Colosseum (kah-luh-SEE-uhm)
czars (zahrz)
Forum : the great public meeting place of Rome
jus gentium (yoos GHEN-tee-uhm)
kaisers (KIY-zurz)
Octavian (ahk-TAY-vee-uhn)
Pax Romana (paks roh-MAH-nuh) : the Roman Peace, or period of stability in the Roman Empire, which lasted nearly two centuries

LEARN

Activity 1: A Peaceful and United Empire *(Online)*

Activity 2: From Republic to Empire *(Offline)*

Instructions

Complete the Reading Guide as you read Chapter 7, from "The Pax Romana" to "Bread and Circuses," pages 377-381. When you have finished, compare your answers with those in the Lesson Answer Key

Activity 3: From Republic to Empire *(Online)*

ASSESS

Lesson Assessment: From Republic to Empire (*Online*)

You will complete an online assessment covering the main points of this lesson. Your assessment will be scored by the computer.

Name Date

Reading Guide

Complete this sheet as you read today's assignment.

1. What was the *Pax Romana*?

2. What evidence indicates that the entire Roman Empire was unified?

3. What did the Romans value above all else?

4. What principles were incorporated into Roman law?

5. What responsibilities did Roman citizens have?

6. Why was the system of roads important to Rome?

7. Describe the imperial capital during the second century A.D.

8. Describe the forum.

Bonus: Russian rulers were called *czars* and German rulers were called *kaisers*. These two words came from a title used by Roman emperors. What is that title?

Student Guide
Lesson 6: The Real Rome

What was life like in Rome? The wealthy had fine food and luxurious homes with indoor plumbing. Even poorer people had access to fancy public baths, because the Romans engineered systems to bring millions of gallons of water into the city. But unemployment was a serious problem. How could the emperor keep thousands of people without jobs from rioting or rebelling? Bread and circuses. Those "circuses" were not minor productions. They were held in a stadium large enough for a hundred thousand people. The Romans even staged mock sea battles in a city arena. At the same time, Rome experienced a golden age for literature as well.

Lesson Objectives

- Define *bread and circuses, Circus Maximus, Colosseum, atrium,* and *aqueduct.*
- Identify the *Aeneid* as the most significant Roman epic poem, and Virgil as its author.
- Analyze Roman art and architecture to find out about life in the Roman Empire.

PREPARE

Approximate lesson time is 60 minutes.

Materials

For the Student

Reading Guide

The Human Odyssey: Prehistory Through the Middle Ages edited by Klee, Cribb, and Holdren

Keywords and Pronunciation

Aeneas (uh-NEE-us)
Aeneid (uh-NEE-id)
Anchises (an-KIY-seez)
aqueduct (AK-wuh-dukt) : a channel that carries abundant supplies of water into the city from the surrounding hills
Ascanius (as-KAN-ee-us)
atrium (AY-tree-uhm) : a large, airy room inside the main entrance of a wealthy Roman home
bread and circuses : free rations and entertainment
Circus Maximus (SUHR-kus MAK-suh-mus) : U-shaped structure enclosing long racetracks where the empire's finest charioteers competed against each other in their two-wheeled chariots
Colosseum (kah-luh-SEE-uhm)
Creusa (kree-OO-suh)
Livy (LIH-vee)
mosaics (moh-ZAY-iks)
Virgil (VUR-juhl)

LEARN

Activity 1: Life in Ancient Rome *(Offline)*

Instructions

Read

Complete the Reading Guide as you read Chapter 7, from "Bread and Circuses" to the end, pages 381-391. When you have finished, compare your answers with those in the Lesson Answer Key.

Activity 2: The Real Rome *(Online)*

ASSESS

Lesson Assessment: The Real Rome (*Online*)

You will complete an online assessment covering the main points of this lesson. Your assessment will be scored by the computer.

Name Date

Reading Guide

Complete this sheet as you read today's assignment.

1. Why did Augustus and the emperors that followed him want to keep the people happy?

2. What was the *Colosseum*?

3. Describe some of the games and spectacles that took place at the Colosseum.

4. What was the *Circus Maximus*?

5. What is an *atrium*?

6. Describe the homes of the wealthy Romans.

7. What is an *aqueduct*?

8. Describe the public baths of Rome.

9. Why did Caesar Augustus want Virgil to compose a story about the founding of Rome?

10. What did Virgil think a hero should exemplify?

Student Guide
Lesson 7: Learning Something New Every Day: Pompeii

Lesson Objectives

- Recognize that historical knowledge changes with new discoveries.
- Identify Pompeii and its archaeological significance.
- Analyze ancient (Pliny's writings) and modern (archaeological evidence) information on Pompeii for examples of daily life there.
- Examine historical documents and archaeological evidence about Pompeii to find out about daily life in the city.
- Demonstrate mastery of knowledge and skills taught in previous lessons.

PREPARE

Approximate lesson time is 60 minutes.

Materials

For the Student

Daily Life in Pompeii

Keywords and Pronunciation

Pompeii (pom-PAY)
Vesuvius (vuh-SOO-vee-us)

LEARN

Activity 1: Life in Pompeii *(Online)*

Activity 2: An Archaeological Dig *(Online)*

ASSESS

Lesson Assessment: Learning Something New Every Day: Pompeii *(Online)*

You will complete an online assessment covering the main points of this lesson. Your assessment will be scored by the computer.

LEARN

Activity 3. Optional: Learning Something New Every Day: Pompeii *(Online)*

Learning Something New Everyday: Pompeii

Daily Life In Pompeii

After reading Pliny's account of the eruption of Vesuvius and joining the recent archaeological dig, decide which source gave you the information listed in the Word Bank. Write the description in the appropriate column. Then add your own descriptions.

Pliny's Account	Archaeological Information

Think About It: How does Pliny's account of Pompeii fit with current archaeological evidence?

Thinking Cap Question: How do new discoveries change our knowledge of history? Cite some examples. (Think about the Iceman, Tut's tomb, etc.)

Student Guide
Lesson 8. Optional: Your Choice

You may use today's lesson time to do one or more of the following:

- Complete work in progress.
- Complete the Beyond the Lesson activity in any lesson in this unit.
- Review the Classical World Time Line in the Resources section.
- Prepare for your state standardized test.
- Go on to the next lesson.

Please mark this lesson complete to proceed to the next lesson in the course.

PREPARE

Approximate lesson time is 60 minutes.

Student Guide
Lesson 9: Rome and Judea

Seventy million people lived in the Roman Empire during the reign of Caesar Augustus. Many people in North Africa, Asia Minor, Europe, and parts of Mesopotamia accepted Roman rule and paid taxes to Rome. Being part of the Roman Empire, after all, meant that you would receive the protection of the most powerful army in the world, enjoy the benefit of public works like aqueducts and baths, and have the opportunity to trade on the finest roads ever built. Why, then, did the people of Judea resist Roman rule? Why were so many of them willing to die rather than be part of the mighty empire?

Lesson Objectives

- Identify Judea, Jerusalem, and Rome on a map.
- Describe the conflicts that led to the Roman control of Judea.
- Explain the tension between Roman rulers and their Jewish subjects in the first century B.C.
- Identify Zealots.

PREPARE

Approximate lesson time is 60 minutes.

Materials

For the Student

Conflicting Ideas

LEARN

Activity 1: One Empire Two Worlds *(Offline)*

Instructions

Read

Answer the following questions in your History Journal as you read Chapter 8, from the beginning to "The Early Life of Jesus," pages 392-396. When you have finished, compare your answers with those in the Lesson Answer Key.

1. What was Judea and where was it in relation to Rome?
2. What is the Torah?
3. What did the Jews learn from the Torah?
4. Why did the people of Judea resist foreign rule?
5. Why was there conflict between the Romans and the Jews?
6. Who were the Zealots?
7. Describe how the Zealots resisted Roman rule and what happened as a result of that resistance.
8. Most Jews thought the Zealots were patriots and heroes, but some Jews were afraid of the Zealots. Why were they afraid of them?
9. Who was Pontius Pilate and how did she handle trouble in Judea?

Use What You Know

Complete the Conflicting Ideas sheet.

ASSESS

Lesson Assessment: Rome and Judea (*Online*)

You will complete an online assessment covering the main points of this lesson. Your assessment will be scored by the computer.

Name Date

Conflicting Ideas

You are an investigative reporter who has traveled back in time to ancient Judea in the year 50 B.C. When you arrive, you notice immediately that there is a lot of tension in the air. The Roman rulers just don't understand why the Jews won't accept their rule and law; after all, other lands and peoples that they have conquered have accepted it. "Interview" the two groups by completing the chart below. For each item already on the chart, write in a corresponding idea or characteristic that represents the other group. The first one has been filled in for you. When you have finished filling in the chart, write an article explaining the tensions between the Roman rulers and their Jewish subjects.

Roman Ideas/Characteristics	Jewish Ideas/Characteristics
Coins had images of men and animals.	The Torah forbade the use of graven images.
	Jews worshiped one God.
They lived according to Roman Law.	
The government was the highest authority.	
	Most Jews viewed Zealots as patriotic heroes.

Name Date

Your Article:

Sequencing Events

Historians have to understand the order in which events happen to get an accurate sense of the relationships between events. Think like a historian and sequence the events that led to the Roman control of Judea.

Number the conflicts that led to Roman control of Judea in correct chronological order. Begin by labeling the first event 1.

_____ Civil war breaks out in Judea.

_____ Nebuchadnezzar forces Hebrews to live in exile in Babylon.

_____ Jews overthrow Greeks.

_____ Rome rules Judea.

_____ Hellenistic culture spreads in Judea.

_____ Persians allow Hebrews to return home.

_____ Assyrians conquer Judea.

_____ Romans come to aid of Hellenized Jews.

_____ Jews become subjects of Alexander the Great.

Student Guide
Lesson 10: Jesus of Nazareth

Jesus was born during a time of unrest in the Roman province of Judea. How did this Jewish boy, raised in the remote town of Nazareth, become one of the most influential people in history? Christians believe he is the Messiah that God promised the Hebrews. Why did Jesus' message appeal so strongly to some people but anger and frighten others?

Lesson Objectives

- Describe the early life of Jesus.
- Summarize Jesus' key teachings.
- Summarize the conflict between Jesus and Jewish leaders and the events that resulted.

PREPARE

Approximate lesson time is 60 minutes.

Materials

For the Student

- Jesus' Key Teachings
- Reading Guide
- The Human Odyssey: Prehistory Through the Middle Ages edited by Klee, Cribb, and Holdren

Keywords and Pronunciation

apostles (uh-PAH-suhls)
baptism : a ritual that symbolized washing away old sins or offenses against God
Capernaum (kuh-PUHR-nay-uhm)
disciples (dih-SIY-puhls)
Galilee (GA-luh-lee)
Judea (joo-DEE-uh)
parables : brief stories that illustrate a moral point
Pharisees (FAIR-uh-seez)

LEARN

Activity 1: Jesus the Teacher *(Online)*

Instructions

Read

As you read, (Chapter 8, from "The Early Life of Jesus" to "The Apostles Set to Work," pages 396-403), complete the Reading Guide. When you have finished, compare your answers with those in the Lesson Answer Key.

Use What You Know

Complete the Jesus' Key Teachings sheet.

ASSESS

Lesson Assessment: Jesus of Nazareth (*Online*)

You will complete an online assessment covering the main points of this lesson. Your assessment will be scored by the computer.

Reading Guide

Complete this sheet as you read today's assignment.

1. Describe what is known about the early life of Jesus.

2. According to the Gospels, what happened to Jesus after he was baptized?

3. Where did Jesus deliver his message and to whom?

4. To Jesus, what was important about the kingdom of God?

5. Who were the Pharisees and why was Jesus so critical of them? What were some of Jesus' criticisms of them?

6. According to Jesus' teachings, how can people show their love for God?

7. Why were some Jews disappointed with Jesus and his teachings?

8. What did Jesus want his apostles to do?

9. What are *parables*?

10. What did the chief priests accuse Jesus of? What happened as a result of those accusations?

11. According to the Gospels, what happened two days after Jesus died?

12. List four or more of the values found in The Sermon on the Mount.

13. Who found Jesus' message appealing? Why?

14. Who found Jesus' message upsetting? Why?

Jesus' Key Teachings

To summarize Jesus' key teachings, complete the web diagram by writing one of his teachings on each of the blank lines. You may add more lines if you would like to.

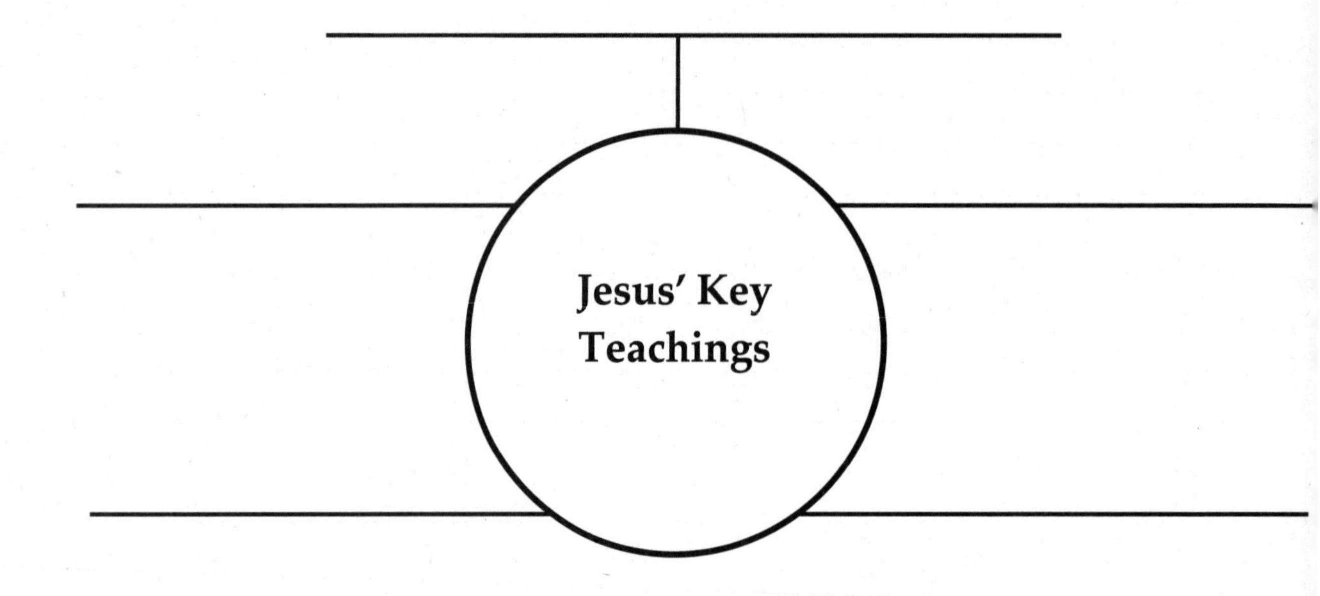

Student Guide
Lesson 11: A New Religion

Jesus' followers set out to create a new religion based on his message of salvation. Despite encountering religious and political opposition, Christianity began to spread throughout the Roman Empire. Paul played an enormous role in the early diffusion of the new ideas.

Lesson Objectives

- Identify core beliefs of Christianity.
- Describe the spread of Christianity in the early first century A.D.
- Define *gentile, Messiah, epistle,* and *catacomb.*
- Identify Peter and Paul as key figures in the early spread of Christianity.

PREPARE

Approximate lesson time is 60 minutes.

Materials

For the Student

Reading Guide

The Human Odyssey: Prehistory Through the Middle Ages edited by Klee, Cribb, and Holdren

Keywords and Pronunciation

Christos (KREES-tohs)
catacombs : a network of underground passages and rooms built by the early Christians and used as burial places and occasional hideaways and meeting places
epistle (ih-PIH-suhl) : long letter
gentile (JEN-tiyl) : a biblical term for a person who is not Jewish
martyr : someone who dies for his or her faith
Messiah (meh-SIY-uh) : the expected king or deliverer of the Jews; the term comes from ancient Hebrew and means, "anointed one"; the word in Greek is Christos
Nero (NEE-roh)
Philippi (FIH-luh-piy)
Thessalonica (theh-suh-LAH-nih-kuh)

LEARN

Activity 1: Spreading the Message *(Online)*

Instructions

Read

As you read, (Chapter 8, from "The Apostles Set to Work" to Chapter 9, "Diocletian's Great Persecution," pages 403-410, and "Faith Underground: The Catacombs," page 411), complete the Reading Guide. When you have finished, compare your answers with those in the Lesson Answer Key.

Activity 2: A New Religion *(Online)*

Activity 3: Focus on Geography *(Online)*

ASSESS

Lesson Assessment: A New Religion (*Online*)

You will complete an online assessment covering the main points of this lesson. Your assessment will be scored by the computer.

LEARN

Activity 4. Optional: A New Religion *(Online)*

Reading Guide

Complete this sheet as you read today's assignment.

1. What did the disciples teach the people?

2. List at least two ideas that became the basis of the Christian faith.

3. Why did Saul hate the followers of Jesus?

4. What is a *martyr*?

5. Describe what happened to Saul on the road to Damascus.

6. Define *gentile.*

7. Why did Saul change his name to Paul?

8. What is the Greek word for *Messiah*?

9. How did Paul answer questions and settle problems for the people he had converted?

10. Why was Paul's life always in danger?

11. What happened to the letters that Paul wrote?

12. To what areas/regions did Paul carry the message of Jesus?

13. Who was Peter and where did he carry the message of Jesus?

14. Who was Nero and how did he treat the Christians?

15. What are catacombs and how did early Christians use them?

Student Guide

Lesson 12: Conflicts for Christians

What was it about the early Christians that inspired fear and anger in Roman rulers? When Roman soldiers began arresting and executing Christians, how did their actions affect the new religion?

Lesson Objectives

- Define *catacombs* and explain their significance.
- Describe the conflicts between Christians and Roman rulers (including persecutions under Nero and Diocletian).
- Compare and contrast Christianity with other world religions.

PREPARE

Approximate lesson time is 60 minutes.

Advance Preparation

- Gather the Comparing Religions and Philosophies chart from Unit 6 (Some Lasting Ideas) Lesson 2 (Relationships and Rulers).

Materials

For the Student

Reading Guide

The Human Odyssey: Prehistory Through the Middle Ages edited by Klee, Cribb, and Holdren

Keywords and Pronunciation

catacombs : a network of underground passages and rooms built by the early Christians and used as burial places and occasional hideaways and meeting places

Diocletian (diy-uh-KLEE-shun)

LEARN

Activity 1: Conflict *(Offline)*

Instructions

Read

Complete the Reading Guide as you read Chapter 9, from "Diocletian's Great Persecution" to the end, pages 410-417. When you have finished, compare your answers with those in the Lesson Answer Key.

Use What You Know

Imagine that you are a reporter for the *Roman Times* newspaper during the reign of Diocletian in the third century A.D. Your assignment is to report on the conflict between the early Christians and the Roman rulers. Before you begin writing, begin thinking like a reporter and gather some information by answering these questions:

1. **Who** is involved in the conflict?
2. **What** happened? (What were the actions and reactions?)
3. **When** did this conflict take place?
4. **Where**?
5. **Why** is there a conflict between the Roman rulers and Christians? Why is the conflict significant?
6. **How** do the people on each side of the conflict respond? How does the response affect people?

Now write your article, beginning with this sentence: "It is a time of trouble in the Roman world."

Comparing Religions and Philosophies

Complete the column for Christianity on the Comparing Religions and Philosophies chart.

ASSESS

Lesson Assessment: Conflicts for Christians (*Online*)

You will complete an online assessment covering the main points of this lesson. Your assessment will be scored by the computer.

LEARN

Activity 2. Optional: Conflicts for Christians *(Online)*

This activity is OPTIONAL. It's provided for enrichment or extra practice, but not required for completion of this lesson. You may skip this activity.

Reading primary-source documents is one of the ways that historians make sense of the past. Read a letter from Pliny the Younger to Emperor Trajan as Pliny first encounters the Christians at

Pliny the Younger: Letter to Trajan

.

Name ____ Date _______________________

Reading Guide

As you read Chapter 9, from "Diocletian's Great Persecution" to the end, pages 410-417, imagine what headlines might have appeared in local Roman newspapers at the time. Fill in the blanks to complete the headlines.

1. Turmoil Grips the ____________ ____________ As the Rule of Law Breaks Down

2. ____________ and ____________ Romans Wonder Why Christians Refuse to Worship Roman Gods

3. Rome Gets a New ____________ Diocletian Attempts to Restore __________ and __________

4. __________ Disobey __________'s Order to ___________ to Roman Gods

5. __________ Soldiers Seize Christian __________, Burn __________, Arrest and Execute __________ __________

6. Efforts to Stamp Out ___________ Fail As __________ Like Valentine Die for Their Beliefs

Student Guide
Lesson 13. Optional: Your Choice

You may use today's lesson time to do one or more of the following:

- Complete work in progress.
- Complete the Beyond the Lesson activity in any lesson in this unit.
- Review the Classical World Time Line in the Resources section.
- Prepare for your state standardized test.
- Go on to the next lesson.

Please mark this lesson complete to proceed to the next lesson in the course.

PREPARE

Approximate lesson time is 60 minutes.

Student Guide
Lesson 14: Empire in Crisis

The Roman Empire was huge. It controlled the land now occupied by more than 40 modern countries. By the second century A.D., the empire extended from North Africa to Britain and from Spain to Mesopotamia. Such a vast empire required strong leadership. Unfortunately, Rome experienced a period of "bad" rulers and internal problems. Invaders began to seriously threaten Roman borders. Would the Roman Empire survive?

Lesson Objectives

- Identify the extent of the Roman Empire at its height and name five modern day countries that now occupy the land that once was part of the Roman Empire.
- Describe the main issues that led to the decline of the Roman Empire.
- Recognize the reasons for Diocletian's decision to divide the empire into two sections.

PREPARE

Approximate lesson time is 60 minutes.

Materials

For the Student

- Reading Guide
- What Went Wrong?

The Human Odyssey: Prehistory Through the Middle Ages edited by Klee, Cribb, and Holdren

History Journal

LEARN

Activity 1: What Went Wrong? *(Offline)*

Instructions

Read

Complete Part 1 of the Reading Guide before you read Chapter 10, from the beginning to "Constantine's Vision and a Move East," pages 419-423. Complete Part 2 as you read.

Use What You Know

Complete the What Went Wrong sheet.

Activity 2: Focus on Geography *(Online)*

ASSESS

Lesson Assessment: Empire in Crisis (*Online*)

You will complete an online assessment covering the main points of this lesson. Your assessment will be scored by the computer.

LEARN

Activity 3. Optional: Empire in Crisis *(Online)*

Name ________________ Date ________________

Reading Guide

Complete Part 1 before you read Chapter 10, from the beginning to “Constantine’s Vision and a Move East,” pages 419-423. Complete Part 2 after you have finished reading.

Part 1

Many different factors led to the rise and fall of ancient empires. The Roman Empire was no exception. By the third century A.D., Rome had forged the largest empire the world had ever known. But the empire’s vast size would pose many problems for its rulers and eventually contribute to its decline.

Think about the problems that an extremely large empire would face. What challenges would its ruler face? What threats, internal and external, would result from overextending an empire? What role would a ruler play in the ability of the empire to deal with these problems and threats?

Write your thoughts on the subject here:

____

____

____

____

____

____

Part 2

1. As you read, list the main problems that led to the decline of the Roman Empire.

- ______________________________
- ______________________________
- ______________________________
- ______________________________
- ______________________________

2. Name two ineffective rulers who were “abysmal” and explain why you think they were terrible emperors.

____

____

Name _______________________________________ Date _______________________

3. Name one good emperor and briefly describe his character (make inferences based on his writings from *Meditations* – see sidebar, page 421). ______________________________

____

____

____

4. Explain why Diocletian decided to split the empire into two sections. Describe the split.

____

____

____

____

____

Name Date

What Went Wrong?

Explore the problems facing the Roman Empire by giving examples of each problem that eventually contributed to the decline of the Empire. The first part of number one has been filled in for you.

1. Poor emperors

- Nero was a brutal, ruthless emperor who was not concerned about his people.
- ______________________________

2. Barbarian invasions

____
____
____
____

3. Demands on the army

____
____
____
____

4. Disease

____
____
____
____

Thinking Cap Question

Which of the problems facing the Roman Empire do you think was the most significant in the fall of the Western Roman Empire and why?

Student Guide

Lesson 15: Barbarians at the Gate

Diocletian had divided the Roman Empire into two separate administrative regions. But soon there were fights over which half would have the real power. Emperor Constantine emerged victorious. He looked to the future in making his decisions, and some of those decisions had an enormous impact on the world.

Lesson Objectives

- Describe the events known as the "fall of Rome."
- Identify Constantine and his achievements.
- Identify reasons for Christianity's appeal to the people of the Roman Empire.

PREPARE

Approximate lesson time is 60 minutes.

Materials

For the Student

- Personality Profile: Constantine
- Reading Guide
- The Human Odyssey: Prehistory Through the Middle Ages edited by Klee, Cribb, and Holdren
- History Journal

Keywords and Pronunciation

Byzantium (buh-ZAN-tee-um)
Chi Rho (kiy roh)
Constantine (KAHN-stuhn-teen)
Constantinople (kahn-stant-n-OH-puhl)
Diocletian (diy-uh-KLEE-shun)
In hoc signo vinces (in hohk SIG-noh WING-kays)
Milan (muh-LAHN)
Momyllus (MAWM-ee-luhs)

LEARN

Activity 1: The First Christian Emperor of the Roman Empire *(Offline)*

Instructions

Read

Complete the Reading Guide as you read Chapter 10, from "Constantine's Vision and a Move East" to the end, pages 424-427.

Personality Profile: Constantine

The choices and actions of some key historical figures have had a significant impact on society. Confucius was one such person. Constantine was another. His decision to legalize Christianity in the Roman Empire in the early fourth century A.D. helped the religion spread quickly.

Complete the Personality Profile: Constantine sheet by using information from your textbook and Grolier's online encyclopedia.

1. Draw (or cut out and paste) a picture of Constantine in the center oval.
2. Fill in the year he was born and the year he died.
3. On the line below that, write "First Christian Emperor of the Roman Empire."
4. In the thought bubble, write something that Constantine might have said just after he issued the Edict of Milan.
5. In the picture frame, illustrate an important event in Constantine's life.
6. In the first square, describe the vision that influenced Constantine.
7. In the second square, write characteristics that describe Constantine and his rule.
8. In the third square, explain how Constantine influenced the growth of Christianity.
9. In the fourth square, tell two things that Constantine is remembered for today.

In your History Journal, use the information from the Personality Profile: Constantine sheet, your textbook, and Grolier's online encyclopedia to write a summary of Constantine's life. Begin your paragraph by describing Constantine's rise to power. Write a concluding sentence explaining Constantine's influence on history.

What If?

Some individuals throughout history have played such an important role that historians often ask questions such as "What if this person had not lived?" "What if this person had done X instead of Y?"

Constantine was one such person. What if he had rejected Christianity? History would certainly have turned out differently. Take a moment and think about this. Speculate a bit about how things might be different if Constantine had rejected Christianity. Write your thoughts in your History Journal.

ASSESS

Lesson Assessment: Barbarians at the Gate (*Online*)

You will complete an online assessment covering the main objectives of this lesson. Your assessment will be scored by the computer.

Name Date 

Reading Guide

Complete this sheet as you read Chapter 10, from "Constantine's Vision and a Move East" to the end, pages 424-427.

After Constantine's Edict of Milan made Christianity a legally recognized faith in the Roman Empire, the religion began to spread faster than ever. List some things about Christianity that appealed to the people of the empire:

- ____
- ____
- ____
- ____

A series of events contributed to a gradual decline of the Roman Empire until, at last, one event heralded the end. List these events that can be collectively considered "the fall of Rome."

- ____
- ____
- ____
- ____
- ____
- ____

Chi-Rho
Christian Symbol for Christ

Name Date

Personality Profile: Constantine

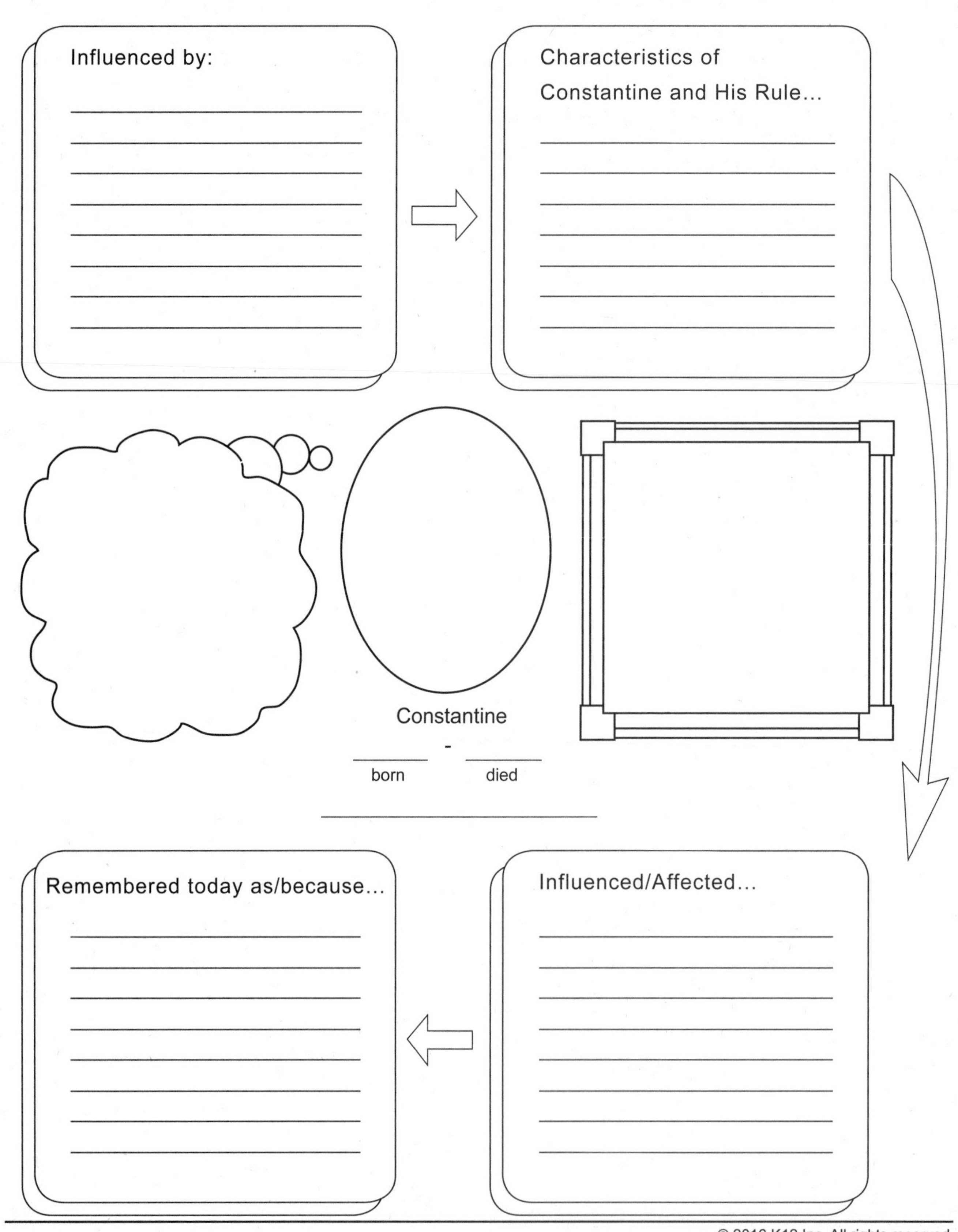

Student Guide
Lesson 16: Who Were They?

You probably know what a *vandal* or *vandalism* is. But do you know where the term *vandal* comes from? Perched along the borders of the Roman Empire were nomadic tribes that the Romans called *barbarians*. The barbarians were actually distinct groups like the Visigoths, the Ostrogoths, the Huns, and (did you guess?) the Vandals. As the strength of the Roman Empire declined, those groups plundered and pillaged Roman villages. The Vandals ransacked Rome so thoroughly that their name still applies to anyone who loots and destroys property.

Lesson Objectives

- Identify at least three barbarian tribes that threatened the Roman Empire in the fourth and fifth centuries A.D.
- Choose one barbarian tribe, tell where they lived, and describe their way of life.
- Identify Attila as the leader of the Huns of central Asia.

PREPARE

Approximate lesson time is 60 minutes.

Materials

For the Student

Barbarians

Roman Times

The Human Odyssey: Prehistory Through the Middle Ages edited by Klee, Cribb, and Holdren

---

LEARN

Activity 1: People of the Barbaricum *(Online)*

Activity 2: News of the Barbarians *(Offline)*

Use the map on page 504 of your book to answer the following questions. This will help you create your newspaper front page.

1. Identify the groups that invaded Western Europe between A.D. 350 and 550.
2. What group of invaders came the greatest distance?
3. What group of invaders came from Asia?
4. Which two groups can you infer were skilled sailors? How do you know?
5. What areas of the Roman Empire were not threatened by barbarian invasions? (Refer to the maps on pages 504 and 423.)

Compare your answers with those in the Lesson Answer Key.

ASSESS

Lesson Assessment: Who Were They? (*Online*)

You will complete an online assessment covering the main points of this lesson. Your assessment will be scored by the computer.

Name Date 

Barbarians

It was the barbarians who stopped the expansion of the Roman Empire. In time, they helped destroy the empire. Explore the barbarians in general, and then choose one group to focus on.

Barbarians: All Groups

The group I will focus on: ____________________

Barbarian Group (i.e., Visigoths, Vandals, Ostrogoths, etc.): ____________________

Social Structure/Culture	Homeland	Methods of Battle	Reasons for Invading

Name Date

Roman Times

Create the front page of a newspaper from the time of barbarian invasions of the Roman Empire in the fourth and fifth centuries A.D. Your front page should include the following:

- A headline about barbarians or a barbarian invasion
- At least one news article (with title) about a specific tribe that invaded the Empire, including where and how they lived (Your completed Barbarians sheet should have most, if not all, of this information organized for you.)
- A special feature article that includes an interview with someone who had dinner with Attila the Hun
- A picture that provides a good visual to one of your articles
- A map that traces the invasions of different groups into the Roman Empire during the fourth and fifth centuries A.D. (Use the completed Barbarian Invasions sheet for help.)

Create your front page on a large (larger than 8 ½" X 11") sheet of paper, newsprint, or construction paper.

Prepare

Almost all newspaper stories start off by answering the questions who, what, when, where, why, and how. Newspaper reporters also interview people to get a balanced point of view. Prepare to write a news story about a recent barbarian invasion by answering the following questions and "interviewing" people for your story. Your Barbarians sheet will help you.

Who?

What?

When?

Where?

Why/How?

Quotations from a Roman citizen:

Quotations from the Roman emperor:

Quotations from a barbarian:

Name Date

Notes from Attila's Dinner

What Attila looked like:

What was served:

How Attila ate:

Other information:

Student Guide
Lesson 17: Unit Review

PREPARE

Approximate lesson time is 60 minutes.

Materials

For the Student

The Human Odyssey: Prehistory Through the Middle Ages edited by Klee, Cribb, and Holdren

History Journal

LEARN

Activity 1: Offline *(Offline)*

Activity 2: Online *(Online)*

Student Guide
Lesson 18: Unit Assessment

You've finished the unit! Now it's time to take the Unit Assessment.

Lesson Objectives

- Identify key events, people, values, and achievements during the time of the Roman Republic.
- Recognize the effects of the Punic Wars on Rome's power on the Italian peninsula and in the Mediterranean.
- Identify the extent of the Roman Empire at its height and the countries that are in that territory today.
- Recognize the role of trade between East and West in moving people, goods, and ideas.
- Recognize political, social, and cultural changes that took place in Rome during the empire.
- Identify the factors that led to the decline of the Roman Empire.
- List examples of the contributions of classical Greece and Rome to modern Western civilization.
- Identify characteristics of climate and terrain in Italy.
- Describe the transition of Rome from republic to empire.
- Identify the origins, beliefs, and important people in the founding and spread of Christianity.

PREPARE

Approximate lesson time is 60 minutes.

Materials

For the Student

Question Review Table

ASSESS

Unit Assessment: Rome: Republic and Empire, Part 1 (*Online*)

Complete the computer-scored portion of the Unit Assessment. When you have finished, complete the teacher-scored portion of the assessment and submit it to your teacher.

Unit Assessment: Rome: Republic and Empire, Part 2 (*Offline*)

Complete the teacher-scored portion of the Unit Assessment and submit it to your teacher.

LEARN

Activity 1: Unit Assessment Review Table *(Online)*

Assessment Date

Unit 10: Rome: Republic and Empire

Before you retake the Unit Assessment, use the table to figure out which activities you should review.

Question Review Table

Circle the numbers of the questions that you missed on the Unit Assessment. Review the activities that correspond with these questions.

Republic and Empire, Part 1

Question	Lesson	Review Activity
1,7	15: Barbarians at the Gate	The First Christian Emperor of the Roman Empire
2	14: Empire in Crisis	What Went Wrong?
3	10: Jesus of Nazareth	Jesus the Teacher
4,11	4: Julius Caesar	Julius Caesar
5	16: Who Were They?	People of the Barbaricum
6	12: Conflicts for Christians	Conflict
8,20	1: A Republic Is Born	Why Rome?
8,9 ,14	2: Celebrating Citizenship	Plebians vs. Patricians
9,10	3: Fighting for Power	Before and After the Punic Wars
11,12,13,18	5: From Republic to Empire	A Peaceful and United Empire
14,15	14: Empire in Crisis	What Went Wrong?
16,17,18	19: Legacies, Part 1	Legacies and Contributions
19	5: From Republic to Empire	Read

Republic and Empire, Part 2

Question	Lesson	Review Activity
1	5: From Republic to Empire	A Peaceful and United Empire
2	11: A New Religion	Spreading the Message

Student Guide
Lesson 19: Legacies, Part 1

Greece and Rome, the classical civilizations that dominated the Mediterranean for more than a millennium, left an enduring legacy, particularly to the Western world. The light of these classical civilizations dimmed after the fall of Rome, but Greek and Roman ideas reemerged centuries later. Many of them continue to shine to this day.

Lesson Objectives

- Review knowledge gained in previous lessons and units.
- Recognize the contributions and legacies of classical Greece and Rome to modern Western civilization.

PREPARE

Approximate lesson time is 60 minutes.

Materials

For the Student

Legacies and Contributions

LEARN

Activity 1: Legacies and Contributions *(Offline)*

Instructions

Review of Legacies/Contributions

As you review the contributions of the ancient Greeks and Romans, do so in the context of "Questions to Ask About a Culture" from Unit 1. Review those questions now--they're in the sidebar on page 48.

After you've reviewed the questions, complete the Legacies and Contributions sheet. Include as many legacies and contributions as you can think of. Skim through your textbook, the Conclusion to Part 3, pages 429 to 435, if you need help remembering what some of them are. The most important column is the last one. Spend a little time thinking about why you included each legacy or contribution.

After you have completed the chart, check the Lesson Answer Key to make sure you included the most important items. Then, select one legacy or contribution to focus on and create a presentation for it.

Presentation

Choose a type of presentation from the bulleted list below and begin working on yours. In the next lesson you'll finish it and present it.

1. Type of Presentation

Think of a creative way to highlight the legacy or contribution you selected. Here are some ideas:

- *Display*
  Use a three-panel display board to create a kiosk-type presentation. As you create your display, imagine that it will be one of many that are set up on a long table. Make yours stand out with interesting images; bold, attention-grabbing headings; and short, to-the-point snippets of text.
- *Slideshow*
  Use Microsoft PowerPoint or similar presentation software to create a slideshow. You can incorporate text, images, animation, sound, and video. Remember that your audience will page through the information in step-by-step manner.
- *Interactive Presentation*
  Use Microsoft PowerPoint or similar software to create a multimedia presentation that the user can view in whatever way suits him. Incorporate text, images, animation, sound, and video. Interactive CD-ROMS are this type of format.
- *Oral Presentation*
  Create an oral presentation that you would give to an audience. Use visuals--posters, models, illustrations, etc. If you wish, dress up as a character to give the presentation. Or, imagine you are a college professor giving a lecture to your world history class, the curator of a museum talking to a group of students, or a historian being interviewed on the History Channel.

2. Regardless of what type of presentation you choose, you need to include, at a minimum, the information from your chart:
   - Name of the legacy or contribution
   - Category (from Questions to Ask About a Culture)
   - Where it comes from (Greece or Rome, and a person, if applicable)
   - A description of the legacy or contribution
   - An explanation of how the legacy or contribution has influenced society, how the world has benefited from it, how it's used today, etc.

Include any other information you want that applies to the contribution.

3. Begin putting together the presentation. If you need more information, do a little research (but don't spend a lot of time researching). Use your book and Grolier's online encyclopedia first. These two sources should contain enough information for your presentation.
4. Do as much work as you can today. You'll finish up in the next lesson.

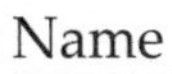

Name Date

Legacies and Contributions

Contribution	Category (from Questions to Ask About a Culture)	Greece or Rome (or both) and Person (if applicable)	Brief Description	Explanation of How It Influenced Later Society (How the World Benefited from It or How It's Used Today, etc.)

Student Guide
Lesson 20: Legacies, Part 2

Lesson Objectives

- Review knowledge gained in previous lessons and units.
- Recognize the contributions and legacies of classical Greece and Rome to modern Western civilization.

PREPARE

Approximate lesson time is 60 minutes.

LEARN
Activity 1: Legacies and Contributions *(Offline)*

Student Guide
Lesson 21. Optional: Your Choice

You may use today's lesson time to do one or more of the following:

- Complete work in progress.
- Complete the Beyond the Lesson activity in any lesson in this unit.
- Review the Classical World Time Line in the Resources section.
- Prepare for your state standardized test.
- Go on to the next lesson.

Please mark this lesson complete to proceed to the next lesson in the course.

PREPARE

Approximate lesson time is 60 minutes.

Student Guide

Unit 11: Empires
Lesson 1: Byzantine Beauty

Constantine moved the capital of the Roman Empire to Byzantium. When the glory that was Rome faded in the West, the Eastern Empire continued to flourish, becoming the Byzantine Empire. Eventually, this empire extended from Spain to the Black Sea and along the north coast of Africa. The Byzantine Empire developed a new culture, exciting art, and remarkable architecture that still inspire awe today. Influences from both West and East came together in the glory and grandeur of the Byzantine Empire.

Lesson Objectives

- Analyze maps to assess the advantages of Byzantium's (Constantinople's) location.
- Recognize that a blend of Eastern and Western elements resulted in a unique Byzantine culture.
- Identify characteristics of Byzantine art.
- Explain the purpose and importance of Justinian's Code.
- Identify Justinian as the sixth-century emperor responsible for developing a code of law.
- Identify Theodora as a powerful empress and Justinian's wife and aide.
- Identify Hagia Sophia as the great architectural achievement of Justinian's reign.

PREPARE

Approximate lesson time is 60 minutes.

Materials

For the Student

The Human Odyssey: Prehistory Through the Middle Ages edited by Klee, Cribb, and Holdren

Keywords and Pronunciation

Byzantine (BIH-zn-teen)
Byzantium (buh-ZAN-tee-um)
Constantine (KAHN-stuhn-teen)
Constantinople (kahn-stant-n-OH-puhl)
Hagia Sophia (HAH-juh soh-FEE-uh)
icon : an image or picture usually painted on wood that depicts holy people or events, such as the birth of Jesus
Justinian (juh-STIH-nee-uhn)
medieval (meh-DEE-vuhl) : an adjective that means “relating to the Middle Ages.”
mosaics (moh-ZAY-iks)
patriarch (PAY-tree-ahrk)
schism (SKIH-zuhm)
Theodora (thee-uh-DOR-uh)
Timbuktu (tim-buhk-TOO)

LEARN

Activity 1: A New Rome *(Online)*

ASSESS

Lesson Assessment: Byzantine Beauty (*Online*)

You will complete an online assessment covering the main points of this lesson. Your assessment will be scored by the computer.

LEARN

Activity 2: Byzantine Beauty *(Offline)*

Instructions

As you read Chapter 1, from "The Emperor Who Never Slept" to "*Strangers from the East*", pages 450-453, answer the following questions in your History Journal.

1. Why was Justinian's Code created? Why was it important?
2. What were Justinian's major accomplishments as emperor?
3. Who was Theodora and what were some of him contributions to the Byzantine Empire?
4. What is the Hagia Sophia?

Activity 3. Optional: Byzantine Beauty *(Online)*

Student Guide
Lesson 2: Justinian and Theodora

Many people helped the Byzantine Empire grow and prosper, but none contributed more than Justinian and Theodora. Acting as a team, the emperor and empress provided forceful leadership and great insight. They expanded the empire and united it through law, art, and architecture. Who were Justinian and Theodora? Read on to learn more.

Lesson Objectives

- Explain the purpose and importance of Justinian's Code.
- Identify Justinian as the sixth-century emperor responsible for developing a code of law.
- Identify Theodora as a powerful empress and Justinian's wife and aide.
- Identify Hagia Sophia as the great architectural achievement of Justinian's reign.
- Recognize the role of trade in the Byzantine Empire.

PREPARE

Approximate lesson time is 60 minutes.

Materials

For the Student

The Human Odyssey: Prehistory Through the Middle Ages edited by Klee, Cribb, and Holdren

Keywords and Pronunciation

Hagia Sophia (HAH-juh soh-FEE-uh)
Justinian (juh-STIH-nee-uhn)
Theodora (thee-uh-DOR-uh)

LEARN
Activity 1: The Emperor and His Empress *(Online)*

ASSESS
Lesson Assessment: Justinian and Theodora (*Online*)

You will complete an online assessment covering the main points of this lesson. Your assessment will be scored by the computer.

LEARN
Activity 2: Justinian and Theodora *(Offline)*

Instructions

Read Chapter 1, from "*Strangers from the East*," to the end, pages 453-457. Be prepared to discuss the role of trade in the Byzantine Empire.

Student Guide

Lesson 3: The Origins of Islam

In the thriving trade center of Mecca, a thoughtful merchant began preaching. He claimed to have had revelations from God and he described a new religion. His words wafted out of Mecca and Medina along the caravan routes that crisscrossed the Arabian Peninsula and out into the Mediterranean world and beyond. His ideas continued to spread, and today there are more than a billion Muslims in the world.

Lesson Objectives

- Recognize the role of trade in the Byzantine Empire.
- Analyze maps to identify geographic characteristics of the Arabian Peninsula.
- Identify key places in the development of Islam.
- Summarize the early life and teaching of Muhammad.
- Define Islam, Muslim, and Hijrah.

PREPARE

Approximate lesson time is 60 minutes.

Materials

For the Student

The Human Odyssey: Prehistory Through the Middle Ages edited by Klee, Cribb, and Holdren

Keywords and Pronunciation

Hijrah (HIJ-ruh) : Muhammad's flight to Medina in A.D. 622, the first year of the Muslim calendar
Mecca (MEH-kuh)
Medina (muh-DEE-nuh)
Muhammad (moh-HAM-uhd) : believed by Muslims to be the last great prophet
Muslim (MOUZ-luhm) : a follower of Islam
Rub' al Khali (roob ahl KHAH-lee)

LEARN

Activity 1: The Rise of Islam *(Offline)*

Check Your Reading

In your History Journal, cite examples from the reading (Chapter 1, from "*Strangers from the East*" to the end, pages 453-457) that would support the following statement: Trade played an important role in the growth and development of the Byzantine Empire.

Read

Read Chapter 2, from the beginning to "The Prophet in Medina," pages 459-466. As you read, answer these questions in your History Journal. When you have finished, compare your answers with those in the Lesson Answer Key.

1. Describe the way of life of the Bedouins of ancient times.
2. What were some of the trade items that the caravans carried? What were some of the places that the caravans visited?
3. What dangers did the caravans face?
4. How did the oases help travelers?
5. Why was Mecca an important city?
6. Describe the early life of Muhammad.
7. What happened to Muhammad when he was in the cave? What did he begin doing afterward?
8. Why did Muhammad move to Medina?

Write a brief definition for each of these terms in your History Journal. When you have finished, compare your definitions with those in the Keywords section of this lesson.

Islam

Muhammad

Muslim

Hijrah

Use What You Know

Imagine you are hosting a television show that features the world's greatest religious leaders of all time. You need to introduce Muhammad to your viewers, but you only have one minute to describe him and summarize his early life and teachings. You need to be both brief and comprehensive. What would you say? Write your introduction and deliver it.

Focus on Geography

Use the map of Average Rainfall in the Middle East on page 461 and your reading to respond to these questions.

1. What body of water lies to the west of Mecca and Medina?
2. Where is the Arabian Sea?
3. What body of water lies east of the Arabian Peninsula?
4. Where is the Arabian Desert?
5. What is Rub' al Khali and where is it located?
6. Which cities or areas on the Arabian Peninsula receive the most amount rainfall?
7. Which cities or areas on the Arabian Peninsula receive the least amount rainfall?
8. How much rainfall does Mecca receive?
9. How much rainfall does Medina receive?

ASSESS

Lesson Assessment: The Origins of Islam (*Online*)

You will complete an online assessment covering the main points of this lesson. Your assessment will be scored by the computer.

Student Guide
Lesson 4: Islam Emerges

Muhammad's teachings were gathered into a book known as the Qur'an. Like the Bible, it is very long and takes years of study to know well. But the main duties that Muhammed wanted every Muslim to obey were summarized in the Five Pillars of Islam.
See if you can name and explain them.

Lesson Objectives

- Describe the events that led to Muhammad's rule over Mecca as the holy city of Islam.
- Identify the Qur'an as the sacred text of Islam.
- Summarize the Five Pillars of Islam.
- Compare and contrast Islam with other major world religions.
- Identify Abu Bakr as the first caliph and Muhammad's friend and father-in-law, and the conflicts during his rule that led to a split in Islam.
- On a map trace the growth of the Muslim Empire.
- List ways in which Islam spread.
- Describe the importance and results of trade in the Muslim Empire.
- Define caliph and jihad.

PREPARE

Approximate lesson time is 60 minutes.

Materials

For the Student

The Five Pillars of Islam

The Human Odyssey: Prehistory Through the Middle Ages edited by Klee, Cribb, and Holdren

Keywords and Pronunciation

Abu Bakr (uh-BOO BAK-ur)
caliph (KAY-luhf) : the title for Muslim rulers after the death of Muhammad
hajj (haj)
Islam (is-LAHM) : a religion based on the teachings of Muhammad
jihad (jih-HAHD) : a struggle on behalf of Islam
mosque (mahsk) : a Muslim place of worship
Qur'an (kuh-RAN) : the sacred book of Islam
Ramadan (RAH-muh-dahn)
Shi'ahs (SHEE-ahs)
Shi'ites (SHEE-iyts)
Sunnis (SOU-neez)

LEARN

Activity 1: The Five Pillars of Islam *(Offline)*

Instructions

Read

As you read Chapter 2, from "The Prophet in Medina" to the end, pages 466-471, answer these questions. When you have finished, compare your answers with those in the Answer Key.

1. How did the people of Medina receive Muhammad?

____

____

____

2. What is the Qur'an? ____________________________________

____

3. What laws did Muhammad give the people to help them live together?

____

____

____

____

4. Why didn't most Jews and Christians follow Muhammad?

____

____

____

____

5. Describe the events that led to Muhammad's rule over Mecca as the holy city of Islam.

____

____

____

____

6. How did Muhammad change the lives and ideas of Arabs?

____

____

____

____

Use What You Know

The Five Pillars of Islam

Complete the Five Pillars of Islam sheet. When you have finished, compare your answers with those in the Answer Key.

Comparing Religions

It is now time for you to complete the Islam section of the Comparing Religions and Philosophies sheet. View the answers in the Answer Key when you have finished.

ASSESS

Lesson Assessment: Islam Emerges (*Online*)

You will complete an online assessment covering the main points of this lesson. Your assessment will be scored by the computer.

LEARN

Activity 2: Islam Emerges *(Offline)*

Read Chapter 3, from the beginning to "The Spread of Faith and Empire," pages 473-477.

Name _______________ Date _______________

The Five Pillars of Islam

Shahadah

____
First Pillar

____
____
____
____
____
____

Salat

____
Second Pillar

____
____
____
____
____
____

Zakat

____
Third Pillar

____
____
____
____
____
____

Name Date

The Five Pillars of Islam

Sawm

Fourth Pillar

Hajj

Fifth Pillar

Student Guide

Lesson 5: Religion and Empire

Lesson Objectives

- Define *caliph* and *jihad.*
- Identify Abu Bakr as the first caliph and Muhammad's friend and father-in-law, and the conflicts during his rule that led to a split in Islam.
- On a map trace the growth of the Muslim Empire.
- List ways in which Islam spread.
- Describe the importance and results of trade in the Muslim Empire.

PREPARE

Approximate lesson time is 60 minutes.

Materials

For the Student

The Human Odyssey: Prehistory Through the Middle Ages edited by Klee, Cribb, and Holdren

---

LEARN

Activity 1: Expanding the Empire *(Online)*

Activity 2: Religion and Empire *(Offline)*

Instructions

Chapter 3, from "The Spread of Faith and Empire" to "The House of Wisdom," pages 477-479

After you read Chapter 3, from "The Spread of Faith and Empire" to "The House of Wisdom," pages 477-479, write two paragraphs in your History Journal. The first paragraph should summarize how Islam spread, and the second paragraph should describe the importance and the results of trade in the Muslim Empire. If you wish, you may also illustrate one event for each paragraph. Compare your thoughts and ideas to those in the Answer Key.

ASSESS

Lesson Assessment: Religion and Empire (*Online*)

You will complete an online assessment covering the main points of this lesson. Your assessment will be scored by the computer.

Student Guide
Lesson 6: Scholars and Storytellers

Suppose there had been a webcam in Baghdad during the Abbasid caliphate. What would visitors have seen? They could easily have explored a research library called the House of Wisdom, visited remarkable buildings, and enjoyed outstanding art. Visitors might have listened to brilliant scientists like Ibn Sina and met the complete mathematician, Al-Khwarizmi. Learning the calligraphy and weaving skills of the Islamic artists might have been challenging, but fun.

As you learn about the art, architecture, science, and math of this era, remember that they were developed more than 1,250 years ago.

Lesson Objectives

- Describe Muslim achievements in science and math.
- Recognize characteristics and examples of Muslim art and architecture.

PREPARE

Approximate lesson time is 60 minutes.

Materials

For the Student

Reading Guide

The Human Odyssey: Prehistory Through the Middle Ages edited by Klee, Cribb, and Holdren

Keywords and Pronunciation

Al-Khwarizmi (al-KHWAHR-iz-mee)
arabesque (air-uh-BESK) : a pattern of winding stems and abstract leaves and flowers
hisab al-jabr (hih-SAB el-JUH-bruh)
Ibn Sina (IB-uhn SEE-nah)
iman (ih-MAHM)
mihrab (mih-RAHB)
minarets (min-uh-RETS)
mosque (mahsk) : a Muslim place of worship
sifr (SIH-fu)

LEARN

Activity 1: Forms of Art and Intellect *(Offline)*

Instructions

Read

Complete the Reading Guide as you read Chapter 3, from "The House of Wisdom" to the end, pages 479-485. Compare your answers with those in the Answer Key.

Activity 2: Scholars and Storytellers *(Online)*

ASSESS

Lesson Assessment: Scholars and Storytellers (*Online*)

You will complete an online assessment covering the main points of this lesson. Your assessment will be scored by the computer.

Name Date

Reading Guide

Complete this sheet as you read today's assignment.

1. What was the House of Wisdom? Where was it located?

2. Who was Al-Khwarizmi? What were some of his most important accomplishments?

3. Who was Ibn Sina? What were some of his accomplishments in the field of medicine?

4. Why didn't Muslim artists make pictures or statues of life-like beings?

5. Define *arabesque*. What word is sometimes included in arabesque designs?

6. What is the primary purpose of Muslim art and what are the major forms?

7. What is a *mosque* and where was the first one?

8. What are *minarets* and what is their purpose?

9. How does a person inside a mosque know the direction of Mecca?

10. Who delivers the sermon in a mosque?

Student Guide
Lesson 7: More Mapping

We can understand history better if we pause to ask ourselves where events happened and why they happened there. Historical events take place in a geographic context. For example, people tend to settle near water and fertile soil. Wars are frequently fought for control of territory. Trade grows more rapidly where travel is easy.

Maps can help us understand the geographic context. Today you'll revisit some of the civilizations that developed in the Mediterranean region and the Middle East and analyze maps to understand the impact of geography. Maps answer questions, but they should also provoke questions.

Lesson Objectives

- Review geographic concepts.
- Use maps to gain information about the Mediterranean region and the Middle East.

PREPARE

Approximate lesson time is 60 minutes.

Materials

For the Student

The Human Odyssey: Prehistory Through the Middle Ages edited by Klee, Cribb, and Holdren

History Journal

LEARN

Activity 1: Learn from Maps *(Offline)*

Instructions

Use What You Know

Imagine you have recently started tutoring a student who needs help with history and geography. You have both worked hard, and now it is time for you to give your student a quiz. Use the maps in your atlas, and the maps in the pertinent chapters in the textbook (see list below) to create the following multiple-choice questions.

1. Write one question about the geography of Greece and its impact on the development of civilization there.
2. Write a question about the impact of geography on the Peloponnesian War.
3. Write a question about the size and location of the Roman Empire.
4. Write a geographic question about the spread of Christianity.
5. The Byzantine Empire spread far and wide once it was clearly established by Constantine. Write a geographic question about the city named for him and the surrounding territory.
6. Write a question related to the geographic growth of the Muslim Empire and any landforms or other features that may have helped or hindered it.

When you have finished, find someone to take your quiz.

The following maps in your textbook may help you create your quiz:
Ancient Greece, page 287
Persian Empire, pages 300-301
Battle of Salamis, page 308
Peloponnesian War, 431-404 B.C., page 329
Alexander's Empire 323 B.C., page 339
Mediterranean World Seventh Century B.C., pages 342-343
Ancient Italy, page 343
Growth of Roman Power, page 360
Rome vs. Carthage, page 362
Roman Empire, page 368
The Roman Empire at Its Height, pages 376-377
Eastern Mediterranean, A.D.30, page 396
Paul's Missionary Travels, page 407

Activity 2. Optional: More Mapping *(Online)*

Student Guide
Lesson 8. Optional: Your Choice

You may use today's lesson time to do one or more of the following:

- Complete work in progress.
- Complete the Beyond the Lesson activity in any lesson in this unit.
- Review the Classical World Time Line in the Resources section.
- Prepare for your state standardized test.
- Go on to the next lesson.

Please mark this lesson complete to proceed to the next lesson in the course.

PREPARE

Approximate lesson time is 60 minutes.

Student Guide
Lesson 9: Mapping Africa

Africa is a huge continent. How big is it? Picture this: you could fit three landmasses the size of the continental United States in it and still have plenty of room left over. This geographically diverse continent contains the world's longest river, largest desert, and some of the wettest places on Earth. Explore the continent as you get ready to delve into its history.

Lesson Objectives

- Locate on a map the Sahara, Kalahari, and Namib deserts, the Nile, Congo, and Niger Rivers; the equatorial rain forest; the savanna and the Sahel.
- Define *rain forest, Sahel, desert,* and *savanna.*
- Use maps to gain information about the physical characteristics of Africa.

PREPARE

Approximate lesson time is 60 minutes.

Keywords and Pronunciation

eucalyp : A dry area, which receives less than 10 inches of precipitation per year.
rain forest : tropical woodland with an annual rainfall of at least 100 inches
savanna : a tropical grassland containing a few scattered trees

---

LEARN

Activity 1: A Journey to Africa *(Online)*

Explore Africa and chart some of the physical features as you travel around the continent.

ASSESS

Lesson Assessment: Mapping Africa (*Online*)

You will complete an online assessment covering the main points of this lesson. Your assessment will be scored by the computer.

Student Guide
Lesson 10: Gold and Salt

Trade gold for salt? Would people actually do that? Why?
Meet the Soninke people of Ghana, then read a story about the trading ritual a Soninke child observed from his hiding place in the bushes.

Lesson Objectives

- Describe the role and importance of trade in Ghana's power.

PREPARE

Approximate lesson time is 60 minutes.

Materials

For the Student

Reading Guide

The Human Odyssey: Prehistory Through the Middle Ages edited by Klee, Cribb, and Holdren

Keywords and Pronunciation

Soninke (soh-NIN-kay)

LEARN
Activity 1: Ghana's Trade *(Offline)*

Instructions

Read

Complete the Reading Guide as you read Chapter 4, from the beginning to “Mali Rising,” pages 487-493. Compare your answers with those in the Lesson Answer Key.

Activity 2: Gold and Salt *(Online)*

ASSESS
Lesson Assessment: Gold and Salt (*Online*)

You will complete an online assessment covering the main points of this lesson. Your assessment will be scored by the computer.

LEARN
Activity 3. Optional: Gold and Salt *(Online)*

Reading Guide

Complete this sheet as you read today's assignment.

1. Describe the location and physical features of the Sudan.

2. Name the two great Sudanese empires in the western part of the region. What led to their wealth?

3. Where was Ghana located?

4. What is a *clan*? What clan populated Ghana?

5. How did Ghana reach the height of its power in the tenth century?

6. How did iron make Ghana powerful?

7. What two items did trade in Ghana focus on?

8. Why would the Soninke people exchange gold for salt?

9. What are some of the other items that were traded in the markets in Ghana?

10. What was *silent trade*?

Student Guide
Lesson 11: A Man Called Mansa Musa

Sundiata was known as the Hungering Lion or Lion King. Although he started out sickly, Sundiata quickly became very powerful. He captured the goldfields of Ghana and guided Mali on to become the most important federation in western Sudan. Decades later another great leader came to power in Mali. Mansa Musa expanded the kingdom and turned Timbuktu, Mali's bustling center of commerce, into the "Pearl of Africa." The Kingdom of Mali, a bright beacon of the times, grew and prospered during the European Dark Ages. While Europe slept, education, trade, culture, and art all flourished in Mali.

Lesson Objectives

- Describe the significance of the legend of Sundiata to Mali's history.
- Identify Mansa Musa as the fourteenth century Muslim ruler of Mali known for his travels.
- Locate on a map the city of Timbuktu and describe its role as a center of trade and education.
- Identify the time period in which the kingdoms of Ghana and Mali flourished.

PREPARE

Approximate lesson time is 60 minutes.

Materials

For the Student

Reading Guide

The Human Odyssey: Prehistory Through the Middle Ages edited by Klee, Cribb, and Holdren

Keywords and Pronunciation

Es-Saheli (es-sah-HEH-lee)

griots (GREE-ohz) : the story-tellers and history-keepers of many western African civilizations

hajj (haj) : a pilgrimage to Islam's holy city of Mecca in Arabia

Ibn Battuta (IB-uhn bat-TOO-tah)

Malinke (muh-LING-kay)

Mansa Musa (MAHN-sah moo-SAH)

Sossos (SOH-sohz)

Sumanguru (soo-mahng-GOO-roo)

Sundiata (soun-JAH-tah)

LEARN

Activity 1: Mali *(Offline)*

Instructions

Read

As you read Chapter 4, from "Mali Rising" to the end, pages 494-501, complete the Reading Guide. When you have finished, you should compare your answers with those in the Answer Key.

Activity 2: A Man Called Mansa Musa *(Online)*

ASSESS

Lesson Assessment: A Man Called Mansa Musa (*Online*)

You will complete an online assessment covering the main points of this lesson. Your assessment will be scored by the computer.

LEARN

Activity 3. Optional: A Man Called Mansa Musa *(Online)*

Name Date

Reading Guide

Complete this sheet as you read today's assignment.

1. What are the people of Mali called?

2. Who was Sundiata? How did the legend of Sundiata affect the Malinke?

3. Describe how Mali took over the gold trade.

4. Who was Mansa Musa? What famous figure in the Qur'an was he named after?

5. Describe Mansa Musa's hajj.

6. How did Mansa Musa's generosity with his gold affect the gold market?

7. Find Timbuktu on the map on page 488 of your textbook. Why was Timbuktu revered as the "Pearl of Africa?"

8. Describe how Timbuktu became an Islamic educational center.

9. Describe Mali after Mansa Musa.

10. Who was Ibn Battuta?

Student Guide
Lesson 12. Optional: Your Choice

You may use today's lesson time to do one or more of the following:

- Complete work in progress.
- Complete the Beyond the Lesson activity in any lesson in this unit.
- Review the Classical World Time Line in the Resources section.
- Prepare for your state standardized test.
- Go on to the next lesson.

Please mark this lesson complete to proceed to the next lesson in the course.

PREPARE

Approximate lesson time is 60 minutes.

Student Guide
Lesson 13: Unit Review

You've finished the unit, and now it's time to review what you've learned. You'll take the Unit Assessment in the next lesson.

PREPARE

Approximate lesson time is 60 minutes.

LEARN
Activity 1: A Look Back *(Online)*

Activity 2: History Journal Review *(Offline)*

Student Guide
Lesson 14: Unit Assessment

You've finished this unit! Now take the Unit Assessment.

Lesson Objectives

- Identify important events, people, and achievements of the Byzantine Empire.
- Describe the origins, beliefs, and major figures in the founding and spread of Islam.
- Identify important events, people, and achievements of the Muslim Empire.
- Assess the role of geography in the growth and power of cities, including Byzantium (Constantinople, Istanbul).
- Analyze maps to identify physical characteristics of Africa.
- Recognize geographic characteristics of southwest Asia.
- Recognize important events, people, and achievements of the African empires of Ghana and Mali.
- Recognize the role of trade in the Byzantine and African Empires.

PREPARE

Approximate lesson time is 60 minutes.

Materials

For the Student

Question Review Table

The Human Odyssey: Prehistory Through the Middle Ages edited by Klee, Cribb, and Holdren

---

ASSESS

Unit Assessment: Empires (*Online*)

You will complete an online assessment covering the main points of this unit. Your assessment will be scored by the computer.

LEARN

Activity 1: Unit Assessment Review Table *(Online)*

Activity 2: Where to Turn? *(Offline)*

Assessment Date

Unit 11: Empires

Before you retake the Unit Assessment, use the table to figure out which activities you should review.

Question Review Table

Circle the numbers of the questions that you missed on the Unit Assessment. Review the activities that correspond with these questions.

Question	Lesson	Review Activity
1,2,3,11	1: Byzantine Beauty	A New Rome
4,5, 8,12,13	4: Islam Emerges	The Five Pillars of Islam
6,9,7,10,25	5: Religion and Empire	Expanding the Empire
14,31	3: The Origins of Islam	The Rise of Islam
15,16,17,18,19	9: Mapping Africa	A Journey to Africa
20,21,22	7: More Mapping	Learn from Maps
23,24,29	2: Justinian and Theodora	The Emperor and His Empress
26	6: Scholars and Storytellers	Forms of Art and Intellect
27,28	11: A Man Called Mansa Musa	Mali
30	10: Gold and Salt	Ghana's Trade

Student Guide

Unit 12: In Western Europe
Lesson 1: Where to Turn?

Wave after wave of land-hungry tribes attacked the Roman Empire and gradually weakened it. The barbarians finally sacked Rome and sent the emperor into exile. What happened when the empire crumbled? Why did Europe become such a dangerous place?

Lesson Objectives

- Explain major cultural and civil consequences of the collapse of Roman civilization.

PREPARE

Approximate lesson time is 60 minutes.

Materials

For the Student

Consequences of the Fall of Rome
The Human Odyssey: Prehistory Through the Middle Ages edited by Klee, Cribb, and Holdren

---

LEARN

Activity 1: Where to Turn? *(Online)*

Activity 2: Examining the Fall of Rome *(Offline)*

Suppose a friend asked you to review a report she had written about the consequences of the collapse of the Roman Empire. You note that the report raises many issues, and you want to be sure your friend has thought about them thoroughly. Use your textbook, Groliers Online, and your own thoughts to examine some of the topics in the report and complete the Consequences of the Fall of Rome sheet.

ASSESS

Lesson Assessment: Where to Turn? (*Online*)

You will complete an online assessment covering the main points of this lesson. Your assessment will be scored by the computer.

Name Date

Examining the Fall of Rome

You've decided to help your friend improve his report "Consequences of the Collapse of Rome". He has made a list of some of the governments' functions to consider. Your task is to look for information in your text, and Groliers Online, and to think about what you know. Then summarize the problems Western Europe faced when Rome fell. The first topic has been completed for you.

1. The government of Rome wrote and enforced laws for the empire.

a. Describe the situation after the fall of Rome	no new laws were written, no one was paid to enforce laws
b. Problems faced in Western Europe	laws gradually disappeared
	law enforcement disappeared and crime increased

2. Soldiers guarded the Roman roads.

a. Describe the situation after the fall of Rome	
b. Problems faced in Western Europe	

3. The government of Rome hired laborers to build and maintain roads and bridges.

a. Describe the situation after the fall of Rome	
b. Problems faced in Western Europe	

4. The government of Rome hired laborers and engineers to build and maintain aqueducts and reservoirs.

a. Describe the situation after the fall of Rome	
b. Problems faced in Western Europe	

Examining the Fall of Rome

5. The Latin language united diverse areas where people spoke local languages; all documents were written in Latin.

a. Describe the situation after the fall of Rome	
b. Problems faced in Western Europe	

6. Now look back at your answers and use the information to write a paragraph describing what life might have been like in Western Europe a hundred years after the fall of the Roman Empire.

____

____

____

____

____

____

____

Student Guide
Lesson 2: Monasteries Carry On

Although many European institutions were crumbling during the dangerous period that followed the fall of Rome, the Christian church carried on scholarly pursuits, provided hospitality for travelers, and assisted the sick and poor. Following rules set by Benedict of Nursia, monasteries focused on work and prayer. They became quiet places of learning and centers of comfort in their communities. Under the leadership of the pope, the church organized the clergy and followers under bishops and archbishops, while monks and nuns carried on the work of the monastic movement.

Lesson Objectives

- Describe the role of the Christian church and the monasteries in spreading Christianity and preserving learning.
- Identify Benedict of Nursia as the fifth-century founder of the Benedictine rule that helped spread monasticism through Europe.
- Describe the basic organizational structure of the Christian church by A.D. 800.
- Identify Charlemagne as king of the Franks in A.D. 800 and list examples of his achievements.
- Locate Charlemagne's empire on a map and identify the countries that are in that area today.

PREPARE

Approximate lesson time is 60 minutes.

Materials

For the Student

Reading Guide

The Human Odyssey: Prehistory Through the Middle Ages edited by Klee, Cribb, and Holdren

Keywords and Pronunciation

Ora et labora (OR-ah et la-BOR-ah)
abbot : the leader of the monastery
Benedict of Nursia (NOUR-see-uh)
Charlemagne (SHAHR-luh-mayn)
Christendom (KRIH-suhn-duhm)
monasticism (muh-NAS-tuh-sih-zuhm) : the monk's way of life, dedicated to prayer and work
Monte Cassino (MAWN-tay kah-SEE-noh)
Munchen (MOUN-chuhn)
Munich (MYOO-nik)
scriptorium (skrip-TOHR-ee-uhm) : a writing room where skilled scribes work

LEARN

Activity 1: Monks and Monasteries *(Offline)*

Instructions

Read

As you read Chapter 5, from "A Matter of Faith" to "Charlemagne and the Faithful Franks," pages 506-510, complete the Reading Guide. When you have finished, compare your answers with those in the Lesson Answer Key.

Activity 2: Monasteries Carry On *(Online)*

ASSESS

Lesson Assessment: Monasteries Carry On (*Online*)

You will complete an online assessment covering the main points of this lesson. Your assessment will be scored by the computer.

LEARN

Activity 3: Monasteries Carry On *(Offline)*

As you read Chapter 5, from "Charlemagne and the Faithful Franks" to "*The Work of Angels*," pages 510-514, list examples that show that Charlemagne was a Christian king devoted to the work of the church and the restoration of unity and order in Europe.

Name Date

Reading Guide

Complete this sheet as you read today's assignment.

1. What institution of the late Roman Empire remained strong and visible? Why?

2. Who were the monks and where did they live?

3. Who was Benedict of Nursia?

4. What is monasticism? What was the *Rule of Saint Benedict*?

5. What does *ora et labora* mean?

6. What two tasks undertaken by monks had a lasting impact on European history?

7. How did monasteries preserve European learning?

8. What is a *scriptorium?*

9. What is the *Book of Kells?*

10. Describe the basic organizational structure of the Christian church in 800 A.D.

Student Guide

Lesson 3: Charlemagne

What determines greatness? In the eighth century, an energetic Frankish king who loved learning and music caught people's attention as he waged war against the Saxons, the Lombards, and finally the Moors. He united under Christianity a vast realm that sprawled across Europe. Once he had established peace, he turned his restless energy to setting up schools and monasteries to encourage education and hope. In recognition of his greatness, on Christmas Day in A.D. 800, the pope crowned Charlemagne emperor of the Holy Roman Empire.

Lesson Objectives

- Identify Charlemagne as king of the Franks in A.D. 800 and list examples of his achievements.
- Locate Charlemagne's empire on a map and identify the countries that are in that area today.

PREPARE

Approximate lesson time is 60 minutes.

Materials

For the Student

The Human Odyssey: Prehistory Through the Middle Ages edited by Klee, Cribb, and Holdren

Keywords and Pronunciation

Charlemagne (SHAHR-luh-mayn)

LEARN

Activity 1: Charlemagne *(Offline)*

Instructions

Compare your list of examples that show Charlemagne was a king devoted to the expansion of Christianity and the restoration of European unity and order with the list in the Lesson Answer Key.

Activity 2: Charlemagne's Empire *(Online)*

Activity 3: Charlemagne *(Offline)*

Instructions

Read

Read Chapter 5, "*The Work of Angels*" to the end, pages 515-519 and then discuss the story with an adult if you have any questions or concerns.

ASSESS

Lesson Assessment: Charlemagne (*Online*)

You will complete an offline assessment covering the main points of this lesson. Your learning coach will score this assessment.

Student Guide
Lesson 4. Optional: Your Choice

You may use today's lesson time to do one or more of the following:

- Complete work in progress.
- Complete the Beyond the Lesson activity in any lesson in this unit.
- Review the Classical World Time Line in the Resources section.
- Prepare for your state standardized test.
- Go on to the next lesson.

Please mark this lesson complete to proceed to the next lesson in the course.

PREPARE

Approximate lesson time is 60 minutes.

Student Guide
Lesson 5: Viking Ventures

At home, on land, or at sea, the Vikings were strong and adventurous. Their ships were light and swift, and helped the Vikings launch surprise attacks along the coasts of Ireland and mainland Europe. What if you had lived back in the time of these fierce Norsemen? Imagine what it would be like to sail on a Viking ship, go on a raid, or attend a boisterous council meeting.

Lesson Objectives

- Identify the geographic and climatic features of Scandinavia that encouraged people to go to sea.
- Recognize characteristics of Norse culture and its legacy.
- Recognize the routes and characteristics of Viking raids and expeditions.

PREPARE

Approximate lesson time is 60 minutes.

Materials

For the Student

Reading Guide

The Human Odyssey: Prehistory Through the Middle Ages edited by Klee, Cribb, and Holdren

History Journal

LEARN

Activity 1: Viking Ventures *(Offline)*

Instructions

Read

Read Chapter 6, from the beginning to the second column of page 527, the sentence that starts "While Rollo and her followers became Christians...", pages 521-527. Complete the Reading Guide as you read. When you have finished, check your answers against those in the Lesson Answer Key.

Activity 2: Focus on Geography *(Online)*

Activity 3: Viking Ventures *(Online)*

ASSESS

Lesson Assessment: Viking Ventures (*Online*)

You will complete an online assessment covering the main points of this lesson. Your assessment will be scored by the computer.

LEARN

Activity 4. Optional: Viking Ventures *(Online)*

Name ______________________________ Date ______________________________

Reading Guide

1. What other name did people call the Vikings? ____________________

2. The region of Northern Europe made up of the modern-day countries of Denmark, Sweden, and Norway is called ____________________.

3. List three physical features of this region.
   - ____________________
   - ____________________
   - ____________________

4. What was the Thing? What did it do?

____

____

____

5. The Vikings originally made their living as ______________, but as the population grew and fertile land became scarce, they turned to ______________ so they could take to the seas as traders.

6. Describe the Viking longship and the advantages of its design.

____

____

____

7. The Vikings originally went to sea for trading, but they soon began raiding the lands they visited. What were the characteristics of a Viking raid?

____

____

____

8. What did King Charles do when the Vikings settled on the coast of Northern France? What was significant about this decision?

____

____

____

Student Guide
Lesson 6: Gods and Leaders

The people we call *Vikings* were rough-and-ready adventurers who made terrifying raids on monasteries and plundered churches and villages. But most Norsemen were farmers, some of whom spent only their summers going "a-viking." The Norse made many cultural contributions that we still use. They developed an alphabet, named the days of the week, and wrote long poems and legends. They sailed their longships far from Scandinavia, and may even have been the first explorers to reach North America some five hundred years before Columbus.

Lesson Objectives

- Recognize characteristics of Norse culture and its legacy.
- Identify Erik the Red and Leif Erikson and their major achievements.

PREPARE

Approximate lesson time is 60 minutes.

Materials

For the Student

The Human Odyssey: Prehistory Through the Middle Ages edited by Klee, Cribb, and Holdren

---

LEARN

Activity 1: Gods and Leaders *(Offline)*

Instructions

Read

Read Chapter 6, from "While Rollo and her followers became Christians..." to the end, pages 527-531. As you read, take some notes about Norse mythology, runes, Erik the Red, and Leif the Lucky.

Activity 2: Focus on Geography *(Online)*

Activity 3: Gods and Leaders *(Online)*

ASSESS

Lesson Assessment: Gods and Leaders (*Online*)

You will complete an online assessment covering the main points of this lesson. Your assessment will be scored by the computer.

LEARN

Activity 4. Optional: Gods and Leaders *(Online)*

Student Guide
Lesson 7: The Structure of Medieval Society

As empires crumbled and bandits and marauders roamed the countryside, who could the people turn to for protection? Powerful landowners, called *lords,* used their land to gain the loyalty of people around them. They granted tracts of land to knights and lesser lords in exchange for military service. At the bottom of the social pyramid were peasants, who grew crops and provided labor in return for protection.

Lesson Objectives

- Explain the reasons for the development of the feudal system.
- Identify the purpose and main principles of the code of chivalry.

PREPARE

Approximate lesson time is 60 minutes.

Materials

For the Student

The Human Odyssey: Prehistory Through the Middle Ages edited by Klee, Cribb, and Holdren

Keywords and Pronunciation

bellatore (beh-lah-TOR-ay)

LEARN

Activity 1: Chivalry Lives! *(Offline)*

Instructions

Read

Read Chapter 7, from the beginning to "Minding the Manor," pages 533-538. Then answer the following questions:

1. What class system developed as local power shifted away from kings into the hands of landowners?
2. How did this system develop, and why did it develop?
3. What groups of people made up the class system?
4. Explain the purpose and principles of the code of chivalry.

Use What You Know

According to your text, "the code of chivalry described an ideal knight as charitable, kind, and loyal." Had there been such an ideal knight, how would she have behaved?

Think about the behavior and duties that the code of chivalry required. Then create a poster that advertises for the ideal knight. Be sure to explain why chivalry is important and also list all the qualities of a chivalrous knight. Illustrate your poster with a drawing of the knight that you would like to find.

Activity 2: The Structure of Medieval Society *(Online)*

ASSESS

Lesson Assessment: The Structure of Medieval Society *(Online)*

You will complete an online assessment covering the main points of this lesson. Your assessment will be scored by the computer.

Student Guide
Lesson 8: Manors

During the early Middle Ages, life in Western Europe was organized along clearly drawn lines of responsibility. Safety and self-sufficiency were foremost. Behind the fortified walls around the manor house, a lord could rule his domain almost like a king in a castle. Peasants lived hard lives in service to the lord of the manor. In return, he gave them plots of land to farm and the protection of his knights. If you had lived during the Middle Ages, where would you have fit in this social pyramid?

Lesson Objectives

- Describe the feudal pyramid and the roles of relationships among the classes.
- Describe the main features of life on a manor.

PREPARE

Approximate lesson time is 60 minutes.

Materials

For the Student

The Human Odyssey: Prehistory Through the Middle Ages edited by Klee, Cribb, and Holdren

---

LEARN

Activity 1: Manors *(Offline)*

Instructions

Read Chapter 7, from "Minding the Manor" to the end, pages 538-541.

Activity 2: Manors *(Online)*

Activity 3: Manors *(Online)*

ASSESS

Lesson Assessment: Manors (*Online*)

You will complete an online assessment covering the main points of this lesson. Your assessment will be scored by the computer.

Student Guide
Lesson 9. Optional: Your Choice

You may use today's lesson time to do one or more of the following:

- Complete work in progress.
- Complete the Beyond the Lesson activity in any lesson in this unit.
- Review the Classical World Time Line in the Resources section.
- Prepare for your state standardized test.
- Go on to the next lesson.

Please mark this lesson complete to proceed to the next lesson in the course.

PREPARE

Approximate lesson time is 60 minutes.

Student Guide
Lesson 10: Christendom

People in Western Europe a millennium ago referred to the world they lived in as *Christendom*. Why? Life in the Middle Ages was guided not by governments as we know them, but by the Christian church, its leaders, and its great thinkers. The church was the great unifying force for both the religious and nonreligious aspects of the daily lives of the people. It owned land, charged taxes, operated courts, and ran schools. All Christians were expected to attend church services weekly and to confess their sins at least once a year to a priest. In a time when many people were haunted by fears of disease, war, and starvation, the church offered them the promise of a better life in heaven. In a hard age, this was a comforting message.

Lesson Objectives

- List examples of the ways in which the Christian church exercised authority, influenced daily life, and offered hope to Europeans during the Middle Ages.
- Identify Thomas Aquinas.

PREPARE

Approximate lesson time is 60 minutes.

Materials

For the Student

Reading Guide

The Human Odyssey: Prehistory Through the Middle Ages edited by Klee, Cribb, and Holdren

Keywords and Pronunciation

Summa Theologica (SOO-muh thee-uh-LOH-jih-kuh)

Thomas Aquinas (uh-KWIY-nuhs)

LEARN

Activity 1: Faith and Logic *(Offline)*

Instructions

Read

Complete the Reading Guide as you read Chapter 8, from the beginning to "Treasures of Faith: The Romanesque Style," pages 543 to 546.

Use What You Know

The Influence of the Church

During the Middle Ages, the Christian church was the great unifying force in Europe. It influenced all aspects of life. Even the calendar used Christ's birth as its starting point.

Imagine that you are creating a game board with different categories of questions. Your category, which heads a list of questions about the Middle Ages, is "Our Daily Bread and Beyond." You must think of answers to three questions that will be in this category:

- How did the Christian church exercise its authority in the Middle Ages?
- How did the Christian church influence daily life in the Middle Ages?
- How did the Christian church offer hope in Europe in the Middle Ages?

You want your producer to have as many answer choices as possible. Review your reading and list as many examples as you can. An example of how the church influenced daily life is that the calendar's starting date was Christ's birthday. Try to think of at least two answers for each question. Group them by question.

What Did He Mean?

Recall that Thomas Aquinas's writings included teachings on reason, logic, and the ideas of Aristotle. Aquinas's most famous work was the *Summa Theologica* (*Summary of Theology*). In this expansive volume, Aquinas explained the logic behind Christian beliefs.

Read aloud the following quotations from this famous philosopher and think about what they might mean. Choose three and rewrite them in your own words or explain what you think they mean.

"To one who has faith, no explanation is necessary. To one without faith, no explanation is possible."

"To live well is to work well, to show a good activity."

"To convert somebody, go and take them by the hand and guide them."

"The test of the artist does not lie in the will with which he goes to work, but in the excellence of the work he produces."

"Peace is the work of justice indirectly, in so far as justice removes the obstacles to peace; but it is the work of charity (love) directly, since charity, according to its very notion, causes peace."

"Justice is a certain rectitude of mind whereby a man does what he ought to do in the circumstance confronting him."

"In order for a war to be just, three things are necessary. First, the authority of the sovereign. Secondly, a just cause. Thirdly, a rightful intention."

"Beware the man of one book."

"The things that we love tell us what we are."

ASSESS

Lesson Assessment: Christendom (*Online*)

You will complete an online assessment covering the main points of this lesson. Your assessment will be scored by the computer.

Name Date

Reading Guide

In the Middle Ages, Western Europeans were held together by the Christian faith. Why do you think the church was able to unify people during this time?

Complete the rest of this sheet while you read Chapter 8, from the beginning to "Treasures of Faith: The Romanesque Style," pages 543 to 546.

One Church for Western Europe

As you read, list all of the ways in which the Christian church influenced life in Western Europe during the Middle Ages. Think about how the church, in its structure and power, affected the average person during his life. How did the church offer hope to people during these times? What powers did the church have?

Thomas Aquinas: A Great Thinker

Read the sidebar on Thomas Aquinas on page 545. Paraphrase what you read in a short paragraph that tells who Thomas Aquinas is and what he is famous for.

Student Guide
Lesson 11: Building on Faith

European cathedrals are much more than places of worship. They are architectural tributes to their builders, and examples of innovative technology. Romanesque churches from the eleventh century are massive, fortress-like structures with thick walls and few windows. Their huge columns and Roman arches give the style its name. In the mid-twelfth century a new style emerged known as the Gothic style. Gothic cathedrals have steep, pointed arches, tall spires, and flying buttresses—graceful stone arches that help support the outer walls, which are much thinner than their Romanesque counterparts. Inside, stained-glass windows and unobstructed space give the sanctuary a light, airy feeling. In medieval Europe, these churches and cathedrals served as safe havens from the tribulations of the times.

Lesson Objectives

- Recognize the characteristics and purposes of Romanesque churches.
- Recognize the characteristics, uses, and construction challenges of Gothic cathedrals.
- Describe the developments in Jewish beliefs resulting from the Babylonian Captivity.

PREPARE

Approximate lesson time is 60 minutes.

Advance Preparation

- If your student wishes to learn more about cathedrals in the Beyond the Lesson activity for this lesson, obtain a copy of the book *Cathedral: The Story of Its Construction* by David Macaulay, Houghton-Mifflin, 1973, from your local library or bookstore.

Materials

For the Student

The Human Odyssey: Prehistory Through the Middle Ages edited by Klee, Cribb, and Holdren

History Journal

Keywords and Pronunciation

Romanesque (roh-muhn-ESK)

LEARN

Activity 1: Building on Faith *(Offline)*

Instructions

The medieval Christian church was powerful. It touched everyone's life in Western Europe. Kings and nobles gave money and land to the church, and the church used some of this money and land to build massive Romanesque churches and soaring Gothic cathedrals.

What were these magnificent structures like? Why were they built, and how were they used? Look for the answers to these questions as you read Chapter 8 from "Treasures of Faith: The Romanesque Style" to "A Command From the Pope," pages 546-549.

When you finish reading:

1. In your History Journal, describe the main challenge faced by those who designed and constructed Gothic cathedrals, and then describe how they overcame this challenge.
2. Return online to complete the lesson.

Activity 2: Building on Faith *(Online)*

Now you're going to use what you learned to analyze some real churches and cathedrals. But first, use the Medieval World Time Line in Resources to answer the following questions:

1. During which century were Romanesque churches first built?
2. When was the Gothic cathedral of Notre Dame completed?

Once you have this information, click From Romanesque to Gothic.

ASSESS

Lesson Assessment: Building on Faith (*Online*)

You will complete an online assessment covering the main points of this lesson. Your assessment will be scored by the computer.

LEARN

Activity 3. Optional: Building on Faith *(Offline)*

This activity is OPTIONAL. It's provided for enrichment or extra practice, but not required for completion of this lesson. You may skip this activity.

If you'd like to know more about cathedrals, you might enjoy a book by famed illustrator David Macaulay. It tells the story of the construction of a fictitious French Gothic cathedral. *Cathedral: The Story of Its Construction* has stunning pictures and many fascinating details.

Student Guide
Lesson 12: Cultures in Conflict

The Crusades began with a request for help in 1071. For nearly 400 years, Muslims had ruled Palestine, a small strip of land along the Mediterranean coast that was once part of the Byzantine Empire. To Jews, Palestine was the "promised land." To Muslims, it was the place where Muhammad's spirit had traveled to heaven. To Christians, it was the site of the birth and death of Jesus. Palestine was considered the Holy Land and Jerusalem its holiest city.

When Muslim warriors began attacking the Byzantine Empire, the emperor asked the pope in Rome for help. If the Byzantine Empire fell, Christians might lose access to the city of Jerusalem, so in 1095 Pope Urban II called for a holy war against the Muslim Turks.

The First Crusade began in 1096 when French nobles headed for the Holy Land, and it ended when the Christian army took the city of Jerusalem. The victory set up a violent tug of war between Christians and Muslims over Palestine until 1291, when the last of the Christian cities in the region fell to the Muslims during the fifth or Last Crusade.

The wars left Christians and Muslims bitter rivals. Christians and Jews were also deeply divided, since the Crusaders had destroyed many Jewish settlements in the conflicts. But the Crusades changed the world in other ways as well. Crusaders brought back new ideas from the East. Greek texts from Eastern libraries came west. Western scholars began translating Muslim works on mathematics, philosophy, and medicine. And goods from the East began making their way to European marketplaces in greater quantities.

Lesson Objectives

- Identify the attitudes, beliefs, and events that led to the Crusades.
- Describe the direct and indirect results of the Crusades.
- Define *Crusades* and *Holy Land.*
- Identify Saladin and Richard the Lion-Heart.

PREPARE

Approximate lesson time is 60 minutes.

Materials

For the Student

Witness to the Crusades

The Human Odyssey: Prehistory Through the Middle Ages edited by Klee, Cribb, and Holdren

Keywords and Pronunciation

Crusades : medieval wars fought by Christians to recapture the Holy Land from the Muslim Turks

Holy Land : a strip of land along the eastern coast of the Mediterranean Sea that is sacred to Jews, Christians, and Muslims, and that includes the city of Jerusalem

Saladin (SAL-uh-din)

LEARN

Activity 1: Cultures in Conflict *(Offline)*

Instructions

As you read, answer these questions:

1. What was happening in Constantinople in 1071?

2. Where did the Byzantine emperor turn for help? Why? What was the result?

3. How did each of the following view the region that included the city of Jerusalem? Why?

Jews

Christians

Muslims

1. Identify:

the Crusades

the Holy Land

Saladin

Richard the Lion-Heart

1. What role did Saladin and Richard play in the Crusades?

2. Describe the direct and indirect results of the Crusades.

Using Primary Sources

When the Byzantine emperor asked for help defending the empire against the Seljuk Turks, Pope Urban II responded with a call for a holy war--a crusade. Thousands of Western European Christians responded. Beginning in 1095, the Crusades continued off and on until 1291, when they ended with the fall of the last Christian cities in Palestine. The Holy Land remained under Muslim rule.

The crusaders traveled to many places over long periods of time. They saw things they had never seen before and they introduced new ideas and culture to the people they came in contact with in the Holy Land and along the way. The impact of the Crusades changed the world forever.

Complete the Witness to the Crusades sheet, which contains excerpts from primary sources that describe events during the Crusades.

ASSESS

Lesson Assessment: Cultures in Conflict (*Online*)

You will complete an online assessment covering the main points of this lesson. Your assessment will be scored by the computer.

LEARN

Activity 2. Optional: Cultures in Conflict *(Online)*

Name Date

Witness to the Crusades

Read the following excerpts from writings by people who witnessed parts of the Crusades. Then answer the questions that follow each selection.

Call to the Crusades: Pope Urban II, 1095 A.D.
Now that you, O sons of God, have consecrated yourselves to God to maintain peace among yourselves more vigorously and to uphold the laws of the Church faithfully, there is work to do, for you must turn the strength of your sincerity, now that you are aroused by divine correction, to another affair that concerns you and God. Hastening to the way, you must help your brothers living in the Orient, who need your aid for which they have already cried out many times.

For, as most of you have been told, the Turks, a race of Persians, who have penetrated within the boundaries of Romania even to the Mediterranean to that point which they call the Arm of Saint George in occupying more and more of the lands of the Christians, have overcome them, already victims of seven battles, and have killed and captured them, have overthrown churches, and have laid waste God's kingdom. If you permit this supinely for very long, God's faithful ones will be still further subjected.

Concerning this affair, I, with suppliant prayer--not I but the Lord--exhort you, heralds of Christ, to persuade all of whatever class, both knights and footmen, both rich and poor in numerous edicts, to strive to help expel that wicked race from our Christian lands before it is too late.

I speak to those present, I send word to those not here; moreover, Christ commands it. Remission of sins will be granted for those going thither, if they end a shackled life either on land or in crossing the sea, or in struggling against the heathen. I, being vested with that gift from God, grant this to those who go.

1. The pope in this passage emphasizes the need to help Eastern Christians. Who are the Eastern Christians and why do they need help?

____

____

2. How would someone profit from becoming a crusader?

____

____

Witness to the Crusades

The Gesta Version: March to Jerusalem, 1099

We left the city on the second day of the week in the month of May and, passing along a narrow and difficult road all day and night, we came to a fortress, the name of which was Botroun. Then we came to a city called Gibilet near the sea, in which we suffered very great thirst, and, thus worn out, we reached a river named Ibrahim. Then on the eve of the day of the Ascension of the Lord we crossed a mountain in which the way was exceedingly narrow, and there we expected to find the enemy lying in ambush for us. But God favoring us, none of them dared to appear in our way. Then our knights went ahead of us and cleared the way before us, and we arrived at a city by the sea which was called Beirut, and thence we went to another city called Sidon, thence to another called Tyre, and from Tyre to the city of Acre.

Use the maps on pages 634-635 to answer the following questions:

3. Note the names of the four cities in the last sentence. In what modern countries was this crusader traveling?

____

4. What is the distance from Sidon to Acre?

____

Henry II, King of England – The Saladin Tithe, 1188

Each person will give in charity one tenth of his rents and movable goods for the taking of the land of Jerusalem; except for the arms, horses, and clothing of knights, and likewise for the horses, books, clothing, and vestments, and church furniture of the clergy, and except for precious stones belonging to the clergy or the laity.

But the clergy and knights who have taken the cross, shall give none of that tithe except from their own goods and the property of their lord; and whatever their men owe shall be collected for their use by the above and returned intact to them.

5. How did King Henry II plan to pay for the cost of sending crusaders from England to Jerusalem?

____

6. What did it mean to "take the cross"?

____

Witness to the Crusades

A Description of Western Peoples by a Muslim Observer, mid-thirteenth century
Frank-land, a mighty land and a broad kingdom in the realms of the Christians. Its cold is very great, and its air is thick because of the extreme cold. It is full of good things and fruits and crops, rich in rivers, plentiful of produce, possessing tillage and cattle, trees and honey. There is a wide variety of game there and also silver mines. They forge very sharp swords there, and the swords of Frank-land are keener than the swords of India.

Its people are Christians, and they have a king possessing courage, great numbers, and power to rule. He has two or three cities on the shore of the sea on this side, in the midst of the lands of Islam, and he protects them from his side. Whenever the Muslims send forces to them to capture them, he sends forces from his side to defend them. His soldiers are of mighty courage and in the hour of combat do not even think of flight, rather preferring death. But you shall see none more filthy than they. They are a people of perfidy and mean character. They do not cleanse or bathe themselves more than once or twice a year, and then in cold water, and they do not wash their garments from the time they put them on until they fall to pieces. They shave their beards, and after shaving they sprout only a revolting stubble.

7. What do the writer's comments reveal about how medieval Muslims might have viewed Christians?

____

____

8. What ideas about Muslims might a Crusader have taken home after spending time in Southwest Asia?

____

____

Student Guide
Lesson 13: Monarchs

Lesson Objectives

- Define *monarch.*
- Describe the Norman Conquest.
- Describe the most important characteristics of the growth of monarchies in Europe during the late Middle Ages.
- Identify William the Conqueror and his achievements.
- Analyze maps for information on England and France.

PREPARE

Approximate lesson time is 60 minutes.

Materials

For the Student

Reading Guide

The Norman Conquest

The Human Odyssey: Prehistory Through the Middle Ages edited by Klee, Cribb, and Holdren

History Journal

LEARN

Activity 1: William the Conqueror: A Strong Monarch *(Offline)*

Instructions

Read

When assigned an event to cover, reporters don't immediately begin writing a story. They first gather information about the event. They interview people and collect background information. As a reporter covering the Norman Conquest, you need to gather information that answers those ever-important questions: *who, what, where, when, why,* and *how.*

The Reading Guide will help you gather and organize information as you read Chapter 9, from the beginning to "Henry II Strengthens the Throne," pages 561-564.

When you have completed the Reading Guide, compare your information with the information in the Lesson Answer Key.

Focus on Geography

As with many important events in history, geography and weather played an important role in the Norman Conquest. Use the atlas in the back of your textbook to help you complete the Norman Conquest sheet.

ASSESS

Lesson Assessment: Monarchs (*Online*)

You will complete an online assessment covering the main points of this lesson. Your assessment will be scored by the computer.

LEARN

Activity 2. Optional: Monarchs *(Online)*

Name Date

Reading Guide

Newspaper reports contain responses to many questions, the most typical of which are *who, what, where, when, why,* and *how.* Suppose you had been a reporter covering the Norman Conquest. How would you have answered those questions in an article about the conquest? There is one additional question to answer: *And so?* In other words, what resulted from this event? Complete this sheet as you read Chapter 9, from the beginning to "Henry II Strengthens the Throne," pages 560 to 564.

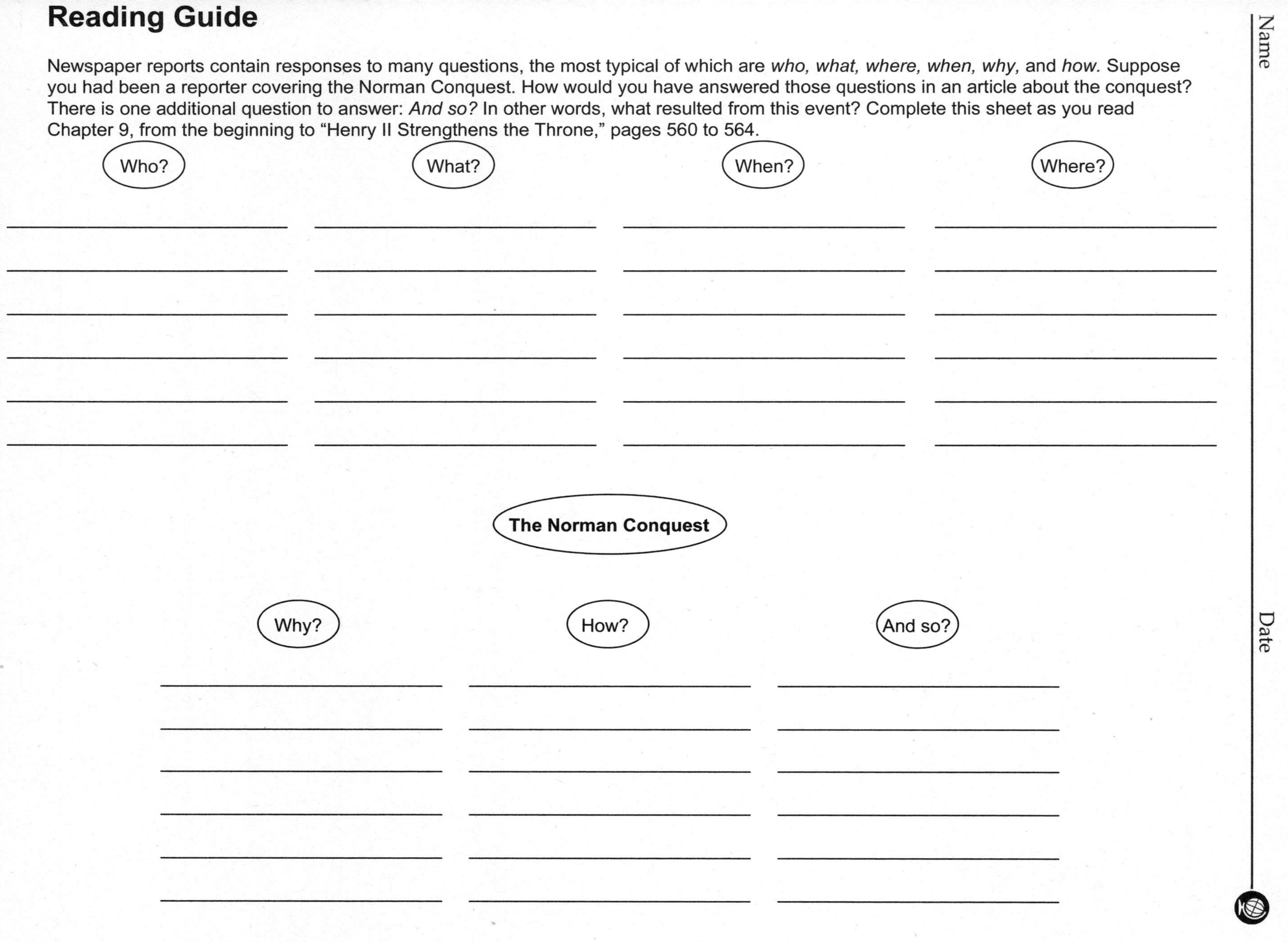

Name Date

The Norman Conquest

Use the map on page 3 of this activity, and the atlas in the back of your textbook to answer the following questions:

After William established his reign in Normandy he set his sights on the fertile lands of England, across the English Channel. One possible reason for his choice was England's proximity to Normandy. The region was also desirable because it has a mild climate and fertile farmlands.

1. England lies along the same latitudes as Denmark and parts of Canada and Russia, but it enjoys a milder climate and a longer growing season. Why is its climate different from other regions at the same latitudes? What kind of climate does England have?

____

____

Ships and men from Brittany, Flanders, Maine, Bologne and other parts of France made up the Norman invasion force. They first gathered near the Norman town of Caen. William had chosen Pevensey, in England, as the landing spot for his forces, and wanted to cross the channel at a location closer to his intended target. His choice for a jumping off point - Saint-Valéry-sur-Somme.

2. As his ships could generally sail only in the direction the wind was blowing, out of which direction did the wind need to blow in order for him to sail his fleet toward Saint-Valéry-sur-Somme? _____________

3. Once his fleet had reached Saint-Valéry-sur-Somme, the jumping off point for the crossing, he had to wait again for the weather to change. Now he needed the wind to blow out of which direction? _____________

All summer, the English had feared an invasion. They had gathered forces around the Pevensey-Hastings area in anticipation of an invasion from Normandy. Around the first week in September, however, they dispersed their fleet and disbanded the army.

4. Why did the English not fear an invasion after the end of summer? (You'll need to do a little extra research outside the book for this one. Here's a hint: It has to do with the weather!)

____

____

5. About how many miles did the Norman invasion fleet have to cross to get from Saint-Valéry-sur-Somme to Pevensey? _____________

6. If the boats in William's fleet averaged four miles an hour, how long would it have taken the invasion force to cross the Channel? ___________

Name _______________________________________ Date _______________________

After William defeated Harold at Hastings, he turned England into a well-organized feudal state where knights pledged their allegiance to him instead of to barons and lords. This was the beginning of strong monarchs in Western Europe.

7. What is a *monarch* and what is the origin of the word? ____________________________

____

Explore

Weather played an important part in the Norman Conquest. More than 800 years later, weather would again play an important role when another invasion force planned to cross the English Channel. Find out how weather influenced the planning of Operations Neptune and Overlord, the D-Day invasion of June 6, 1944, at http://www.metoffice.gov.uk/learning/library/publications/historical-facts.

Name Date

The Norman Conquest

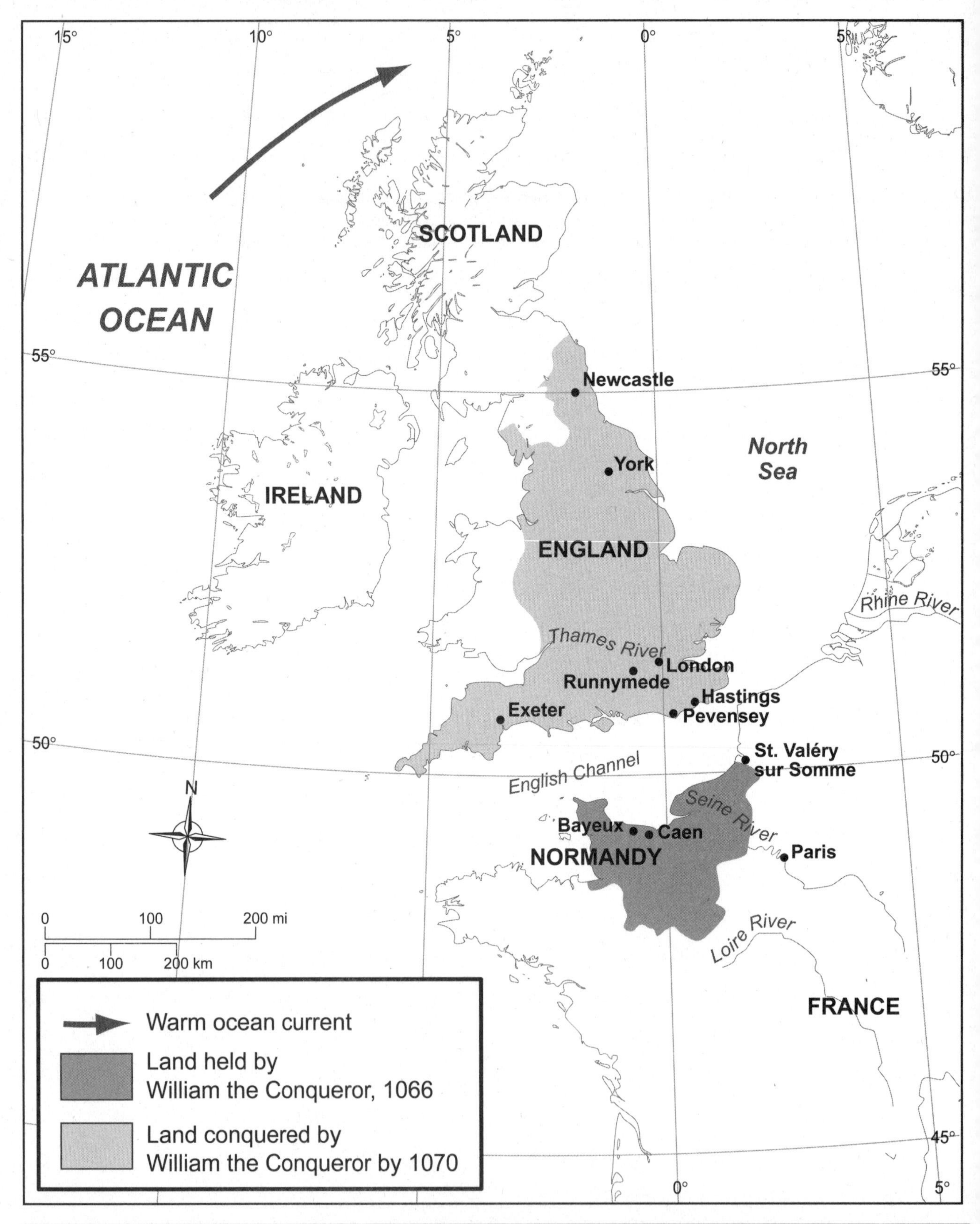

Student Guide
Lesson 14: New Ideas of Justice

Lesson Objectives

- Define *common law* and *jury.*
- Recognize ways in which monarchs consolidated power.
- Identify Henry II and his legacy.

PREPARE

Approximate lesson time is 60 minutes.

Materials

For the Student

The Human Odyssey: Prehistory Through the Middle Ages edited by Klee, Cribb, and Holdren

Keywords and Pronunciation

Aquitaine (A-kwuh-tayn)

Henry II : the great-grandson of William I who gave England a new system of justice that included courts, juries, common law, and uniform treatment of legal cases

---

LEARN

Activity 1: New Ideas of Justice *(Offline)*

Activity 2: New Ideas of Justice *(Online)*

Activity 3: Understanding Eleanor of Aquitaine *(Online)*

ASSESS

Lesson Assessment: New Ideas of Justice (*Online*)

You will complete an online assessment covering the main points of this lesson. Your assessment will be scored by the computer.

Student Guide
Lesson 15: Limiting Power

The Magna Carta was written in 1215, but its influence stretched far beyond its time. English barons forced King John to sign the Magna Carta, which formally recognized the nobles' ancient rights and limits on taxation. The nobles insisted that copies of the document be made so it could be read aloud in every county in the kingdom. The Magna Carta made legal and official the idea that no one in England, not even the king, had absolute power. With the signing of the Magna Carta, the journey toward constitutional government had begun.

Lesson Objectives

- Explain why the Magna Carta was written and describe its key arguments.
- Explain the Magna Carta's legacy to democratic government.
- Analyze excerpts from the Magna Carta to assess its impact on future political thought.

PREPARE

Approximate lesson time is 60 minutes.

Materials

For the Student

Examining the Magna Carta

The Human Odyssey: Prehistory Through the Middle Ages edited by Klee, Cribb, and Holdren

---

LEARN
Activity 1: The Great Charter *(Offline)*

Instructions

Read and Check Your Reading

Read Chapter 9 from "The Magna Carta" to the end, pages 566-569. Then answer the following questions about this important document:

1. Why did the nobles demand that King John sign the Magna Carta?
2. What did the Magna Carta say about taxes?
3. Why did King John agree to sign the Magna Carta?
4. Why was the Magna Carta important to future generations?

Use What You Know

Examining the Magna Carta

The Magna Carta is one of the most important documents ever written, so it is important for you to understand it. In this activity you will read excerpts from the Magna Carta. Each excerpt is followed by a series of questions to help you decode the language. Here's a good study hint: read the questions first. Complete the Examining the Magna Carta sheet.

ASSESS

Lesson Assessment: Limiting Power (*Online*)

You will complete an online assessment covering the main points of this lesson. Your assessment will be scored by the computer.

LEARN

Activity 2. Optional: Limiting Power *(Online)*

Name ____ Date ______________________

Examining the Magna Carta

Understanding the Magna Carta, a primary source document, can be a challenge. In decoding difficult texts it is often a good idea to read sections aloud and summarize them as you go. Below are several excerpts that highlight the main ideas of the Magna Carta. For each excerpt you should:

- Read the text aloud.
- Follow the instructions below the excerpt and answer the questions to help you break the information into pieces that you can summarize.

Excerpt One, from the Preamble
"Know ye that we, unto the honour of Almighty God, and for the salvation of the souls of our progenitors and successors, Kings of England, to the advancement of holy Church, and amendment of our Realm, of our meer and free will, have given and granted to all Archbishops, Bishops, Abbots, Priors, Earls, Barons, and to all freemen of this our realm, these liberties following, to be kept in our kingdom of England for ever."

It may surprise you to learn that the Magna Carta did not apply to everyone. But the term "freemen" in this sentence would eventually refer to all Englishmen. The Magna Carta set a precedent for written guarantees of rights. Read the questions below, then re-read this very long sentence from the Magna Carta and answer the questions.

1. What is the simple subject of the sentence (the person, place, thing, or idea that is doing the action)?

   ____

2. What is the verb in the sentence (the action)?

   ____

3. What is the direct object of the sentence (answers the question "what")?

   ____

4. Who will receive the liberties promised by the Magna Carta and how long will they last?

   ____

   ____

5. Who is making this promise?

   ____

Examining the Magna Carta

6. Restate the sentence in simpler terms:

____

____

____

Excerpt Two, Section 14

"A Freeman shall not be amerced [punished] for a small fault, but after the manner of the fault; and for a great fault after the greatness thereof, saving to him his contenement [means of making a living]; and a Merchant likewise, saving to him his Merchandise...And none of the said amerciaments [punishments] shall be assessed, but by the oath of honest and lawful men of the vicinage [area or neighborhood]. Earls and Barons shall not be amerced [punished] but by their Peers, and after the manner of their offence."

According to this section:

7. Who can punish a freeman?

____

8. Who can punish Earls and Barons?

____

9. Restate the idea of the passage in simpler terms:

____

____

____

Excerpt Three, Section 21

"No Sheriff nor Bailiff of ours, or any other, shall take the Horses or Carts of any man to make carriage, except he pay the old price limited, that is to say, for carriage with two horse, x.d. a day; for three horse, xiv.d. a day. Nor we, nor our Bailiffs, nor any other, shall take any man's wood for our Castles, or other our necessaries to be done, but by the licence [permission] of him whose wood it shall be."

10. What kind of action by government officials does this passage address?

____

11. What does this passage guarantee?

____

____

Examining the Magna Carta

Excerpt Four, Section 29

"No Freeman shall be taken, or imprisoned, or be disseised [denied] of his Freehold [land], or Liberties, or free Customs, or be outlawed, or exiled, or any otherwise destroyed; nor will we pass upon him, nor condemn him, but by lawful Judgment of his Peers...."

According to the passage:

12. Who has the power to punish, imprison, or fine a freeman?

____

Excerpt Five, Section 34

"No Man shall be taken or imprisoned upon the Appeal of a Woman for the Death of any other, than of her husband."

13. What situation does this passage address?

____

14. What does this passage say would happen if someone was murdered who was not the woman's husband?

____

____

Excerpt Six, Section 8

"No widow shall be compelled to marry, so long as she wishes to remain without a husband. But she must give security that she will not marry without royal consent, if she holds her lands of the Crown, or without the consent of whatever other lord she may hold them of."

15. Restate in simpler terms:

____

____

16. What can you infer from this section and the one before about the rights of women?

____

____

Examining the Magna Carta

Thinking Cap Questions

1. What do we call the group of "honest and lawful men of the neighborhood" that decide guilt today?

   ____

2. What American documents have some similarities to the Magna Carta?

   ____

3. What examples of the importance of written law have you seen in earlier eras?

   ____

   ____

Student Guide
Lesson 16: Unit Review

PREPARE

Approximate lesson time is 60 minutes.

LEARN
Activity 1: A Look Back *(Online)*
Instructions

In this unit you learned about the fall of the Roman Empire, barbarians invasions, societal arrangements meant to provide protection and safety, and wars between Christians and Muslims. How did people survive this dangerous time? Eventually, they developed new systems of government and new ideas about power and justice.

Student Guide
Lesson 17: Unit Assessment

Lesson Objectives
- Recognize how the fall of Rome affected culture and civilization in Western Europe.
- Describe the role of the Christian church, including monasteries and individuals, in preserving learning in Europe and in spreading Christianity.
- Identify important events, individuals, and groups in the development of a new social structure in Western Europe between A.D. 500 and 1000.
- Identify important characteristics of European culture in the Middle Ages.
- Recognize important contributions and legacies of medieval England to the development of democracy.
- Describe key causes, results, events, and individuals of the Crusades.
- Identify geographic characteristics of Western Europe.
- Use maps to trace the routes of the Barbarian invasions.
- Identify important events and people in the development of monarchies in Western Europe during the late Middle Ages.
- Describe the structure and role of feudalism.

PREPARE
Approximate lesson time is 60 minutes.

Materials
For the Student

Question Review Table

ASSESS
Unit Assessment: In Western Europe, Part 1 (*Online*)
Complete the computer-scored portion of the Unit Assessment. When you have finished, complete the teacher-scored portion of the assessment and submit it to your teacher.

Unit Assessment: In Western Europe, Part 2 (*Offline*)
Complete the teacher-scored portion of the Unit Assessment and submit it to your teacher.

LEARN
Activity 1: Unit Assessment Review Table *(Online)*

Assessment Date

Unit 12: In Western Europe

Before you retake the Unit Assessment, use the table to figure out which activities you should review.

Question Review Table

Circle the numbers of the questions that you missed on the Unit Assessment. Review the activities that correspond with these questions.

In Western Europe, Part 1

Question	Lesson	Review Activity
1	1: Where to Turn?	Check Your Reading
2,5,19	2: Monasteries Carry On	Monks and Monasteries
3,11	3: Charlemagne	Check Your Reading Charlemagne's Empire
4,6,8,9,16	12: Cultures in Conflict	Read
7	14: New Ideas of Justice	Understanding Eleanor of Aquitaine
10	10: Christendom	Faith and Logic
12,13,14,15	5: Viking Ventures	Focus on Geography
17,21	13: Monarchs	William the Conqueror: A Strong Monarch
18	11: Building on Faith	Read
20	15: Limiting Power	The Great Charter

In Western Europe, Part 2

Question	Lesson	Review Activity
6	2: Monasteries Carry On	Monks and Monasteries
1, 2, 3	5: Viking Ventures	Focus on Geography
7	15: Limiting Power	The Great Charter
4,5	7: The Structure of Medieval Society	Chivalry Lives!

Student Guide

Unit 13: From East Asia to Western Europe Again

Lesson 1: A New Dynasty

China, the longest continuous civilization in the world, entered a golden age under the Tang dynasty. The Chinese produced exceptional poetry, paintings, and porcelain, and their inventions--like the compass and fireworks--changed the world. Even when fierce Mongol invaders took over China's government and, for a time, ruled the largest empire in the world, Chinese civilization lived on. Meanwhile in Europe, wars and plague brought calamity and change.

Lesson Objectives

- List examples of ways in which governments unite nations.
- Identify the Sui dynasty (as the family of rulers who reunited China in the sixth and seventh centuries) and its main achievements.
- Define *bureaucracy*.
- Describe the role of the Grand Canal in uniting China and in ending the Sui dynasty.

PREPARE

Approximate lesson time is 60 minutes.

Materials

For the Student

- Linking China: The Grand Canal
- Reading Guide
- The Human Odyssey: Prehistory Through the Middle Ages edited by Klee, Cribb, and Holdren

Keywords and Pronunciation

bureaucracy (byur-AH-kruh-see) : a group of officials who help run a government or other organization
Chang'an (chahng-en)
Han (hahn)
Hangzhou (hahng-JOH)
Huang He (hwahng hou)
Qin Shi Huangdi (chin shur hwahng-dee)
Song (soong)
Sui (sway)
Sui dynasty : the family of rulers who reunited China in the sixth and seventh centuries
Tang (tahng)
Wendi (wen-DEE)
Xi´an (shee-ahn)
Yangdi (YAHNG-dou)

LEARN

Activity 1: Restoring an Empire *(Offline)*

Read

Read Chapter 10, from the beginning to "A Golden Age Under the Tang Dynasty," pages 571-575. As you read, answer the questions in the first section of the Reading Guide, China in the Sui Dynasty.

Then, think back to other cultures you've studied. You've learned about the rise and fall of many great empires and civilizations. Recall some of the cultures and rulers you've studied to answer the questions in the second section of the Reading Guide, Think About It. Look through your History Journal to find information from previous lessons to help you answer the questions.

When you have finished the Reading Guide, compare your answers to those in the Lesson Answer Key.

Focus on Geography

The Grand Canal was a remarkable feat of engineering. The interconnecting waterways cover a distance of 1,200 miles and unite China from north to south. Complete the Linking China: The Grand Canal sheet to see what you recall about the canal's impact on China.

ASSESS

Lesson Assessment: A New Dynasty (*Online*)

You will complete an online assessment covering the main points of this lesson. Your assessment will be scored by the computer.

LEARN

Activity 2. Optional: A New Dynasty *(Online)*

Name ______________________________ Date ______________________________

Reading Guide

China in the Sui Dynasty

1. Write a definition or short description of:

   bureaucracy

   ____

   Sui dynasty

   ____

Answer the following questions:

2. In the seventh century, how did China differ from Europe in size, organization, and government?

   ____

   ____

3. What steps did Emperor Wendi take to unify China?

   ____

   ____

   ____

   ____

   ____

   ____

4. Describe the Grand Canal.

   ____

   ____

5. How did the Grand Canal help unite China?

   ____

   ____

   ____

6. How did the building of the Grand Canal contribute to the end of the Sui dynasty?

   ____

   ____

Reading Guide

Think About It

Answer the following questions:

7. What dynasties, governments, rulers, or empires come to mind when you think of large areas that were united under one rule?

8. What are some strategies or general practices that rulers throughout history have used to unite diverse people under one rule? In other words, what have rulers done to hold their empires together?

9. Do you see any common or repeated reasons that great empires declined?

Name Date

Linking China: The Grand Canal

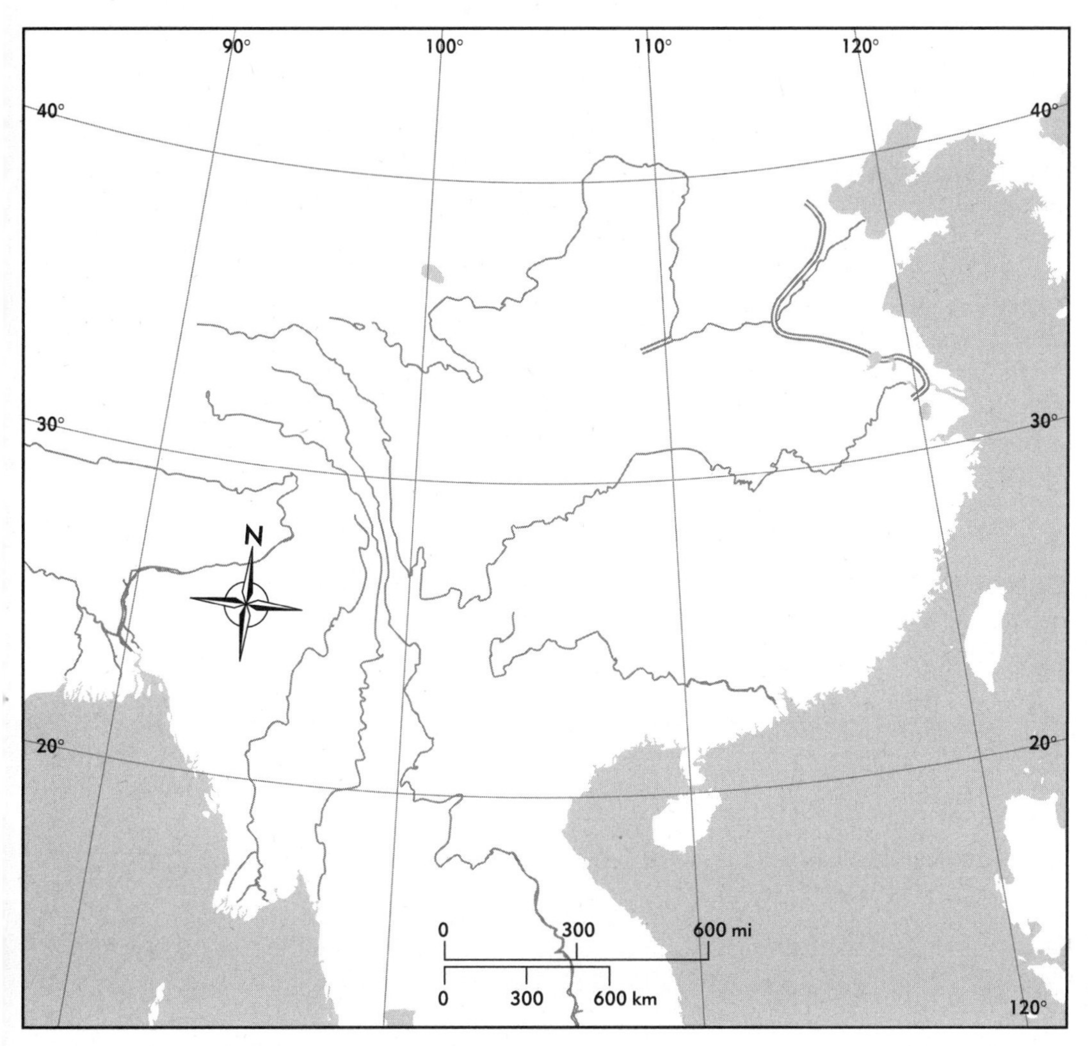

1. Using the chapter and atlas maps, label the following places on the map above. Keep in mind that latitude and longitude coordinates are very helpful in transferring information from one map to another.

a. Yellow (Huang He) River
b. Yangtze River
c. Beijing
d. Hangzhou
e. Chang'an
f. Grand Canal

Linking China: The Grand Canal

2. What two present-day cities does the Grand Canal connect?

____

3. What two rivers does the Grand Canal connect?

____

4. In what direction do China's major rivers flow?

____

5. In what direction does the Grand Canal run?

____

6. Think back to what you learned about the unification of Egypt thousands of years ago. The Grand Canal has been called the "artificial Nile." Explain why this name is appropriate for the Grand Canal.

____

____

____

____

Student Guide
Lesson 2: Changing the Earth

Lesson Objectives

- Explain why people build canals and describe the challenges in building them.
- List examples of major canals around the world.
- Review the geographic concept of human-environment interaction.
- Identify the reign of the Tang dynasty as a golden age for China.
- Identify the Tang era as the high point of trade on the Silk Road.
- Trace on a time line critical events of the Tang and Song dynasties.
- Recognize internal and external reasons for the fall of the Song dynasty.

PREPARE

Approximate lesson time is 60 minutes.

Materials

For the Student

The Human Odyssey: Prehistory Through the Middle Ages edited by Klee, Cribb, and Holdren

History Journal

Keywords and Pronunciation

Sui (sway)

LEARN

Activity 1: Changing the Earth *(Online)*

Human-Environment Interaction: Canals

Answer the questions to explore why people interact with the environment by building canals. Use the atlas in your textbook if you need help locating the canals.

1. Why do people try to change their natural environment?
2. What two large bodies of water does the Panama Canal link?
3. The Suez Canal is sometimes considered the boundary between what two continents?
4. Ships traveling through the Suez Canal save thousands of miles on their route between what two bodies of water?
5. Through what modern nation does the Suez Canal pass?
6. Use the maps to locate the Erie Canal and the St. Lawrence Seaway. What do you think was the goal of these two projects? Hint: Look at the location of the two waterways.
7. Summarize the purpose(s) behind great canal-building projects such as the Grand Canal, the Panama Canal, the Suez Canal, and the Erie Canal.
8. What were some of the challenges in building large canals such as Grand Canal, the Panama Canal, the Suez Canal, and the Erie Canal?
9. Explain how canal building is an example of human interaction with the environment. Think about the ways people adapt to their environment and the ways they modify their environment.

Activity 2: Changing the Earth *(Online)*

Activity 3: Changing the Earth *(Offline)*

A New Canal?

Imagine that you have been chosen to develop a new canal system. Before you choose where to build your canal, you must formulate a plan and ask questions of people who have built canals before.

1. In your History Journal, formulate three or four questions you might want to ask before choosing your location and beginning your project.
   - Keep in mind that canal building takes imagination, courage, and hard work.
   - Be sure to ask questions that will help you identify your purpose and the challenges you will face.
2. Use your atlas or the online maps in Grolier's online encyclopedia to pinpoint a logical area to build the canal. In your History Journal, name the location and answer the questions you developed in Question 1.

ASSESS

Lesson Assessment: Changing the Earth (*Online*)

You will complete an online assessment covering the main points of this lesson. Your assessment will be scored by the computer.

LEARN

Activity 4: Changing the Earth *(Offline)*

Read Chapter 10 from "A Golden Age Under the Tang Dynasty" to the end, pages 576-581.

Student Guide
Lesson 3: A Golden Age

Lesson Objectives

- Identify the reign of the Tang dynasty as a golden age for China.
- Identify the Tang era as the high point of trade on the Silk Road.
- Trace on a time line critical events of the Tang and Song dynasties.
- Recognize internal and external reasons for the fall of the Song dynasty.

PREPARE

Approximate lesson time is 60 minutes.

Materials

For the Student

The Human Odyssey: Prehistory Through the Middle Ages edited by Klee, Cribb, and Holdren

Tang and Song

Keywords and Pronunciation

Chang'an (chahng-en)
Mongols (MAHNG-guhls) : mounted warriors from central Asia who conquered northern China
Song (soong)
Tang (tahng)
Xuanzong (shoo-en-dzawng)

LEARN

Activity 1: A Golden Age *(Online)*

Activity 2: Focus on Geography *(Online)*

A Chinese proverb describes porcelain as "whiter than jade and thinner than paper." Click Porcelain to find out more about this prized export of China.

Activity 3: A Golden Age *(Offline)*

ASSESS

Lesson Assessment: A Golden Age (*Online*)

You will complete an online assessment covering the main points of this lesson. Your assessment will be scored by the computer.

LEARN

Activity 4. Optional: A Golden Age *(Online)*

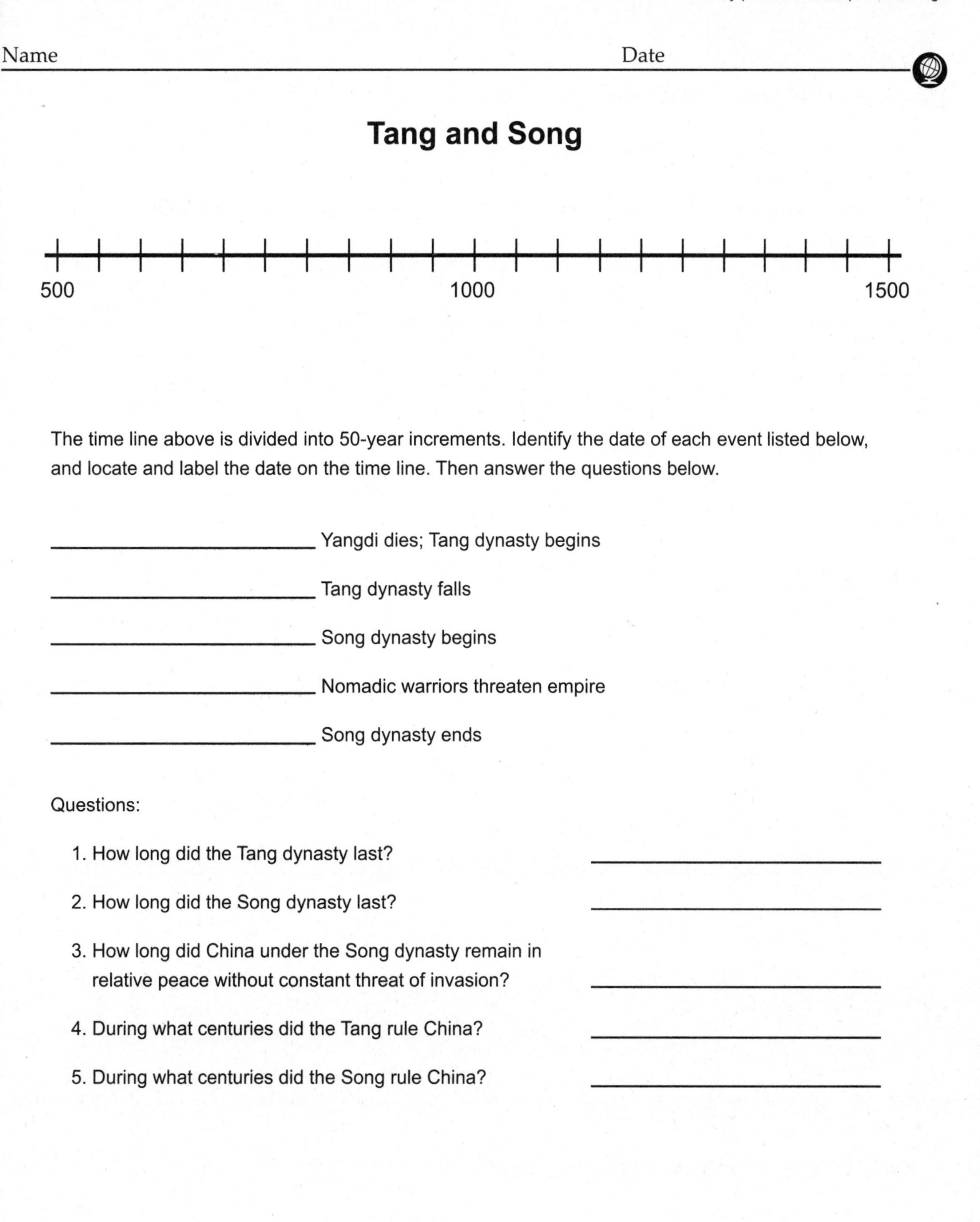

Name ______________________ Date ______________________

Tang and Song

The time line above is divided into 50-year increments. Identify the date of each event listed below, and locate and label the date on the time line. Then answer the questions below.

______________________ Yangdi dies; Tang dynasty begins

______________________ Tang dynasty falls

______________________ Song dynasty begins

______________________ Nomadic warriors threaten empire

______________________ Song dynasty ends

Questions:

1. How long did the Tang dynasty last? ______________________
2. How long did the Song dynasty last? ______________________
3. How long did China under the Song dynasty remain in relative peace without constant threat of invasion? ______________________
4. During what centuries did the Tang rule China? ______________________
5. During what centuries did the Song rule China? ______________________

Student Guide
Lesson 4: Remarkable Achievements

Lesson Objectives

- List examples of cultural and political innovations and inventions in China under the Tang and Song dynasties.
- Analyze art and technologies of China for information on the culture and values.
- Identify the Mongols.
- Describe the Mongols' nomadic way of life and the reasons for it.
- Recognize geographic features of Mongolia and surrounding regions.

PREPARE

Approximate lesson time is 60 minutes.

Materials

For the Student

The Human Odyssey: Prehistory Through the Middle Ages edited by Klee, Cribb, and Holdren

Analyzing Art and Artifacts

History Journal

LEARN
Activity 1: Remarkable Achievements *(Online)*

Activity 2: Analyzing Art and Artifacts *(Online)*

ASSESS
Lesson Assessment: Remarkable Achievements (*Online*)

You will complete an online assessment covering the main points of this lesson. Your assessment will be scored by the computer.

LEARN
Activity 3: Remarkable Achievements *(Offline)*

Activity 4. Optional: Remarkable Achievements *(Online)*

Remarkable Achievements

Analyzing Art and Artifacts

Analyze each image and jot down some notes about what you observed. Then, use your observations to make some deductions about culture and values during the Tang and Song dynasties. The first image has been done for you.

Observations Under each description, write what you observed about each artwork or artifact. Look for details in each image.	**Prior Knowledge** Describe what you know about the object or the time period it comes from.	**Inferences** What does the art or object tell you about the values and culture? In other words, what can you infer about the culture by looking at the image?
Horse-and-rider figurines They are small ceramic sculptures. The horses look strong and well bred. The artist included saddles, bridles, and other details.	Horses were imported from Persia. Nobles played polo—a game from the West—riding Persian horses. Artisans refined the art of making ceramics, such as porcelain, which became valuable all over the world.	Horses were important to the military and to the noble classes. A fine horse was probably a status symbol. People liked art that portrayed real life, and they valued attention to detail.
Tricolored pot with phoenix head		
Two-humped Bactrian camels		
Civil service exam		
Landscape showing village amidst rivers and mountains		
Early papermaking		
Chinese compass, 220 B.C.		
Ancient Chinese musical instruments		

Thinking Cap Question

Reread the two-paragraph description of China's capitol of Chang'an on Page 576, starting with "Meanwhile China's capitol…"

What connection do you see between the characteristics of life in Chang'an and the artistic and technological innovations produced in China during this time?

Student Guide
Lesson 5. Optional: Your Choice

You may use today's lesson time to do one or more of the following:

- Complete work in progress.
- Complete the Beyond the Lesson activity in any lesson in this unit.
- Review the Classical World Time Line in the Resources section.
- Prepare for your state standardized test.
- Go on to the next lesson.

Please mark this lesson complete to proceed to the next lesson in the course.

PREPARE

Approximate lesson time is 60 minutes.

Student Guide
Lesson 6: The Mongols

Lesson Objectives

- Identify the Mongols.
- Describe the Mongols' nomadic way of life and the reasons for it.
- Recognize geographic features of Mongolia and surrounding regions.
- Identify Genghis Khan and the methods he used to gain power.
- Identify Kublai Khan and the characteristics of his rule.
- Recognize the extent of the Mongol empire and the countries that lie within its ancient borders today.

PREPARE

Approximate lesson time is 60 minutes.

Materials

For the Student

Steppe Geography

The Human Odyssey: Prehistory Through the Middle Ages edited by Klee, Cribb, and Holdren

---

LEARN
Activity 1: The Mongols *(Online)*

Activity 2: Focus on Geography *(Online)*

Activity 3: Working with Maps *(Offline)*

ASSESS
Lesson Assessment: The Mongols (*Online*)

You will complete an online assessment covering the main points of this lesson. Your assessment will be scored by the computer.

LEARN
Activity 4: The Mongols *(Offline)*

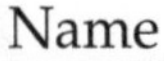

Name ______________________________ Date ______________________

Working with Maps

Steppe Geography

Answer the following questions:

1. Look at the World Political Map on pages 624-625 in your textbook and find Mongolia in Asia. What latitude line runs through the center of Mongolia?

   ____

2. Turn to the Climate Zones map on page 640. What is Mongolia's dominant climate?

   ____

3. Now look at the Terrestrial Biomes map on page 641. What is Mongolia's dominant biome?

   ____

4. You'll notice that the same climate and biome stretch in a band all the way across Asia to the Black Sea. Where else in the world do you see large areas of steppe and temperate prairie?

   ____________________ ____________________

   ____________________ ____________________

5. At about what latitude do these regions lie in the Northern Hemisphere? ______________

   In the Southern Hemisphere? ____________________

6. Now turn to the World Physical map on pages 622-623. The kind of land you have been looking at is a steppe. The region of South America that has a similar climate and biome is called the ______________. The steppe region of the United States and Canada is known as the ______________ ______________.

7. The dry grasslands of Asia, Australia, Africa, South America, and North America border or partially surround ______________ , which have an even drier climate.

Thinking Cap Question

8. You have read that the Mongols were nomads who followed herds of yaks and goats across the treeless steppes, carrying their homes (gers) with them. How does this way of life compare to that of the early people of the American Great Plains?

   ____

   ____

   ____

Student Guide
Lesson 7: Conquering Khans

The Mongol Empire didn't last as long as some other empires, but it was the largest land empire in all of history. How did the Mongols conquer such a vast territory, and what was the empire like?

Lesson Objectives

- Identify Genghis Khan and the methods he used to gain power.
- Identify Kublai Khan and the characteristics of his rule.
- Recognize the extent of the Mongol empire and the countries that lie within its ancient borders today.

PREPARE

Approximate lesson time is 60 minutes.

Materials

For the Student

The Human Odyssey: Prehistory Through the Middle Ages edited by Klee, Cribb, and Holdren

---

LEARN

Activity 1: Conquering Khans *(Online)*

Activity 2: Focus on Geography *(Offline)*

Instructions

Geography of the Khan Empire

1. Locate the Mongol Empire on the map on pages 588-589 of your textbook. Use the map and the atlas in the back of the book to identify present-day countries that lie within the territory that Kublai Khan controlled.
2. What was the distance from the easternmost edge of the empire to the westernmost border?
3. What was the empire's distance from north to south along the 60° E longitude line?
4. Do you know how to estimate square miles to find the total area of a country or region? Multiply the empire's distance from east to west by the distance from north to south. How many square miles did the Mongol Empire encompass?
5. According to the 2004 World Almanac, the United States covers 3,535,000 square miles. How much larger was Kublai Khan's empire?
6. Identify five mountain ranges the Mongol Empire encompassed. Look at several maps--there are more than five possible answers.
7. What kinds of climates did the empire include?
8. What parts of Asia did the Mongols fail to control?

Activity 3: Conquering Khans *(Online)*

Genghis Khan was the first leader to unite the Mongol tribes into one nation, but his grandson Kublai Khan expanded the empire to encompass all of China. Find out how Kublai Khan ruled this huge territory this as you read Chapter 11 from "Kublai Khan: Conqueror and Builder" to the end, pages 588-595.

Activity 4: Conquering Khans *(Online)*

ASSESS

Lesson Assessment: Conquering Khans (*Online*)

You will complete an online assessment covering the main points of this lesson. Your assessment will be scored by the computer.

LEARN

Activity 5. Optional: Conquering Khans *(Online)*

Student Guide
Lesson 8: A World Traveler

Curiosity and a desire for new products lead to exploration. In the thirteenth century it was mainly Italian merchants who established trade with the Chinese. One young Italian ventured far beyond the rest. Out of his journey came one of the greatest "travelogues" ever written--Marco Polo's *A Description of the World.* Marco Polo's account of his adventures inspired future explorers, including one of the most celebrated of all--Christopher Columbus.

Not long after Marco Polo made his legendary journeys, another traveler kept a detailed record of his own adventures. Click World Traveler to find out about this famous adventurer and writer.

Lesson Objectives

- Identify Marco Polo.
- Analyze excerpts of Marco Polo's writings to gain information on travel in the thirteenth century.

PREPARE

Approximate lesson time is 60 minutes.

Materials

For the Student

The Human Odyssey: Prehistory Through the Middle Ages edited by Klee, Cribb, and Holdren

---

LEARN

Activity 1: A World Traveler *(Online)*

Instructions

1. Visit the websites listed online.

2. Create your travel brochure to get people interested in following part of Marco Polo's route. Write short narratives describing historical and/or interesting sites that a tourist might enjoy visiting. Consider using some of Marco Polo's own words from the websites. Illustrate some features that you think might entice people to travel that part of the route. For example, if your brochure includes Sumatra you might draw the "unicorn of Sumatra"--a rhinoceros. Finally, provide a map of the route. To make the brochure:
   - Prepare a letter-size sheet of paper by folding it twice--once horizontally and once vertically. This will give you several small areas and one large area inside the brochure.
   - From your notes, choose the information you want to include.
   - Decide where you will put different facts that travelers need to know. For example, you might include information about accommodations on the back of the brochure.
   - Try to balance text with illustrations. Remember, your goal is to entice travelers to visit the distant lands.
   - Create an attractive, colorful cover for your brochure.

3. Then, in your History Journal, make a brief list of information for tourists who want to know about difficulties they might face when traveling Marco Polo's route. This list might include places they would encounter harsh climate, rough terrain, or other obstacles.

ASSESS

Lesson Assessment: A World Traveler (*Online*)

You will complete an online assessment covering the main points of this lesson. Your assessment will be scored by the computer.

LEARN

Activity 2. Optional: A World Traveler *(Online)*

This activity is OPTIONAL. It's provided for enrichment or extra practice, but not required for completion of this lesson. You may skip this activity.

Go back and revisit any of the websites to learn more about Marco Polo's travels and observations.

Student Guide

Lesson 9: How Many Years of War?

When Marco Polo returned from Asia, Europe seemed to be enjoying a period of peace and prosperity. But within three decades, the picture had changed completely. Europeans faced famine, war, and devastating disease.

Lesson Objectives

- Summarize the story of Joan of Arc.
- Describe the causes of the Hundred Years' War.
- Explain how advances in technology affected the conduct of the war.
- Recognize the results of the Hundred Years' War.

PREPARE

Approximate lesson time is 60 minutes.

LEARN

Activity 1: How Many Years of War? *(Offline)*

Instructions

Read Chapter 12, Europe's Calamitous Fourteenth Century, from the beginning to "The Black Death," pages 597-601. As you read, answer the following questions.

1. What happened in Europe during the 1200s that seemed to put Europe on track for a bright future?

    ____

    ____

2. What three things happened during the fourteenth century that led historians to call it "the calamitous fourteenth century"?

    ____

    ____

    ____

3. What caused the Hundred Years' War?

    ____

    ____

4. What developments in technology and war tactics changed the way people fought wars during the fourteenth century?

    ____

    ____

5. What was the final outcome of the Hundred Years' War?

    ____

    ____

Activity 2: Looking at Art *(Online)*

Instructions

La Pucelle! **by Frank Craig**

1. Describe the action you see in the painting.

____

____

2. Who is the central figure? How does the artist draw your eye to the central figure?

____

____

____

____

3. How does the artist convey strength and/or weakness? Good and/or evil?

____

____

____

____

4. Do you think Joan looks heroic? Explain.

____

____

5. Frank Craig completed *La Pucelle!* in 1907. Is it a primary source on the Hundred Years' War? Why or why not?

____

____

____

____

Activity 3: How Many Years of War? *(Online)*

ASSESS

Lesson Assessment: How Many Years of War? (*Online*)

You will complete an online assessment covering the main points of this lesson. Your assessment will be scored by the computer.

Student Guide
Lesson 10: Plague!

Despite famine and war, Europe's population grew and prospered after 1100, but in the mid-1300s, something happened that shook society to its foundations. In 1347, a mysterious disease from Asia entered Italy and swept through Western Europe. Historians estimate that one-third to one-half of Europe's population died from the plague. How did the loss of so many people affect medieval Europe? How did society change?

Lesson Objectives

- Explain how the Black Death started and describe its effects on Europe.
- Recognize the consequences of the plague on Europe's social structure.
- Explain how Europe changed and how it stayed the same after the plague.

PREPARE

Approximate lesson time is 60 minutes.

Materials

For the Student

The Human Odyssey: Prehistory Through the Middle Ages edited by Klee, Cribb, and Holdren

History Journal

Keywords and Pronunciation

Messina (meh-SEE-nah)

LEARN

Activity 1: Plague! *(Offline)*

Read Chapter 12, from "The Black Death" to the end, pages 601-603.

Focus on Geography

Use the map of the Plague's Progress on page 602 of your textbook to answer the following questions:

1. Describe where the plague spread and name some of the places that it directly affected. How long did it take to spread to those areas?

2. You have learned how goods, innovations, and ideas spread from one place to another. How does the spread of the Black Death illustrate this idea?

3. Thinking Cap: Do diseases still move from one part of the world to another?

Activity 2: Plague! *(Offline)*

Instructions

Your three diary entries about your grandmother's stories should include the following information:

1. A few facts about the Black Death from your grandmother's description of a neighbor who died of the plague, and why she thought the plague happened.
2. Some differences between your life and your grandmother's early life as a serf, such as: How does your family earn a living? How do your neighbors earn a living? Are you better off than your grandmother was at your age? If so, in what ways? Why?
3. A comparison of your life and your grandmother's. What is different? What has stayed the same?
4. Your last entry should include your thoughts about how your world would be different if the first ship of sick sailors had never docked in Messina. What might your life have been like if the plague had never reached Europe?

ASSESS

Lesson Assessment: Plague! (*Online*)

You will complete an online assessment covering the main points of this lesson. Your assessment will be scored by the computer.

Student Guide
Lesson 11: Unit Review

You've finished the unit, and now it's time to review what you've learned. You'll take the Unit Assessment in the next lesson.

Lesson Objectives

- Demonstrate mastery of important knowledge and skills in this unit and the previous unit.

PREPARE

Approximate lesson time is 60 minutes.

LEARN
Activity 1: A Look Back *(Online)*

Online Review

Review the following:

- Canals
- Quick Check: The Tang and Song Dynasties
- Exchanges Along the Silk Road
- Ideas, Innovations, and Inventions of China
- Quick Check: The Mongols
- Code Breaker: Geographic Concepts
- Quick Check: The Khans

History Journal Review

Review what you've learned in this unit by going through your History Journal. You should:

- Look at activity sheets, Personality Profiles, maps, the travel brochure, and Reading Guides you completed for the unit.
- Review unit Keywords.
- Read through any writing assignments you completed during the unit.
- Review any offline lesson assessments you took.
- Skim through the chapters in *The Human Odyssey* that you read in this unit.

Student Guide
Lesson 12: Unit Assessment

You've finished the unit! Now it's time to take the Unit Assessment.

Lesson Objectives

- Identify important events, characteristics, and individuals of the Mongol Empire.
- Recognize important events and achievements of the Sui, Tang, and Song dynasties.
- Recognize key causes, events, and people of the Hundred Years' War.
- List examples of ways in which the Black Plague changed Europe.
- Recognize the extent of the Mongol Empire and the countries in that territory today.
- Identify geographic features of the Asian steppe.
- Assess ways in which governments attempt to unite nations.
- Recognize the geographic concept of movement as it relates to disease.
- Describe the concept of human-environment interaction as it relates to the building of canals.

PREPARE

Approximate lesson time is 60 minutes.

Materials

For the Student

Question Review Table

ASSESS

Unit Assessment: From East Asia to Western Europe Again, Part 1 (*Online*)

Complete the computer-scored portion of the Unit Assessment. When you have finished, complete the teacher-scored portion of the assessment and submit it to your teacher.

Unit Assessment: From East Asia to Western Europe Again, Part 2 (*Offline*)

Complete the teacher-scored portion of the Unit Assessment and submit it to your teacher.

LEARN

Activity 1: Unit Assessment Review Table *(Online)*

If you earned a score of **less than 80%** on the Unit Assessment, complete the activity.

If you earned a score of **80% or greater**, you may skip this activity.

Let's prepare to retake the Unit Assessment:

- Identify the questions that you answered incorrectly.
- Complete the appropriate review activities listed in the table.

Assessment Date

Unit 13: From East Asia to Western Europe Again

Before you retake the Unit Assessment, use the table to figure out which activities you should review.

Question Review Table

Circle the numbers of the questions that you missed on the Unit Assessment. Review the activities that correspond with these questions.

From East Asia to Western Europe Again, Part 1

Question	Lesson	Review Activity
1,3,5,6	7: Conquering Khans	Check Your Reading
2	1: A New Dynasty	Restoring an Empire
4,7	9: How Many Years of War?	Looking at Art
8	3: A Golden Age	Check Your Reading
9,10,11,12,13	1: A New Dynasty 3: A Golden Age	Restoring an Empire Check Your Reading
14	10: Plague!	Read Use What You Know
15,16,17,18	9: How Many Years of War?	Read

From East Asia to Western Europe Again, Part 2

Question	Lesson	Review Activity
6	1: A New Dynasty 3: A Golden Age	Restoring an Empire Check Your Reading
1,2,3,4,5	6: The Mongols	Check Your Reading

Student Guide

Unit 14: Seeking the Silk Road
Lesson 1: Summing Up

Most people who lived during the Middle Ages never traveled more than a mile or two from home. But as trade and war brought diverse regions into contact with one another, economic, religious, scientific, and cultural ideas gradually spread. Revisit the Middle Ages—the period that connects classical civilizations and modern history.

Lesson Objectives

- Review knowledge gained in previous units/lessons.
- Summarize the work and influence of Confucius.
- Summarize the most important achievements of the Roman Republic.
- Identify the origins, beliefs, and important people in the founding and spread of Christianity.
- Recognize the role of trade in the Byzantine Empire.
- On a map trace the growth of the Muslim Empire.
- Identify important events, people, and achievements of the Byzantine Empire.
- Identify important events, people, and achievements of the Muslim Empire.
- Recognize important events, people, and achievements of the African empires of Ghana and Mali.
- Recognize the role of trade in the Byzantine and African Empires.

PREPARE

Approximate lesson time is 60 minutes.

Materials

For the Student

Looking Back on the Middle Ages

The Human Odyssey: Prehistory Through the Middle Ages edited by Klee, Cribb, and Holdren

Keywords and Pronunciation

Renaissance (REH-nuh-sahns)

LEARN

Activity 1: Revisiting the Middle Ages *(Offline)*

Read

As you read the Conclusion to Part 4, pages 605 to 611, complete the Looking Back on the Middle Ages sheet. When you have finished, check your answers in the Lesson Answer Key.

Activity 2: Summing Up *(Online)*

ASSESS

Lesson Assessment: Summing Up (*Online*)

You will complete an online assessment covering the main points of this lesson. Your assessment will be scored by the computer.

Name Date

Looking Back on the Middle Ages

As you read, complete the chart to review what you've studied. Add other information from your reading and your memory. The first one is completed for you.

	Location	Trade	Beliefs	Accomplishments	Other
Byzantine Empire	Asia Minor and the eastern Mediterranean	crossroads for trade; merchants from Europe, Asia, and Africa traded furs, gold, salt, honey, wheat, barley, silk, ivory, porcelain, spices	home of many faiths, but mainly Eastern Orthodox Christianity, which split from the Western church in 1054 and is led by a patriarch	scholars preserved texts; Justinian's Code helped unifiy the empire; built the Hagia Sophia and other churches; Byzantine art thrived and consisted of mosaics, frescoes, and icons	capital city is Constantinople; Justinian began the silk industry in the West and built an enormous underground aqueduct
Islamic Empire					
African Empires					

Name Date

Looking Back on the Middle Ages

As you read, complete the chart to review what you've studied. Add other information from your reading and your memory. The first one is completed for you.

	Location	Trade	Beliefs	Accomplishments	Other
Chinese Empires					
Western Europe					

Student Guide

Lesson 2: The Big Picture

The cultures of the Middle Ages left diverse legacies. Their influence is still visible today.

Lesson Objectives

- Demonstrate knowledge gained in previous lessons about the Middle Ages.
- Recognize major factors that led to the development of the four river-valley civilizations of Mesopotamia, Egypt, the Indus Valley, and China.
- Summarize the most important achievements of the Roman Republic.
- Identify important events, people, and achievements of the Byzantine Empire.
- Identify important events, people, and achievements of the Muslim Empire.
- Recognize important events, people, and achievements of the African empires of Ghana and Mali.

PREPARE

Approximate lesson time is 60 minutes.

Materials

For the Student

Map of the Middle Ages

The Human Odyssey: Prehistory Through the Middle Ages edited by Klee, Cribb, and Holdren

art supplies - poster board

colored pencils or markers

History Journal

LEARN

Activity 1: Medieval Times *(Online)*

Use What You Know

The Middle Ages Map

- Print the The Middle Ages Map.
- Locate and identify the following: Byzantine Empire, Islamic Empire, African empires, Western Europe, and Chinese empires. Write the names in the appropriate locations. Color each region or empire and color the legend to match.
- What have you learned about the Middle Ages? In your History Journal, make a short list of what comes to mind when you think about each place you studied. What made each of these empires or regions unique? What characterized each one? Consider geographic factors such as place and climate, cultural features such as art and architecture, and human factors or individual people. For additional help, review what you wrote on the Looking Back on the Middle Ages sheet from the Summing Up lesson.

Say It with Pictures

- Create a collage on poster board highlighting the achievements, culture, history, and/or geography of each of the five empires or regions. Refer to your History Journal notes.

1. Glue the Middle Ages map in the center of your poster board.
2. Mark off five distinct areas on the poster board surrounding the map.
3. In each area you marked off, draw or cut and paste images of what you most associate with that place. You may use pictures from previous lessons.

- Draw lines to connect the images to their correct locations.

ASSESS

Lesson Assessment: The Big Picture (*Online*)

You will complete an online assessment covering the main points of this lesson. Your assessment will be scored by the computer.

Name Date

The Middle Ages

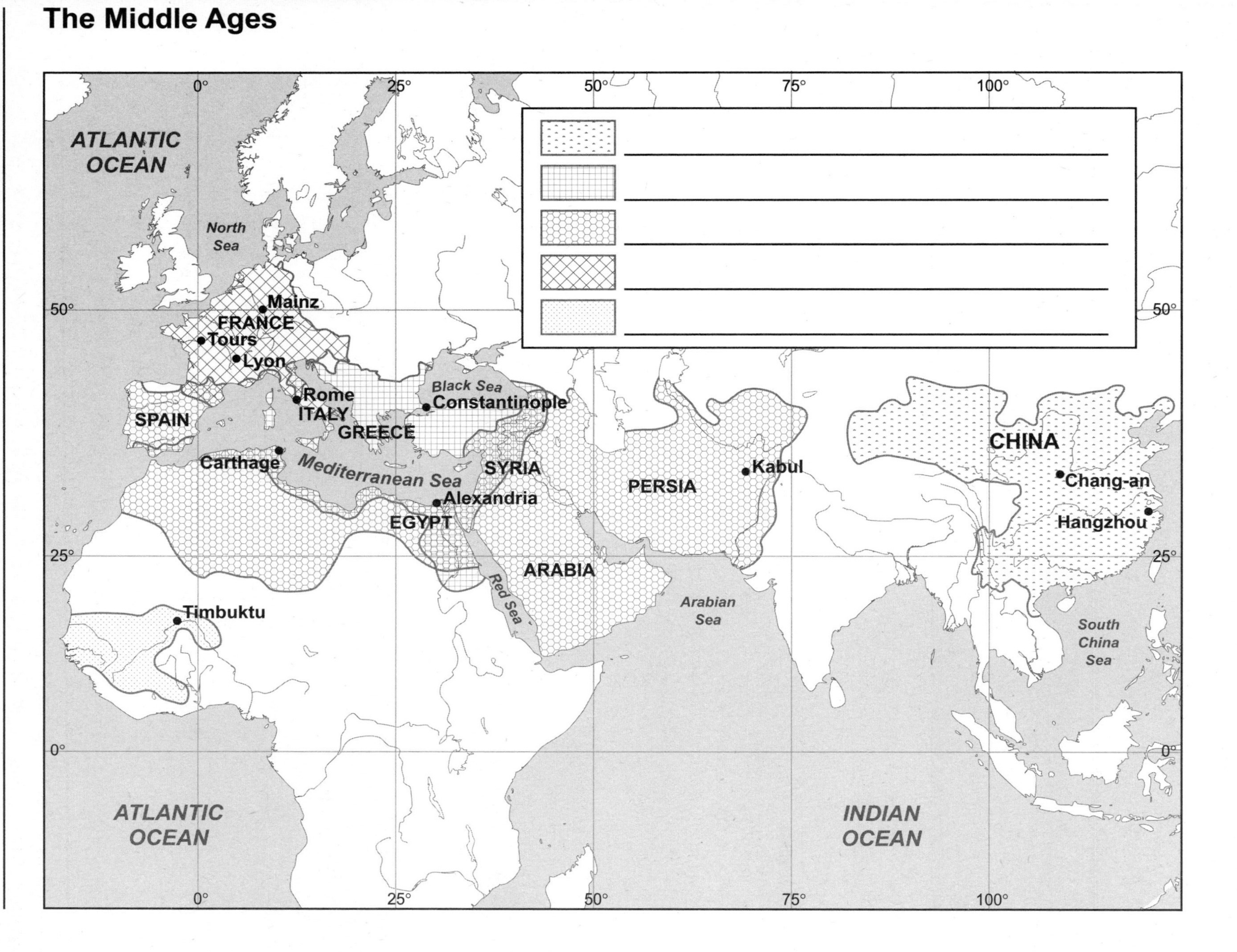

Student Guide
Lesson 3: Trade, Trade, Trade

In the days of the Egyptian pharaohs, how did ideas move from place to place? How did Islam find its way to England? How did Greek citizens learn about Persian and North African cultures?

Lesson Objectives

- Review knowledge gained in previous lessons.
- Conduct research in preparation for writing a research report.
- Describe the emerging importance of trade on the Silk Road.
- Describe the role of trade between Rome and the East (the Silk Road).
- Identify the Tang era as the high point of trade on the Silk Road.

PREPARE

Approximate lesson time is 60 minutes.

Materials

For the Student

Along the Silk Road

The Human Odyssey: Prehistory Through the Middle Ages edited by Klee, Cribb, and Holdren

History Journal

LEARN

Activity 1: Trading Along the Silk Road and Beyond *(Offline)*

Instructions

Use What You Know

Along the Silk Road and Beyond

- Go back to earlier chapters in your textbook to identify goods, ideas, people, and other items that traveled along the Silk Road in different time periods.
- Complete the Along the Silk Road sheet by listing goods or ideas that moved over the route, where they came from, and where they went in each of the time periods shown (there may be an overlap of goods and ideas in different time periods). Don't try to list everything. Some suggestions of where to look are:
- Part 2: Chapters 2, 4, and 5
- Part 3: Chapter 4
- Part 4: Chapters 1, 3, 4, 10, 11, and 12
- Compare your answers with those in the Lesson Answer Key.

Activity 2: Brainstorming Research Topics *(Online)*

ASSESS

Lesson Assessment: Trade, Trade, Trade (*Online*)

You will complete an online assessment covering the main points of this lesson. Your assessment will be scored by the computer.

Name Date

Along the Silk Road

Second Century B.C. to Sixth Century A.D.		
What	**From**	**To**
ivory, jade, ceramics		Persia and the Mediterranean region
glass, wine, perfumes, linen, woolen goods	Europe	
	Afghanistan	Asia, North Africa
language, laws, art, architecture, science, philosophy		Asia, North Africa
Spices		Persia and the Mediterranean region
Eastern ideas and philosophies		
Christianity		
	Russia	China

Name Date

Along the Silk Road

Second Century B.C. to Sixth Century A.D.		
What	**From**	**To**
silkworm	China	
Seventh to Tenth Centuries A.D.		
What	**From**	**To**
paper	China	
Islam		Europe, Africa, Asia
math, physics, astronomy	Byzantine Empire, Egypt, Persia, India	
Buddhism		Central Asia, China, Korea
music, musical instruments, dances		China

Name Date

Along the Silk Road

Eleventh to Fourteenth Centuries A.D.		
What	**From**	**To**
plague and other diseases		Europe
	Ghana (Africa)	Arabian Peninsula
salt	Sahara	
clothing, cloth, silk		Ghana
compass, gunpowder, paper money, movable type		Europe
Marco Polo		China, Asia

Student Guide
Lesson 4: Finding Information

By now you should have chosen a topic you want to write about. But before you start to look for information on the topic, you'll need to narrow it down and point yourself in the right direction by asking questions that you would like to answer. Then it will be time to take notes and prepare bibliography cards.

Lesson Objectives

- Review knowledge gained in previous lessons.
- Conduct research in preparation for writing a research report.

PREPARE

Approximate lesson time is 60 minutes.

Materials

For the Student

Narrowing a Topic

Taking Notes

The Human Odyssey: Prehistory Through the Middle Ages edited by Klee, Cribb, and Holdren

---

LEARN

Activity 1: Research *(Offline)*

Instructions

Narrow Your Topic

You want a good working topic for your paper--one that is neither too broad nor too narrow. To help you focus in on your topic, complete the Narrowing a Topic sheet.

Next you'll start your research. But don't jump right into reference books and websites! First, point yourself in the right direction by asking questions that you would like to answer about your topic. On a separate sheet of paper (or on the back of the Narrowing a Topic sheet), make a list of questions. That way, you will not be trying to use every source that has to do with a topic that is too broad.

Save your questions to use as you begin researching. They will help you develop subtopics (the smaller parts of the main topic). Below is an example of a main topic and some possible subtopics.

Topic: Decline of the Silk Road

Possible Subtopics:

- The end of the Mongol Empire
- New technologies
- New trade routes

Write a Thesis Statement

A *thesis statement* is a sentence that states the main idea of an essay or report. It helps you keep that idea in mind as you plan, research, and write your report.

Write a thesis statement for your research report on a note card. Keep in mind that this statement may not be your final one. You may want to revise it as you research. Keep your thesis statement with your other note cards so you can refer to it as needed.

Take Good Notes

When writing a research paper, it is important to take good notes and to list your sources.

- Print and read the Taking Notes sheet.
- Be sure to complete bibliography cards and note cards as you research.

ASSESS

Lesson Assessment: Finding Information (*Online*)

You will complete an online assessment covering the main points of this lesson. Your assessment will be scored by the computer.

Name Date 

Narrowing a Topic

Below is an example of how to narrow your topic.

My possible topic is:

the history of flight

What more in particular about this topic would I like to know?

I would like to know about the different kinds of flight and how flight began and grew to what it is today.

What more in particular about this topic would I like to know?

Some of the different kinds of flight are air travel, space travel, and balloons.

What more in particular about this topic would I like to know?

I think I need to choose just one kind of flight. Space flight is recent. I always think of the Wright brothers for airplanes. I don't know anything about balloons.

My narrowed topic is:

balloon flights because I would like to learn about how they started and how they are used today

Keep in mind that your topic so far is a working topic, not a final one. You can change it if you need to, after you have done more thinking and research.

Name Date

Narrowing a Topic

My possible topic is:

What more in particular about this topic would I like to know?

What more in particular about this topic would I like to know?

What more in particular about this topic would I like to know?

My narrowed topic is:

Keep in mind that your topic so far is a working topic, not a final one. You can change it if you need to, after you have done more thinking and research.

Name Date 

Taking Notes

Bibliography Cards and Note Cards
You will find it easier to write your research report if you take plenty of good notes. You will be able to pick and choose from among your cards to use the information that best develops your topic. To take good notes, you will need to use a separate note card for each piece of information.

Before you begin taking notes, be sure you have a bibliography card for the source you are using. Here is an example of a bibliography card from an Internet website:

Name of Site:
"NOVA Online: Balloon Race Around the World"
URL: http://www.pbs.org/wgbh/nova/balloon
Date Visited: September 4, 2003
Date Created: October 2000

Then write the following information on your note card:

- At the top left of the card, write the subtopic.
- At the top right, list the name of the website or author and screen or page number of the source.
- In the main text of the note, **summarize** the information; that is, take down the important points. You may either **paraphrase**, or quote directly from the source. If you quote directly, make sure to write the exact words and put them in quotation marks. When you write your report, you will need to give credit to any sources you quote or to any paraphrases in which you change only a few words.

Name Date

Here is an example of a completed note card:

Subtopic **Source information**

Piccard's historic flight	NOVA, screen 1
"To fly non-stop around the world in a balloon was one of aviation's last great challenges—a challenge that was finally met on March 20, 1999 by Bertran Piccard of Switzerland and Brian Jones of Britain."	

Note Card

Main Text:
- Important information
- Quotations

Using Your Own Words

Some of your research report may consist of quotations from sources. Quotations must be placed in quotation marks and given proper credit.

Most of your research report should be in your own words. What does "your own words" mean? It means:
- You must change the wording in a major way.
- You should usually change the sentence structure.

You are not allowed to:
- Copy the exact words of a source and pretend the words are your own
- Just change a few minor words from the source

If you pretend that someone else's words are your own, you are committing a dishonest act called **plagiarism**.

Student Guide
Lesson 5: Finding More Information

Lesson Objectives

- Review knowledge gained in previous lessons.
- Conduct research in preparation for writing a research report.

PREPARE

Approximate lesson time is 60 minutes.

LEARN

Activity 1: More Research *(Offline)*

ASSESS

Lesson Assessment: Finding More Information (*Online*)

You will complete an online assessment covering the main points of this lesson. Your assessment will be scored by the computer.

Student Guide
Lesson 6: Showing What You've Learned

Complement your research report by developing a visual that illustrates or represents your chosen topic. Then continue your research if you need to, and begin to prepare an outline for your paper.

Lesson Objectives

- Review knowledge gained in previous lessons.
- Conduct research in preparation for writing a research report and for creating a visual.
- Conduct research in preparation for writing a research report.

PREPARE

Approximate lesson time is 60 minutes.

Materials

For the Student

Formal Outline

The Human Odyssey: Prehistory Through the Middle Ages edited by Klee, Cribb, and Holdren

---

LEARN

Activity 1: Completing Your Research *(Offline)*

Instructions

Create a Visual for the Research Report

Many research reports include one or more visual items. These visuals convey information about the topic to enhance the report.

1. Brainstorm ideas for a visual that will complement your research report and show what you've learned. Write your ideas on a sheet of notebook paper. For example, if you have chosen Music of the Silk Road as your topic, you might create pictures (with captions) of several types of instruments that traveled the Silk Road. If you chose the Geography of the Silk Road, you might create a colored map that illustrates the geographic features of the Silk Road or images of surrounding land such as deserts, mountains, rivers, and plains.
2. Develop your visual.

Finish Up Research

If you think you need additional information for your report, now's the time to find it!

Plan the Research Report

By now you should have all the information for your research report on your note cards. Now it's time to plan your report.

1. Read over your notes and arrange the cards into separate stacks according to their content. For example, if your topic was the Decline of the Silk Road, then all cards with information about the end of the Mongol Empire would be in one stack, cards with information related to new technologies in another, and cards with information about new trade routes would be in a third stack.
2. As you begin to plan for writing your research paper, how do you know what to include and what to leave out? The key is unity. In a good research report, every piece of information should be related to the main topic. Details that are interesting but stray from the topic should not be included. Remove any note cards that give information that strays from the topic.
3. You will follow the classic essay pattern of an introduction with a thesis statement followed by the main body of supporting paragraphs, and finally, a conclusion. Revisit your thesis statement. Make sure it matches the notes you've taken. If you find that it does not quite fit the information, rewrite the thesis statement so it reflects your research. Remember your thesis statement will form the core of your introductory paragraph.
4. Begin to outline the paragraphs of the main body of the report by following the pattern on the Formal Outline sheet. Remember that an outline is the skeleton of a research report. If parts of your outline aren't covered well in your notes, go back now and try to find more information for those sections. If you do not finish the outline in this lesson, you can finish it in the next lesson.

ASSESS

Lesson Assessment: Showing What You've Learned (*Online*)

You will complete an online assessment covering the main points of this lesson. Your assessment will be scored by the computer.

Name Date

Formal Outline

A **formal outline** consists of at least three levels of headings: **main topics**, **subtopics**, and **specific facts**.

Main topics follow Roman numerals and periods.

Subtopics follow capital letters and periods.

Specific details follow Arabic numerals and periods.

More information about the specific details follows lowercase letters and periods.

Sample Formal Outline Pattern:

I. First Main Topic
    A. First Subtopic
        1. First Specific Detail
        2. Second Specific Detail
        3. Third Specific Detail
    B. Second Subtopic
        1. First Specific Detail
        2. Second Specific Detail
            a. More information about this detail
            b. More information about this detail
            c. More information about this detail
    C. Third Subtopic
        1. First Specific Detail
        2. Second Specific Detail
            a. More information about this detail
            b. More information about this detail
II. Second Main Topic
    A. First Subtopic
        1. First Specific Detail
        2. Second Specific Detail
    B. Second Subtopic
(etc.)

Student Guide
Lesson 7: Writing About What You've Learned

If you have not finished your outline and visual, complete them now and then write the first draft of your research paper.

Lesson Objectives

- Conduct research in preparation for writing.
- Write the first draft of a research report.

PREPARE

Approximate lesson time is 60 minutes.

Materials

For the Student

Model Citations

LEARN

Activity 1: Writing the First Draft *(Offline)*

Instructions

Complete the Research and Visual

1. Continue to work on your outline if you did not finish it in the previous lesson. Remember that an outline is the skeleton of a research paper. If your notes do not cover all parts of your outline, go back now and try to find more information for those parts. If you can't find information, remove those parts from your outline.
2. If you have not finished creating the visual for your research report, do so now.

Begin the First Draft

1. Now it's time to write the first draft of your research report. Research reports are a little different from other kinds of essays. One key difference is that in a research report you must document your sources. Whenever you use a direct quotation from a source or whenever you state a fact that is not common knowledge, you must provide a reference, or *citation,* that shows where you got that information.

- The format for citations within a report is simple--you list the citation in parentheses after the fact or quotation it documents. This is called "parenthetical documentation." The citation should include the website name or author's last name and the screen or page number where you found the information. Here is an example of a quotation with a citation: "To fly non-stop around world in a balloon was one of the aviation's last great challenges--a challenge that was finally met on March 20, 1999 by Bertran Piccard of Switzerland and Brian Jones of Britain."
- If you give the author's name in your own passage, your citation should show only the page number. For example, "As author Aaron Percefull says…" (25).

1. Here are a few reminders as you begin to write your draft:

- Use a writing style that is appropriate for serious information and for your intended audience.
- Try to maintain a consistent tone and voice to go with your informational style.
- Follow the classic essay pattern consisting of these elements: introduction with a thesis statement, supporting paragraphs, and conclusion.
- Each paragraph should have a main idea of its own, with a topic sentence and supporting details.
- As you write, follow your outline. You don't have to start by writing the first paragraph of the report, however. You may write the body of the report first, or even the conclusion.
- Whether you are writing by hand or typing your report, double space to leave room for revisions.

1. At the end of your report, you will need to provide the complete reference to any materials you used in a "Works Cited" page.

A Works Cited page includes all the sources you cited in the text of your report. If you took notes on a source but did not actually use it, don't list it on the Works Cited page. To create the Works Cited page, review your report and locate all the citations. Then gather the bibliography cards you made for the sources. Arrange the cards into categories (such as books, periodicals, Internet sources, etc.) and alphabetize the sources in each category. For each source, write out a full citation in the correct form as shown on the Model Citations sheet.

ASSESS

Lesson Assessment: Writing About What You've Learned (*Online*)

You will complete an online assessment covering the main points of this lesson. Your assessment will be scored by the computer.

Name Date

Model Citations

Here are some model Works Cited entries that you can follow.

- Notice that titles of books are italicized, and titles of articles are in quotation marks.
- Dates are written in the order of day-month-year.
- Use page numbers when the source is part of a larger work, such as an article from a magazine.
- Notice the capitalization and punctuation of each notation also.

Books
Percefull, Aaron W. *Balloons, Zeppelins, and Dirigibles*. New York: Franklin Watts, 1983.

Periodicals
"2002 Laureate Awards." *Aviation Week and Space Technology* 21 April 2003: 41.

Encyclopedia Articles
Piccard, Don. "Balloon." *World Book Multimedia Encyclopedia*. CD-ROM. Chicago: World Book, 1999.

Internet Sources
"Balloon Race Around the World." *NOVA Online*. Oct. 2000. WGBH Educational Foundation. 4 Sept. 2003 <http://www.pbs.org/wgbh/nova/balloon/>

If you need more models, consult a language handbook.

Student Guide
Lesson 8: Writing Well

Congratulations! You have completed the first draft of your research report. Now it's time to check over your draft for ways to improve it, and then complete your research report.

Lesson Objectives

- Write the final draft of a research report.

PREPARE

Approximate lesson time is 60 minutes.

Materials

For the Student

- Checklist for Proofreading a Research Report
- Checklist for Revising a Research Report

LEARN

Activity 1: Completing Your Research Report *(Offline)*

Instructions

Revising a research report involves several steps. First you need to revise for content and for style and form. Then you need to proofread your paper.

1. Make a title page for your research report and include your name on a separate line.
2. Read back through your whole research paper. Did you stay on the topic? Are all your ideas clearly written? Use the Checklist for Revising a Research Report to guide you as you read your paper.
3. Do you see any spelling, grammar, or punctuation mistakes? Use the Checklist for Proofreading a Research Report to guide you as you proofread your paper.
4. Make your corrections to your essay, and then copy your revised essay onto clean loose-leaf paper or print from the computer after you have made your revisions.
5. Add the visual that you developed to your research paper.

If you're unable to complete your research report, you'll have time to finish proofreading and rewriting it in the next optional lesson.

ASSESS

Lesson Assessment: Writing Well (*Online*)

You will complete an online assessment covering the main points of this lesson. Your assessment will be scored by the computer.

Name ______________________________ Date ______________________________

Checklist for Revising a Research Report

Revising for Content

☐ Does my report fulfill its purpose of providing information on my specific, chosen topic?	If not, can I fix the problem by either adding relevant information or deleting irrelevant information? ______________________________
☐ Does my report follow the pattern of organization I chose?	If not, where does it go astray? What changes should I make to get it back on course? ______________________________
☐ Is every point in my outline covered in my paper, in the same order as in the outline?	If not, what do I need to add or move? ______________________________
☐ Does my introduction identify the topic in an interesting way?	If not, how can I make the introduction more effective? ______________________________
☐ Does every paragraph in the body of my report help support the thesis statement?	If not, what do I need to add or remove? ______________________________
☐ Does my conclusion tell the reader what I learned from my research, and does it leave the reader with something to think about?	If not, how can I strengthen my conclusion? ______________________________

Name ______________________________ Date ______________________________

Revising for Style and Form

☐ Does each of my sentences tell a complete thought?	If not, how can I complete the sentences?
☐ Does my report use a consistent, appropriate voice and tone?	If not, what word choices need to be changed? Do I need to rethink my report's voice or tone?
☐ Are all my sentences clear and understandable?	If not, how can I improve the style of my report?
☐ Are my word choices vivid and exact?	If not, how can I improve the style of my report?
☐ Does each sentence in the report contribute to the unity of the paragraph that contains it?	If not, what steps, such as deleting passages, should I take to improve unity?
☐ Do my sentences and paragraphs move logically from one to the next?	If not, where can I add transitions?
☐ Have I cited my sources, using the exact words of quotations?	If not, what sources haven't I cited?

Name ______________________________ Date ______________________________

Checklist for Proofreading a Research Report

Questions for Proofreading	Notes About My Research Report
☐ Are all words spelled correctly? Have I looked up the spellings of words when I am not sure?	
☐ Are all names and dates in my report correct and consistent?	
☐ Are all names of people and places capitalized correctly?	
☐ Does each sentence begin with a capital letter and end with a mark of punctuation?	
☐ In quotations, have I used the exact words of the speaker or writer and placed them within quotation marks?	
☐ Are all the citations within the text in proper form?	
☐ Are all the entries on my Works Cited page in proper form? Have I checked the capitalization and punctuation?	
☐ Are my pages numbered?	
☐ Is the title of the report spelled and capitalized correctly? Is my name included on a separate line?	

Student Guide
Lesson 9. Optional: Your Choice

You may use today's lesson time to do one or more of the following:

- Complete work in progress.
- Complete the Beyond the Lesson activity in any lesson in this unit.
- Review the Classical World Time Line in the Resources section.
- Prepare for your state standardized test.
- Go on to the next lesson.

Please mark this lesson complete to proceed to the next lesson in the course.

PREPARE

Approximate lesson time is 60 minutes.

Student Guide

Unit 15: Finishing
Lesson 1: Conclusions

Lesson Objectives

- Demonstrate mastery of knowledge gained in previous lessons.
- Identify the invention of the wheel as a major contribution of Mesopotamian civilization.
- List examples of the relationship between geography and the rise and fall of civilizations.
- Summarize the work and influence of Confucius.
- Identify fundamental teachings of Hinduism about many gods, the caste system, and reincarnation.
- Identify important accomplishments, beliefs, people, and events of the Hebrew people.
- Identify Pericles.
- Identify Socrates, Plato, and Aristotle and their key ideas and achievements.
- Identify Alexander the Great.
- Compare Julius Caesar and Cincinnatus and their relationship to societal changes.
- Summarize Jesus' key teachings.
- Identify Constantine and his achievements.
- Identify key events, people, values, and achievements during the time of the Roman Republic.
- Explain the purpose and importance of Justinian's Code.
- Identify Theodora as a powerful empress and Justinian's wife and aide.
- Recognize ways in which monarchs consolidated power.
- Analyze excerpts from the Magna Carta to assess its impact on future political thought.
- Explain why people build canals and describe the challenges in building them.
- List examples of cultural and political innovations and inventions in China under the Tang and Song dynasties.
- Identify Genghis Khan and the methods he used to gain power.
- Summarize the story of Joan of Arc.
- Compare and contrast Christianity with other world religions.
- Analyze artifacts to describe human creativity.

PREPARE

Approximate lesson time is 60 minutes.

Materials

For the Student

The Human Odyssey, Volume 1, Quiz

The Human Odyssey: Prehistory Through the Middle Ages edited by Klee, Cribb, and Holdren

LEARN

Activity 1: The Main Ideas *(Offline)*

Activity 2: The Details *(Online)*

ASSESS

Lesson Assessment: Conclusions (*Online*)

You will complete an online assessment covering the main points of this lesson. Your assessment will be scored by the computer.

Name _______________________________________ Date _______________________

The Human Odyssey, Volume 1, Quiz

Create a quiz that covers the most important ideas and concepts from Volume 1 of *The Human Odyssey: Prehistory Through the Middle Ages*. You need to include at least 10 items on the quiz. They can be multiple choice, true/false, matching, fill in the blank, or short answer. Include the answer(s) for each item. For help, refer to your reading selection, "The Ongoing Human Odyssey," pages 615–621, and the five main headings in the text.

Your test items should focus on the *main* concepts and ideas in the book. Avoid test items that ask about supporting details.

The following is an example of a main concept, and would be an acceptable item for your quiz:

____________ has determined where and how people live.

a. religion
b. government
c. geography (correct answer)
d. astronomy

Avoid test items like this one, which ask about details.

The people of ____________ learned to use the land for grazing sheep and growing olives.

a. Sumer
b. Egypt
c. Greece (correct answer)
d. Rome

Student Guide
Lesson 2: End-of-Course Review: Units 9 and 10

You've finished! Now it's time to pull together what you have learned this semester. You've learned a lot, so we'll review it unit by unit. Let's start by taking a look at the Classical Greece and Rome: Republic and Empire units.

Lesson Objectives

- Demonstrate mastery of important knowledge and skills taught in the Classical Greece unit.
- Demonstrate mastery of important knowledge and skills taught in the Rome: Republic and Empire unit.

PREPARE

Approximate lesson time is 60 minutes.

Materials

For the Student

History Journal

LEARN

Activity 1: Online *(Online)*

Activity 2: Offline *(Offline)*

Review what you learned this semester by going through your History Journal. You should look at:

- Completed activity sheets, including Reading Guides
- Printouts of online activities (Personality Profiles, Flash Cards, Code Breakers, and Slide Shows)
- Maps
- Keywords and definitions
- Offline assessments

Student Guide
Lesson 3: End-of-Course Review: Units 11, 12, and 13

Let's continue pulling together what you have learned this semester. You've learned a lot, so we'll review it unit by unit. Today we'll take a look at the following units: Empires, In Western Europe, and From East Asia to Western Europe Again.

Lesson Objectives

- Demonstrate mastery of important knowledge and skills taught in the Empires unit.
- Demonstrate mastery of important knowledge and skills taught in the In Western Europe unit.
- Demonstrate mastery of important knowledge and skills taught in the From East Asia to Western Europe Again unit.

PREPARE

Approximate lesson time is 60 minutes.

Materials

For the Student

History Journal

LEARN

Activity 1: Online *(Online)*

Activity 2: Offline *(Offline)*

Review what you learned this semester by going through your History Journal. You should look at:

- Completed activity sheets--including Reading Guides
- Printouts of online activities (Personality Profiles, Flash Cards, Code Breakers, Slide Shows, Quick Checks)
- Maps
- Keywords and definitions
- Offline assessments

Student Guide
Lesson 4: End-of-Course Final Review

You've finished! Now it's time to pull together what you have learned this semester. You've looked back at what you have learned this semester in a unit by unit review. Now you'll have one more opportunity to do a final review of the semester before taking the End-of-Course Assessment, Part 1.

Lesson Objectives

- Demonstrate mastery of important knowledge and skills taught in the Classical Greece unit.
- Demonstrate mastery of important knowledge and skills taught in the Rome: Republic and Empire unit.
- Demonstrate mastery of important knowledge and skills taught in the Empires unit.
- Demonstrate mastery of important knowledge and skills taught in the In Western Europe unit.

PREPARE

Approximate lesson time is 60 minutes.

Materials

For the Student

History Journal

LEARN

Activity 1: Online *(Online)*

Activity 2: Offline *(Online)*

History Journal Review

To help you prepare for the offline portion of the End-of-Course Assessment you should look at activity sheets and charts that:

- compare religions
- explain the role of the Christian church
- explain some strategies or general practices that rulers throughout history have used to unite people
- explain the legacy of classical Greece and Rome to modern western civilization

Student Guide
Lesson 5: End-of-Course Assessment, Part 1

Lesson Objectives

- Recognize the values, government, and way of life in Greece.
- Identify democratic reformers and their accomplishments in Athens.
- Describe the main accomplishments and characteristics of the Persian Empire and its leaders.
- Summarize the main events of the First and Second Persian Wars.
- Recognize the main characteristics of Greek theater.
- Identify Aeschylus, Sophocles, and Euripides and their contributions to literature.
- Describe the main cause of the Peloponnesian War.
- Explain the main reasons for Athens' defeat in the Peloponnesian War.
- Recognize the results of the Peloponnesian War.
- Define *philosophy, monarchy, aristocracy, democracy,* and *anarchy.*
- Identify Socrates, Plato, and Aristotle and their key ideas and achievements.
- Identify Alexander the Great.
- Compare and contrast characteristics of Sparta and Athens.
- Describe characteristics of Greek art, architecture, and literature.
- Define *paterfamilias, rex, patrician,* and *republic.*
- Describe important changes that took place in Rome after the end of the Punic Wars.
- Summarize the achievements of Julius Caesar.
- Identify the extent of the Roman Empire at its height and name five modern day countries that now occupy the land that once was part of the Roman Empire.
- Describe the main issues that led to the decline of the Roman Empire.
- Identify Constantine and his achievements.
- Identify key events, people, values, and achievements during the time of the Roman Republic.
- Define Pax Romana and forum.
- Describe the transition of Rome from republic to empire.
- List examples of the contributions of classical Greece and Rome to modern Western civilization.

PREPARE

Approximate lesson time is 60 minutes.

ASSESS

Semester Assessment: End-of-Course Assessment, Part 1, Online Assessment (*Online*)

Complete the computer-scored portion of the End-of-Course Assessment. When you have finished, complete the teacher-scored portion of the assessment and submit it to your teacher.

Student Guide
Lesson 6: End-of-Course Assessment, Part 2

Lesson Objectives

- Describe the Aryan migration and how it led to the development of Hinduism.
- Identify the founder of Buddhism.
- Describe the fundamental teachings of Buddhism about the search for Nirvana, the way to live a good life, and reincarnation.
- Name the religion of the ancient Hebrews.
- Summarize the basic beliefs of Judaism.
- Identify core beliefs of Christianity.
- Identify the origins, beliefs, and important people in the founding and spread of Christianity.
- Analyze maps to assess the advantages of Byzantium's (Constantinople's) location.
- Identify characteristics of Byzantine art.
- Explain the purpose and importance of Justinian's Code.
- Identify Justinian as the sixth-century emperor responsible for developing a code of law.
- Identify the Qur'an as the sacred text of Islam.
- Summarize the Five Pillars of Islam.
- Identify Abu Bakr as the first caliph and Muhammad's friend and father-in-law, and the conflicts during his rule that led to a split in Islam.
- Define *rain forest, Sahel, desert,* and *savanna.*
- Describe the role and importance of trade in Ghana's power.
- Identify Mansa Musa as the fourteenth century Muslim ruler of Mali known for his travels.
- Describe the origins, beliefs, and major figures in the founding and spread of Islam.
- Identify important events, people, and achievements of the Muslim Empire.
- Describe the role of the Christian church and the monasteries in spreading Christianity and preserving learning.
- Identify Charlemagne as king of the Franks in A.D. 800 and list examples of his achievements.
- Identify Erik the Red and Leif Erikson and their major achievements.
- Explain the reasons for the development of the feudal system.
- Recognize the characteristics, uses, and construction challenges of Gothic cathedrals.
- Describe the direct and indirect results of the Crusades.
- Describe the Norman Conquest.
- Define *common law* and *jury.*
- Explain the Magna Carta's legacy to democratic government.
- Identify important events, individuals, and groups in the development of a new social structure in Western Europe between A.D. 500 and 1000.
- Describe key causes, results, events, and individuals of the Crusades.
- Identify important events and people in the development of monarchies in Western Europe during the late Middle Ages.
- List examples of cultural and political innovations and inventions in China under the Tang and Song dynasties.

- Identify Kublai Khan and the characteristics of his rule.
- Identify Marco Polo.
- Explain how the Black Death started and describe its effects on Europe.
- Recognize key causes, events, and people of the Hundred Years' War.
- List examples of ways in which the Black Plague changed Europe.
- List examples of the ways in which the Christian church exercised authority, influenced daily life, and offered hope to Europeans during the Middle Ages.
- List examples of ways in which governments unite nations.
- Assess ways in which governments attempt to unite nations.

PREPARE

Approximate lesson time is 60 minutes.

ASSESS

Semester Assessment: End-of-Course Assessment, Part 2, Offline Assessment *(Offline)*

Complete the teacher-scored portion of the End-of-Course Assessment and submit it to your teacher.

Student Guide
Lesson 7. Optional: Your Choice

You may use today's lesson time to do one or more of the following:

- Complete work in progress.
- Complete the Beyond the Lesson activity in any lesson in this unit.
- Review the Classical World Time Line in the Resources section.
- Prepare for your state standardized test.
- Go on to the next lesson.

Please mark this lesson complete to proceed to the next lesson in the course.

PREPARE

Approximate lesson time is 60 minutes.